'Benedetta Voltolini's book is an insightful and inspiring read, essential for all those with an interest in European integration, European foreign policy, interest groups and the Israeli–Palestinian conflict. Uncovering the role of non-state actors in EU policy towards the Israeli–Palestinian conflict has been long over-due. Voltolini has done a superb job at opening up this new avenue of research.'
— **Nathalie Tocci**, *Deputy Director IAI and Special Advisor to the EU High Representative*

'The book plunges into the fascinating and poorly known universe of lobbying on the Israeli–Palestinian conflict. Private actors from both sides of the conflict do not co-opt policy-makers, but their actions shape how issues are understood and communicated. By analysing commercial and humanitarian policies, the book demonstrates that non-state actors contribute significantly to areas that we associate more commonly with high politics and diplomatic relations. A must-read for anyone who wants to know how the European Union's foreign policy is made.'
— **Cornelia Woll**, *Professor of Political Science, Sciences Po Paris*

I0127761

Lobbying in EU Foreign Policy-making

This book examines lobbying in EU foreign policy-making and the activities of non-state actors (NSAs), focusing on EU foreign policy on the Israeli–Palestinian conflict. It sheds light on the interactions between the EU and NSAs as well as the ways in which NSAs attempt to shape EU foreign policies. By analysing issues that have not yet received systematic attention in the literature, this book offers new insights into lobbying in EU foreign policy, EU relations surrounding the conflict and the EU's broader role in the peace process.

The book will be of key interest to scholars and students of political science, international relations, EU politics, EU foreign policy-making, Middle East studies and the Israeli–Palestinian conflict.

Benedetta Voltolini is Lecturer in International Relations at the Department of Political Science, Maastricht University, the Netherlands.

Routledge / UACES Contemporary European Studies

Edited by Federica Bicchi, London School of Economics and Political Science, Tanja Börzel, Free University of Berlin, and Mark Pollack, Temple University, on behalf of the University Association for Contemporary European Studies.

The primary objective of the new Contemporary European Studies series is to provide a research outlet for scholars of European Studies from all disciplines. The series publishes important scholarly works and aims to forge for itself an international reputation.

Lobbying in EU Foreign Policy-making

The case of the Israeli–Palestinian conflict

Benedetta Voltolini

Routledge
Taylor & Francis Group

LONDON AND NEW YORK

First published 2016
by Routledge

2 Park Square, Milton Park, Abingdon, Oxon OX14 4RN
711 Third Avenue, New York, NY 10017, USA

Routledge is an imprint of the Taylor & Francis Group, an informa business

First issued in paperback 2017

British Library Cataloguing in Publication Data
A catalogue record for this book is available from the British Library

Library of Congress Cataloging in Publication Data

Voltolini, Benedetta.
Lobbying in EU foreign policy-making : the case of the Israeli-Palestinian
conflict / Benedetta Voltolini.
pages cm. – (Routledge/UACES contemporary European studies; 28)
1. European Union countries–Foreign relations–Decision making.
2. Lobbying–European Union countries. 3. Pressure groups–European
Union countries. 4. European Union countries–Foreign relations–Israel.
5. Israel–Foreign relations–European Union countries. 6. European
Union countries–Foreign relations–Middle East. 7. Middle East–Foreign
relations–European Union countries. 8. Arab-Israeli conflict–1993-
I. Title. II. Title: Lobbying in European Union foreign policy-making.
JZ1570.V65 2015
341.242'2095694–dc23
2015007785

ISBN: 978-1-138-84814-6 (hbk)
ISBN: 978-1-138-03901-8 (pbk)

Typeset in Times New Roman
by Cenveo Publishers Services

Contents

List of figures and tables

Figures

Tables

Acknowledgements

This book is the result of a long research journey, which allowed me to meet, talk with and learn from a number of people. Without their help, this book would not have seen the light of day. All mistakes or imprecisions remain my sole responsibility.

First, I would like to thank Federica Bicchi and Karen E. Smith, who provided stimulating crucial feedback and intellectual inputs that pushed me to constantly improve my work and progress towards becoming a researcher. I am also grateful to all those who took the time to comment on my work, either at conferences, via email or by chatting with me. While it is impossible to mention all of them, I would like to thank Nathalie Tocci, Esra Bulut Aymat, Cornelia Woll, Ulrich Sedelmeier and two anonymous reviewers, who commented on this research project at different stages; I greatly appreciate their sharp and insightful comments.

I am also indebted to all those public officials and non-state actor representatives who took the time to explain to me the intricacies of EU foreign policy and lobbying, and who had the patience to answer all my questions. Without their help this book would not exist. Anonymity was granted to all of them, but I would like to openly thank Charles Shamas for his invaluable help in explaining to me the legal aspects of the Israeli–Palestinian conflict and of EU foreign policy, and Z. S. at the European Parliament for the numerous chats and lunches we shared. Over the years they have taught me a lot about how the EU's world works.

I would also like to thank the editors of the Routledge/UACES Contemporary European Studies Series for their feedback, the Routledge team, Carol Ross and Daniela Lai for their editorial support. This research was made possible thanks to the financial and/or logistical support of the Department of International Relations at the London School of Economics and Political Science (United Kingdom), the European Union Institute for Security Studies (France), the Centre for European Political Studies (Belgium), the Kollegsforschungsgruppe on Transformative Power Europe at the Freie Universität Berlin (Germany), the MaxPo Centre and the LIEPP at Sciences Po Paris (France) and Maastricht University (Netherlands). These places all provided an inspiring and stimulating research environment and I am grateful to all the people who made my research stay there a very enjoyable experience.

My friends have always been a great support: they cheered me up in the difficult moments and shared with me a lot of lovely experiences over the years. I also thank all the people who entered my life during this journey at different times, in different manners and for different periods. Last, but not least, I would have not been able to pursue this research without the support of my family. My grandfather Mario and my great aunt Riccarda passed away before the end of this project, but they have played a big role in it and they have taught me some important life-lessons. My mother has been a constant presence over the years and her love, patience, encouragement and understanding have helped me to face the numerous challenges of the past years. Olivier, who entered my life towards the end of this project, made the last 'miles' of this research journey a much happier and richer experience. His patience, support and love helped me to reach the conclusion of this book, which is dedicated to him.

List of abbreviations

ACAA	Agreement on Conformity Assessment and Acceptance of Industrial Products
AFET	Committee on Foreign Affairs
ALDE	Alliance of Liberals and Democrats of Europe
BDS	Boycott, Divestment and Sanctions
CEPR	Council for European–Palestinian Relations
CIDSE	Coopération Internationale pour le Développement et la Solidarité (International Cooperation for Development and Solidarity)
DG AGRI	Directorate-General for Agriculture and Rural Development
DG DEVCO	Directorate-General for International Cooperation and Development
DG ENTR	Directorate-General for Enterprise and Industry
DG RELEX	Directorate-General for External Relations
DG SANCO	Directorate-General for Health and Consumers
DG TAXUD	Directorate-General for Taxation and Customs Union
DIW	Deutsche-Israelische Wirtschaftsvereiningung
EAEPC	European Association of Euro-Pharmaceutical Companies
EC4I	European Coalition for Israel
ECCP	European Coordination of Committees and Associations for Palestine
ECJ	European Court of Justice
EEAS	European External Action Service
EFI	European Friends of Israel
EFPIA	European Federation of Pharmaceutical Industries and Associations
EIDHR	European Instrument for Democracy and Human Rights
EMHRN	Euro-Mediterranean Human Rights Network
EMP	Euro-Mediterranean Partnership
ENP	European Neighbourhood Policy
EP	European Parliament
EPP	European People's Party

FIDH	Fédération internationale des ligues des droits de l'Homme (International Federation for Human Rights)
FoE	Friends of the Earth
GUE/NGL	European United Left/Nordic Green Left
HoM	Heads of Mission
IEPN	Israeli–European Policy Network
INTA	Committee on International Trade
ITRE	Committee on Industry, Research and Energy
MEP	Member of the European Parliament
MEPP	Middle East Peace Process
MP	Member of Parliament
NGO	Non-Governmental Organisation
NSA	Non-State Actor
OPTs	Occupied Palestinian Territories
PA	Palestinian Authority
PLO	Palestinian Liberation Organisation
S&D	Socialists and Democrats
TEC	Treaty Establishing the European Community
UfM	Union for the Mediterranean
UN	United Nations
UNGA	United Nations General Assembly
UNHRC	United Nations Human Rights Council
UNSC	United Nations Security Council
Verts/ALE	The Greens/European Free Alliance

Introduction
'Embedded' lobbying in EU foreign policy

The iconic images of the Israeli–Palestinian conflict portray Israeli and Palestinian leaders shaking hands or issuing condemnation, generally with international leaders in the background. This picture of officials as the sole drivers of peace negotiations and conflict rounds is, however, misleading and a vast literature on the role of the Israeli lobby in the USA has challenged this view in the case of American foreign policy. Nothing of the sort has been done in the case of the European countries, though, and for long the impression was that this was not the case on the European side of the Atlantic. I began to doubt this version in 2008, when I was interviewing an official in the Council of the European Union (EU). As he quite openly reported, he was frequently contacted by the pro-Israel lobby, which was trying to influence EU policies and positions. A couple of years later, in an interview with the representative of a non-governmental organisation (NGO) working on the promotion of relations between the EU and Israel, I was told how easy it is for his organisation to have high-level contacts with EU Commissioners and senior staff, instead of approaching desk officers, whom he considered easily approachable but not important enough. And I was not told much about the activities of his organisation for fear that my research might disrupt their actions and damage their strategy. In the same period, I met the representative from another NGO working on the promotion of human rights who was very sceptical about the extent of her organisation's influence on EU policies due to their limited resources and the existence of strong counter-lobbying. At this stage I wondered how much influence non-state actors (NSAs) really have and, if they do have influence, how they succeed in shaping EU foreign policy on Israel and Palestine.

As we know from Baumgartner and Leech (1998: xviii) in relation to the US context, '[w]ithout a good understanding of the role of interest groups, our understanding of the functioning of our political system cannot possibly be complete'. While they are not the only factor explaining policy outcomes, NSAs play a significant role in policy-making. Foreign policy is no exception. Lots of ink has been spilled on how various groups influence American decisions, ranging from the power of the Cuban lobby (Haney and Vanderbush 1999) to the famous and controversial Mearsheimer and Walt (2006) article, in which the authors claimed that the 'Israel lobby' is a key factor to understand US policy towards the Middle East. While the extent to which NSAs shape US foreign policy remains a contested point, much attention has been paid to their actions (see, for instance, Organski 1990; Trice 1976; Paul and Paul 2009). This has, however, not been the case for the EU, a system which is in many ways considered similar to the US one.

Following Mearsheimer and Walt's argument, David Cronin (2011) claims that the Israel lobby has also reached Europe and, while not being comparable to its American counterpart in terms of strength and power, has significantly grown over the past few years. While Cronin's argument is controversial and overstated, cases of EU lobbying concerning the Israeli–Palestinian conflict are also echoed in newspapers. As *EUobserver* reported on 10 March 2010, European Jewish groups heavily lobbied the European Parliament on the text of a resolution in support of the Goldstone Report, the UN's fact-finding mission report following Operation Cast Lead in Gaza in December 2008–January 2009 (Phillips 2010). Similarly, in October 2012 the European Coordination of Committees and Associations for Palestine (ECCP), an umbrella organisation of solidarity movements across Europe, launched a campaign to persuade the EU not to approve the EU–Israeli Agreement on Conformity Assessment and Acceptance of Industrial Products (ECCP 2012). These examples are also supported by the words of an EU official (Interviewee 11), who argued that a large number of NSAs lobby the EU on the Israeli–Palestinian conflict, in a more persistent and extensive way than on any other controversial issue in the Mediterranean region, such as the Western Sahara–Morocco case. Given these among many other examples of lobbying efforts aimed at influencing EU foreign policy towards the Israeli–Palestinian conflict, it is worth asking whether *NSAs matter in EU foreign policymaking towards the Israeli–Palestinian conflict*. Put differently, *do NSAs have an impact on EU foreign policy?*

Questions about who influences whom and who wins/loses in politics have been central to political science for decades, given that they are linked to issues of democracy, legitimacy and equal representation. The role of NSAs and their impact on policies has also been widely discussed in the EU context, but lobbying in EU foreign policy has received extremely limited attention by scholars. This policy area is generally considered as an issue of high politics, which is still in the hands of member states and, as such, does not give rise to lobbying actions (e.g., Coen and Richardson 2009). However, empirical evidence shows that this is not the case (cf. Dembinski and Joachim 2008; Joachim and Dembinski 2011; Voltolini 2012). Thus, this book aims to shed light on lobbying in EU foreign policy and, to this purpose, investigates *who these NSAs are, what and how they lobby* and *in what venues and at what level they carry out their activities.*

In empirical terms, these questions will be answered in the exploratory case study of EU foreign policy towards the Israeli–Palestinian conflict. To be precise, EU 'foreign policy' is here understood as 'the sum of what the EU and its member states do in international relations' (Hill 1998: 18). It thus includes declarations, decisions and actions in different areas, namely economic relations, developmental policies and all those areas that have external impact, not being limited to the Common Foreign and Security Policy (CFSP) and Common Security and Defence Policy (CSDP).[1] As for the definition of NSAs, this book draws on and adapts the definition provided by Beyers *et al.* (2008), which conceives of NSAs as individuals or groups that conduct activities aimed at influencing the policy-making process and display three key features.[2] First, they have a minimum level of organisation (which can be very formal like an NGO, or more loose like solidarity movements);[3] second, they are autonomous of the government (autonomy does not mean that they cannot receive public funding, but simply that the government does not play a role in the running of the NSA); and, third, they aim to play a role in EU foreign policy-making (but do not aim at any governing position).[4] As will be shown in Chapter 3, business actors, NGOs, solidarity movements, think tanks, the media and individuals are included in the analysis. Political parties, trade unions, cultural associations and criminal organisations are not part of the dataset.[5]

Lobbying in EU foreign policy towards the Israeli–Palestinian conflict will be analysed by tackling three interrelated questions. First, it is asked *what role, if any, NSAs play in EU foreign policy-making towards the Israeli–Palestinian conflict*. The concept of role allows us to understand who these actors are and how they act, encapsulating, at the same time, the idea that they are embedded in the social context and that lobbying is based on social interactions between the policy-makers and NSAs. Distinguishing among roles will help us to understand NSA–EU forms of interaction and how they reciprocally define themselves in these relations. More specifically, three types of roles will be identified in the following chapters, namely the dialogue-builder, the voice-articulator and the opponent.

The second question addressed in the book asks *what types of instruments NSAs rely on in their lobbying activities*, thus focusing on how NSAs lobby. Given the informational nature of lobbying in the EU (i.e., provision of information), ideational tools and, more specifically, frames are central to the analysis. Frames can be defined as 'a way of selecting, organising, interpreting and making sense of a complex reality to provide guideposts for knowing, analysing, persuading and acting' (Rein and Schön 1993: 146). It will be shown that NSAs rely on different types of frames (defined as technical, mixed and political frames), which lead to different forms of contribution to EU policies. The roles played by NSAs are the basis on which frames are developed and travel from NSAs to the EU (and vice versa). Focusing on this aspect will therefore lead to a better understanding of how NSAs get involved in the EU foreign policy-making process.

Finally, given the multi-level nature of the EU and the important role that member states play in EU policy-making, it is crucial to examine what links exist between the national and EU levels as far as lobbying is concerned. The concept of level is useful not only to analyse 'where' NSAs lobby, but also to understand whether NSAs based in member states take the EU level into account and, if so, how. In other words, *how are the EU and national levels linked when NSAs lobby on foreign policy issues?* By providing an overview of how NSAs rely (or not) on the national level to influence EU policies, this book tackles a central question related to the multi-level governance structure of the EU and the fundamental role that member states play in policy-making. Investigating this aspect will not only explain the differences between the national and European arenas, but it will also shed light on the level of integration of EU foreign policy and how lobbying has been Europeanised.

What I will show in the book is that NSAs matter and are key players in EU foreign policy-making. I will demonstrate how the participation of NSAs in the EU's policy-making process is shaped by the role they play and the frames they use. While NSAs at the national level tend to adopt an adversarial attitude that does not favour dialogue between them and policy-makers, and to frame their discourse in political terms, NSAs lobbying the EU have a different approach. They tend to play a more consensual role, which does not challenge the EU's actorness but contributes to the formulation of policies towards Israel and Palestine. Through interactions, NSAs and EU institutions produce new frames that are translated into the policy-making process. The more NSAs' lobbying relies on technical frames, the more significant their role in the policy process is. Finally, the book argues that, while there is a partial Europeanisation of lobbying, the EU and national levels tend to remain quite 'disentangled' from each other. Integration between lobbying in the EU and national arenas exists only to a limited extent, showing that EU and national foreign policies are still running on relatively separate and complementary tracks.

The framework I propose for investigating lobbying in EU foreign policy touches upon issues that are often discussed in the literature on interest groups, but reinterprets them through constructivist insights. Instead of adopting the predominant rationalist view that NSAs and EU institutions have fixed preferences and engage in exchange relations, I am interested in the embeddedness of actors who can only make sense of the world through social interactions. A constructivist view understands the social world as the result of structures and processes based on intersubjective and collective meaning construction. Interactions are the basis through which actors create and transfer knowledge about events and situations. In other words, knowledge is shaped by 'the context of and with reference to collective or intersubjective understandings, including rules and language' (Adler 2002: 100).

Metaphorically, NSAs' lobbying can be compared to the actions on the stage of a theatre. These actions are all interconnected and each player depends on the others in order to perform their part. The performance is not just the exact reproduction of the written text, but the result of the interactions among actors, who interpret the story and adapt to each other when developing the script. Moreover, the script cannot be performed by each single actor individually; rather, the interactions among them are a necessary condition for the performance to take place. The identities and behaviours of the characters are shaped not only by each actor's interpretation of the role, but also by the stage on which they act and the interactions that are developed on it. The script provides the boundaries within which the performance develops (see Goffman 1971).

This book can be read in different ways. It can be seen as an attempt to tell a story that combines the literature on EU foreign policy and on lobbying, with a focus on the Israeli–Palestinian conflict. From an empirical perspective, not only does the book offer an original mapping of NSAs involved in EU foreign policy towards Israel and Palestine, it also provides an in-depth analysis of three EU policies towards Israel and Palestine. By doing so, it covers aspects of EU foreign policy-making that have largely gone unnoticed and have not been investigated in a systematic and precise way in the literature (more specifically, the case of the rules of origin of Israeli settlement products, the issue surrounding the Goldstone Report following the conflict in Gaza, and the EU–Israel Agreement on Conformity Assessment and Acceptance of Industrial Products). It also enriches the literature on lobbying in the EU by investigating an under-researched policy area.

This book can also be read in light of the theoretical debates with which it engages. It discusses one of the key questions in the study of politics: who influences whom and who wins/loses in politics. NSAs are indeed part and parcel of policy-making and need to be taken into account in the analysis of policy processes. While this book does not make the claim that NSAs hold ultimate power, it does stress the importance of investigating them when analysing EU foreign policy-making in order to avoid simplified understandings of these processes. Moreover, this book engages with the debate on the role of ideational factors in policy-making and aims to introduce an alternative approach to the rational-choice view in the discussion of lobbying. By relying on insights from the constructivist literature and taking the view that frames result from socially produced knowledge, this book departs from the mainstream analysis of lobbying and sheds lights on social interactions, the centrality of knowledge and embeddedness. The discussion of levels of lobbying also touches upon the broader debates on Europeanisation and EU integration. To what extent have interest groups been affected by the process of EU integration in the field of foreign policy? Are the EU and national levels linked to each other when it comes to lobbying activities? While there is evidence that NSAs have been Europeanised, as direct lobbying takes place at the EU level and there are also several umbrella organisations that put forward the interests of their members, lobbying at the national level is often focused on national foreign policies and internal debates, thus missing a European dimension and links to what happens in Brussels. In this sense, EU integration in foreign policy is still lagging behind compared to other policy areas. It is not just a matter of being active at the EU level; integration should also be mirrored in the discourses and activities that take place in member states.

This book is structured as follows. Chapter 1 will introduce the analytical framework used in this research. It explains the three main analytical dimensions (roles, frames, levels) and how they are employed in the empirical chapters. The two following chapters provide an overview of the 'policy' and 'actors' fields. On the one hand, Chapter 2 analyses the evolution of EU foreign policy towards the Israeli–Palestinian conflict: it shows how the EU has reached a common position towards the conflict, so that disagreement among member states is limited by the overarching framework provided by EU foreign policy. At the same time, the policies and tools at the EU's disposal to engage with Israel and Palestine have increased over time, thus granting new powers and roles to various actors. Chapter 3, on the other hand, gives insights on the trends in the population of NSAs interested in EU foreign policy towards the Israeli–Palestinian conflict by relying on the original dataset mentioned above. Chapters 4 to 6 are devoted to the empirical analysis of the case studies: the case of the rules of origin in EU–Israel trade relations (Chapter 4), the events related to the Goldstone Report (Chapter 5) and the policy process leading to the ACAA between the EU and Israel (Chapter 6). Given that the focus of these chapters is predominantly on the EU level (although a brief section on the national level will be present in each chapter), Chapter 7 complements this analysis by looking in depth at the national level to tackle the third question of the book, with specific focus on the cases of the United Kingdom, France and Germany. Finally, the concluding chapter pulls the threads of the thesis together by comparing and summarising the findings. Conclusions about lobbying in EU foreign policy and the implications for further research are also advanced.

Notes

1 Some scholars consider foreign policy as the Common Foreign and Security Policy (CFSP), while others share the extended definition that encompasses external relations. On the different definitions of EU foreign policy, see Carlsnaes (2007) and Tonra (2000).
2 For other definitions of non-state actors or interest groups, see Alston (2005); Arts (2003); Josselin and Wallace (2001); Kollman (1998).
3 In the case of NSAs classified as individuals (see Chapter 3), they are listed as NSAs because they carry out systematic lobbying although they are not part of an organisation. They act independently, have a clear agenda and have the same intentions as other NSAs.
4 The Palestinian Authority (PA) is considered as a state actor, as it is the body in charge of the government of the West Bank and Gaza Strip following the agreement between the Palestine Liberation Organisation (PLO) and Israel with the Oslo Accords. While the PA has carried out extensive lobbying on the issue of the recognition of Palestine as a member of the UN, these actions are viewed as lobbying by a state.
5 Chambers of commerce, when included, are considered as NSAs, because they do not run for election and are generally funded by their members.

References

Adler, Emanuel. 2002. 'Constructivism and International Relations'. In *Handbook of International Relations*, edited by Walter Carlsnaes, Thomas Risse and Beth A. Simmons. London: SAGE. 95–118.
Alston, Philip, ed. 2005. *Non-State Actors and Human Rights*. Oxford: Oxford University Press.
Arts, Bas. 2003. *Non-State Actors in Global Governance: Three Faces of Power*. 4. Bonn: Max Planck Institute for Research on Collective Goods.

Baumgartner, Frank R. and Beth L. Leech. 1998. *Basic Interests: The Importance of Groups in Politics and Political Science*. Princeton, NJ: Princeton University Press.

Beyers, Jan, Rainer Eising and William Maloney. 2008. 'Researching Interest Group Politics in Europe and Elsewhere: Much We Study, Little We Know?' *West European Politics* 31 (6): 1103–28.

Carlsnaes, Walter. 2007. 'European Foreign Policy'. In *Handbook of European Union Politics*, edited by Knud Erik Jørgensen, Mark A. Pollack and Ben Rosamond. London: SAGE. 545–60.

Coen, David and Jeremy Richardson, eds. 2009. *Lobbying the European Union: Institutions, Actors and Issues*. Oxford: Oxford University Press.

Cronin, David. 2011. *Europe's Alliance with Israel*. London: Pluto Press.

Dembinski, Matthias and Jutta Joachim. 2008. 'Von Der Zusammenarbeit Europäischer Regierungen Zum Europäischen Regieren? Nichtregierungesorganisationen in Der EU-Außenpolitik'. *Forschungsjournal NSB* 21 (2): 42–51.

ECCP, European Coordination of Committees and Associations for Palestine. 2012. 'The EU–Israel ACAA Agreement: Legally Flawed, Encouraging Impunity'. http://www.eccpalestine.org/the-eu-israel-acaa-agreement-legally-flawed-encouraging-impunity/

Goffman, Erving. 1971. *The Presentation of Self in Everyday Life*. Harmondsworth: Penguin.

Haney, Patrick J. and Walt Vanderbush. 1999. 'The Role of Ethnic Interest Groups in US Foreign Policy: The Case of the Cuban American National Foundation'. *International Studies Quarterly* 43 (2): 341–61.

Hill, Christopher. 1998. 'Closing the Capabilities-Expectations Gap'. In *A Common Foreign Policy for Europe?*, edited by John Peterson and Helene Sjursen. London: Routledge. 18–38.

Joachim, Jutta and Matthias Dembinski. 2011. 'A Contradiction in Terms? NGOs, Democracy, and European Foreign and Security Policy'. *Journal of European Public Policy* 18 (8): 1151–68.

Josselin, Daphne and William Wallace. 2001. *Non-State Actors in World Politics*. Basingstoke: Palgrave.

Kollman, Ken. 1998. *Outside Lobbying: Public Opinion and Interest Group Strategies*. Princeton, NJ: Princeton University Press.

Mearsheimer, John J. and Stephen M. Walt. 2006. 'The Israel Lobby and US Foreign Policy'. *London Review of Books* 28 (6): 3–12.

Organski, Abramo F. K. 1990. *The 36 Billion [Dollar]Bargain: Strategy and Politics in US Assistance to Israel*. New York: Columbia University Press.

Paul, David M. and Rachel Anderson Paul. 2009. *Ethnic Lobbies and US Foreign Policy*. London: Lynne Rienner.

Phillips, Leigh. 2010. 'Despite Heavy Lobbying, EU Parliament Endorses Goldstone Report'. *EUobserver* 10 March. http://euobserver.com/foreign/29650

Rein, Martin and Donald Schön. 1993. 'Reframing Policy Discourse'. In *The Argumentative Turn in Policy Analysis and Planning*, edited by Frank Fischer and John Forester. Durham, NC/London: Duke University Press. 145–66.

Tonra, Ben. 2000. 'Mapping EU Foreign Policy Studies'. *Journal of European Public Policy* 7 (1): 163–9.

Trice, Robert H. 1976. *Interest Groups and the Foreign Policy Process: US Policy in the Middle East*. Beverly Hills: SAGE.

Voltolini, Benedetta. 2012. *The Role of Non-State Actors in EU Policies towards the Israeli–Palestinian Conflict*. Occasional Paper 99. Paris: EU ISS.

1 Exploring lobbying in EU foreign policy-making

The aim of this book is to understand how non-state actor (NSAs) participate in the EU's foreign policy-making process and what influence they have on EU foreign policy, in particular in the case of the Israeli–Palestinian conflict. This research topic fits within the broader interest in political science and International Relations about who influences whom and who wins/loses in politics. These questions indeed raise concerns in terms of democracy, legitimacy of policies and power of different types of actors (either states or NGOs and business groups). Understanding who participates in the policy-making process, how different actors act and whom they target is also of central interest in the case of the European Union (EU), where the engagement with NSAs, such as business groups, NGOs, think tanks and solidarity movements, has become part and parcel of the policy-making process. EU foreign policy is no exception to this trend, where a plethora of NSAs constantly aim at being involved in and indeed shaping EU foreign policies.

The main argument of the book is that NSAs are crucial actors in EU foreign policy-making and manage, in different ways, to influence EU policies. NSAs' participation in and their impact on EU foreign policy-making depends on how they interact with EU and national institutions, on the ideational tools they use and whom they target when lobbying. Three aspects are therefore fundamental in the understanding of lobbying in the EU's foreign policy-making process. First, it is crucial to investigate the *role* played by NSAs, namely who these actors are and what they do. The concept of role provides us with an analytical tool to encapsulate different forms of social interactions between NSAs and the EU, and to highlight how NSAs are embedded in specific contexts. On the basis of the forms of social interactions, three roles will be identified in this chapter, namely the dialogue-builder, the voice-articulator and the opponent. Second, it is important to explore how they act – that is, how NSAs try to influence EU policies. Here the concept of *frames* – defined as 'a way of selecting, organising, interpreting and making sense of a complex reality to provide guideposts for knowing, analysing, persuading and acting' (Rein and Schön 1993: 146) – helps to shed light on the ideational element through which lobbying is conducted and how new information and knowledge can enter the policy process. Roles represent the basis on which frames travel and get developed. Third, the *level* (national or

European) at which lobbying takes place (and thus whom NSAs target) is indispensable to understanding lobbying in EU foreign policy, given the multi-level character of the EU and the crucial role that member states play in it. What we observe is that NSAs interacting with the EU in a consensual way, which does not challenge the EU's actorness, and relying on technical frames tend to be more involved in the policy-making process and have an impact on EU policies towards Israel and Palestine. In contrast, NSAs tend to adopt an adversarial attitude and to frame their discourse in political terms at the national level. Moreover, lobbying activities at the two levels tend to be disentangled, with scant integration between the two arenas.

This chapter delineates in greater detail the analytical framework that is used to investigate lobbying in EU foreign policy, and is organised as follows. First, I will summarise the main trends in the literature on EU foreign policy and on lobbying. By situating my theoretical argument within these debates, I will also develop the analytical framework that will be used in the rest of the book. In particular, I will show that constructivist insights, highlighting that the world is socially thick and that knowledge gets developed and travels through social interactions, could help us form a complete picture of lobbying in EU foreign policy. This is followed by development of the three elements that form the analytical framework of the book. In the second section I will focus on the roles played by NSAs and how different types of role matter in lobbying the EU. I will then turn to frames in the third section and explore the relevance of framing processes in lobbying efforts. Finally, in the fourth section I will discuss lobbying in the context of the EU's multi-level system and how NSAs' activities vary accordingly. Before the concluding section will pull the threads together and pave the way for the empirical analysis in the chapters to follow, the methodology and research design adopted will be presented.

EU foreign policy and non-state actors

The literature on EU foreign policy and that on lobbying and NSAs have not talked to each other a great deal. These two sets of literature have developed separate research patterns, with different areas of interest and limited exchanges. On the one hand, the literature on EU foreign policy has focused on institutional actors such as member states or institutions, while that on NSAs has almost exclusively investigated all areas of EU policies but foreign policy. On the other hand, the literature on EU foreign policy has progressively seen an increased dialogue among different theoretical perspectives, which can be summarised as a debate between rationalists and constructivists. In contrast, the literature on EU lobbying has been mainly dominated by a rational-choice approach, whereby lobbying has been conceived as a strategic exchange between the EU and interest groups in the pursuit of their pre-given interests. Even when considering ideational factors, such as frames, the idea of strategy as a rational calculation, encapsulated in the idea of spinning, has been preponderant.

In preparing the ground for the framework that I will present in the following pages, it is important to offer a brief overview of the most salient aspects of these sets of literature and see how we can combine the two 'stories' that the literature on EU foreign policy and on lobbying tell separately.

Theorising EU foreign policy

The study of EU foreign policy has undoubtedly grown since its beginnings, not only in quantity but also in terms of the disciplinary perspectives on which it has been based. The main focus of discussion has for a long time been on the existence and/or definition of a European foreign policy (for overviews, see Nuttall 2000; Carlsnaes 2007), to what extent and in what ways the EU is an actor on the international stage (e.g., Manners 2002; Dûchene 1973; K. E. Smith 2005; Bull 1982; Damro 2012; Tocci 2008). While these debates are still ongoing, many scholars have also shifted the discussion to other issues, such as the impact of EU foreign policy (e.g., Ginsberg 1999; Tocci 2007) or the conditions that determine its effectiveness (e.g., da Conceição-Heldt and Meunier 2014; Bouris 2012; Niemann and Bretherton 2013). Moreover, increasing attention has been paid to EU foreign policy-making, with the specific aim of identifying who performs EU foreign policy, in which ways, and how the policy process works (e.g., Bicchi 2010; Vanhoonacker and Pomorska 2013; Davis Cross 2010).

Despite numerous insights from different disciplines such as International Relations, Comparative Politics, Governance Studies and Policy Analysis, it can be argued that there are two main explanations of EU foreign policy-making: rationalist and constructivist approaches (cf. Bicchi 2007). This debate reflects similar trends in International Relations (cf. Checkel and Moravcsik 2001) as well as in public policy (Fischer and Forester 1993; Goldstein and Keohane 1993; Béland and Cox 2011a). From a rationalist or rational-choice view, which has long been the dominant paradigm in the literature on EU foreign policy (S. Smith 2000), individuals are the basic unit of analysis (methodological individualism) and all explanations can be reduced to the properties of individual actors. These, following what March and Olsen (1998) call the 'logic of consequentiality', aim to maximise their exogenously determined and fixed preferences in a context in which they face strategic and institutional constraints (Pollack 2007). Therefore, cooperation among member states at the EU level is seen more as the response to systemic factors and/or reflecting the interests of EU member states, who negotiate and bargain in order to promote their national interests (Hyde-Price 2006, 2008; Hoffmann 2000; Moravcsik 1998).

In contrast, constructivists, regardless of the strand to which they belong,[1] share the view that reality and knowledge are socially constructed; that is, the social world is the result of structures and processes based on intersubjective and collective meanings (Berger and Luckmann 1966; Adler 2002) and that agents and structures are mutually constituted (Giddens 1979, 1984) – that is, they are ontologically dependent on each other and are involved in the production of social phenomena (Wendt 1987, 1998, 1999). Actors' preferences are socially defined and their actions conform to a 'logic of appropriateness', according to which they 'follow rules that associate particular identities to particular situations, approaching individual opportunities for action by assessing similarities between current identities and choice dilemmas and more general concepts of self and situations' (March and Olsen 1998: 951). As a result, actors behave on the basis of the social environment they are embedded in, internalising the norms, rules and principles of action of each specific context. This process, leading to compliance with the rules of a given community and to the progressive adoption of certain behaviours independently from material gains or sanctions, is defined as 'socialisation' (Checkel 2005).

Not only have constructivist approaches offered an alternative explanation to the rational-choice view of EU foreign policy-making, they have also opened up the space for the investigation of new issues such as identity, actorness and, more generally, the role of ideational factors in the policy-making process (e.g., Tonra 2003; Tonra and Christiansen 2004; Jørgensen 2004; Knodt and Princen 2003; Lucarelli and Manners 2006; Bretherton and Vogler 2006). Several scholars have shown the relevance of constructivist insights to explain the process of institutionalisation of foreign and security policy via socialisation (M. E. Smith 2004a, 2004b), to show how new EU initiatives in foreign policy are the result of the social construction of knowledge by EU actors (Bicchi 2007) and how normative commitments shape EU external policies (e.g., Manners 2002; Sedelmeier 2003, 2005). This interest in ideational factors has also fostered the study of epistemic communities (e.g., Davis Cross 2013; Faleg 2012) and of communities of practice (Bicchi 2011) in shaping EU foreign policy. Moreover, various scholars have also discussed how there is a need to expand our understanding on the ways in which interactions take place. Instead of assuming, as rationalists do, that EU foreign policy is the result of bargaining among member states who aim to maximise their goals, it has been convincingly shown that actors also rely on different forms of interaction defined as arguing (Risse 2000), persuasion (Checkel 2001) and communicative action (Niemann 2004; Sjursen 2006). Actors thus aim to achieve a common understanding and agreement by convincing their counterparts of the validity of their arguments, by persuading the others on the basis of shared values and by engaging in a process of knowledge construction (Bicchi 2014).

In the past 15 years scholars have aimed to combine rationalist and constructivist approaches or, at least, to identify possible complementarities between these paradigms. In particular, it has been argued that these two alternative explanations are not incompatible, as they investigate different aspects. Following this view, actors behave strategically (rationalist account) on the basis of a set of preferences that are socially constructed (constructivist approach) (Fearon and Wendt 2002). For example, Finnermore and Sikkink (1998) see rationality and norms as intertwined in what they call a 'strategic social construction', arguing that a staged approach allows for rational explanations to be the basis of social knowledge and vice versa. This stance in favour of a 'middle ground approach' has also trickled down into research on EU foreign policy. For instance, Youngs

(2004: 415) argues that 'instrumentalist security-oriented dynamics persist within the parameters set by norms defining the EU's identity'. Strategically oriented actors thus act within a normative context, which influences their preferences and identities. Similarly, in her explanation of EU Mediterranean policy Bicchi (2007) relaxes some of the conditions of radical constructivism as far as deter-minism and the absence of cognitive uncertainty are concerned, and proposes a middle-way approach that she calls 'ideational intergovernmentalism'. Elgström (2000) goes in a similar direction by suggesting that the normative component leading to the definition of preferences and common norms is linked to a process of negotiation, in which strategic actions prevail. Another combination of the two paradigms is offered by Schimmelfennig and Sedelmeier's (2005) research on EU enlargement. In their view, rationalist and constructivist explanations tend to work in a complementary way, as rationalist accounts have proven insufficient to account for the decision to enlarge in 2004. While Schimmelfennig (2001) adopts a thin rationalist approach, according to which norms are instrumentally used by actors, in what he calls 'rhetorical action', Sedelmeier's (2005) argument links a thinner constructivist approach to rationalist accounts that include the role of non-material factors, by distinguishing between the regulative and constitutive effects of norms and identities. While regulative effects only influence the behaviour of actors, constitutive norms shape the identities and preferences of the actors involved. In the case of the eastern enlargement, 'the regulative norm provided the necessary condition, which, in combination with strategic behaviour by the policy advocates and the support of some actors motivated by material self-interests, led EU policy towards eastern enlargement' (ibid.: 127).

While debates on the merit of one or the other approach continue, it is clear that the constructivist approach has broadened the field of investigation of EU foreign policy and has increased the relevance of ideational factors as well as social interactions so that a more complete picture of the policy process can be traced. Despite these important insights, the literature on EU foreign policy remains concentrated on states, governmental actors and institutions, leaving the role of NSAs under-researched.[2] Even the work on epistemic communities and communities of practice still attributes a central role to institutional actors. In contrast, scholars have not paid great attention to the role of NSAs, except for some works done on the implementation of EU external policies. In this regard, it has been highlighted how the EU engages with NSAs in conflict resolution or aid policies, especially on the ground (Jünemann 2002; Tocci 2011).

Non-state actors in the EU: a rational-choice field of study?

The literature on interest groups in the EU is characterised by two features. First, this literature has flourished in recent years, but the focus has been on all areas of EU policy-making except foreign policy. Second, this literature has predomi-nantly been characterised by a rational-choice perspective. NSAs and institutions are assumed to be rational and utility-maximising actors, who react and modify their strategies and tactics on the basis of the institutional context in which they act in order to increase their chances of success (e.g., Baumgartner *et al.* 2009; Klüver 2013b). This aspect becomes particularly evident when looking at the way in which scholars working on lobbying treat ideational factors and interaction processes (e.g., Chalmers 2011; Klüver *et al.* 2015).

On the one hand, these trends reflect more general features that can be found in the literature on US interest groups, which has a much longer and established tradition (e.g., Baumgartner and Leech 1998; Baumgartner *et al.* 2009; Hojnacji *et al.* 2012; R. Smith 1995). On the other hand, and unlike in the US literature on interest groups, limited attention has been paid to the field of foreign policy. In the US literature, numerous scholars have investigated the relationship between the state and society and how domestic and transnational dynamics put in motion by NSAs are relevant to explain the foreign policy of states (Skidmore and Hudson 1993; Hill 2003; Hudson 2007; McCormick 1998; Müller and Risse-Kappen 1993; Stoddard 2006; Stone 2000; Abelson 2002; Parmar 2004). Most research agrees that NSAs are able to influence US foreign policy-making and identifies which conditions and factors make this possible (e.g., T. Smith 2000; Paul and Paul 2009; Hägel and Peretz 2005). In this context, the work on ethnic groups has highlighted different variables that explain the impact of NSAs on US policies, ranging from the resources at disposal of these actors, the salience of an issue and the coalition unity (e.g., Rogers 1993) to structural factors such as the level of assimilation into American society (e.g., Uslaner 1995). For example, the Cuban lobby has been able to attain its goals thanks to its organisational model and its incorporation into the formal foreign policy apparatus (e.g., Haney and Vanderbush 1999), while the success of the Japanese lobby is determined by reliance on insiders to the US system, such as American intellectuals or former officials (e.g., Hrebenar and Clive 1995). Others have shown the role of the Israel lobby in shaping US foreign policy in the Middle East, although there is significant disagreement as to the degree of influence that this lobby manages to exert (Organski 1990; Spiegel 1987; Goldberg 1990; Trice 1976; Slater 2009; Miller 2008; Mearsheimer and Walt 2006, 2007, 2009).

Following the expansion of EU competences after the Single European Act in the 1980s, the literature on interest groups in the EU has flourished (see Greenwood 2003; Coen 2007; Beyers *et al.* 2008; Coen and Richardson 2009; Eising 2008). Relying on the findings and theoretical insights of the US literature, the literature on the EU has progressively expanded, so that there is now a 'fusion of US and EU interest group studies' (Baumgartner and Mahoney 2008: 1255). As said, this is evident in the predominant rational-choice perspective that scholars studying lobbying in the EU adopt as well as in the methods they have recently started to employ. Various aspects have been analysed over the past few decades, including patterns of mobilisation and the formation of alliances (e.g., Mahoney 2007a; Klüver 2013b), access to EU institutions (e.g., Bouwen 2002a, 2002b, 2004a, 2004b), venue-shopping (e.g., Princen and Kerremans 2008; Saurugger 2002, 2009), lobbying strategies (Beyers 2004; Bouwen and McCown 2007), the Europeanisation of interest groups and interest intermediation (Klüver 2010; Beyers and Kerremans 2007, 2012; Dür and Mateo 2010, 2012; Grossman and Saurugger 2006; Schmidt 1999; Green Cowles 2001; Eising 2009; Fairbrass 2003) and the professionalisation of NSAs (Klüver and Saurugger 2013). Despite the centrality of the issue, less has been written on the influence that interest groups have on EU policies, due to the difficulty in measuring influence and establishing causality between NSAs' actions and the final policy outcomes (Dür 2008a; Klüver 2009, 2013a). Moreover, changes are also evident in terms of methods, with a recent call for shifting from descriptive and exploratory research based on case studies to confirmatory theory-testing (Coen 2007; Beyers *et al.* 2010; Coen and Richardson 2009). This has led to an increase in the number of studies based on large-N samples and statistical analyses (Klüver 2013a; Mahoney 2008). While this new avenue can be promising, it is too early to reach definitive conclusions about the confirmatory nature of these studies, which are still at an initial stage.[3]

In contrast to the US literature, that on lobbying in the EU has not taken into consideration the more political aspects of EU foreign policy. Most research has been concentrated on those policies where EU competence is exclusive or concurrent, like environmental policy (e.g., Bugdahn 2008; Bunea 2013; Gullberg 2008; Richards and Heard 2005), anti-dumping policy (De Bièvre and Eckhardt 2011) and agricultural policy (e.g., Pappi and Henning 1999). A few scholars have taken into consideration external economic policies (Gerlach 2006; Woll 2007; Trommer 2011; Dür and De Bièvre 2007a, 2007b). Only a few works have been carried out in the domain of common foreign and security policy, such as on the emergence of the Code of Conduct for arms control in the EU (Dembinski and Joachim 2008) and on the small arms regime (Anders 2003).

Lobbying in the EU has been mainly conceived as an exchange between two parties due to their mutual resource dependence. According to Bouwen (2002a), NSAs require access to EU institutions and EU officials need NSAs to fulfil their institutional duties. EU institutions are indeed often understaffed and in need of legitimacy (Bouwen 2002a, 2004a), so that information coming from NSAs is of fundamental importance. In exchange for access, NSAs provide EU officials with information on technical issues, citizen preferences, economic aspects, etc.[4] Because it is generally based on the provision of information and expertise, the interaction between NSAs and EU officials is generally defined as 'informational lobbying' (Chalmers 2011; Broscheid and Coen 2003).

While the factors explaining influence, access or success of lobbying range from the type of information provided (Bouwen 2002a, 2004a) to resources (Klüver 2012), strategies (Chalmers 2013; Bouwen and McCown 2007; Beyers 2004) or institutional constraints (Broscheid and Coen 2003), the vast majority of studies share the underlying assumption that NSAs and EU institutions are rational actors that aim to maximise their goals on the basis of fixed preferences. EU institutions work as constraints or facilitators for NSA lobbying, while NSAs adapt their strategies and behaviours to increase their chance of influencing EU policies. The rational-choice approach becomes particularly evident in the treatment of information, which can be equated to material factors (i.e., goods to be exchanged). Similarly, frames and framing process are strategically used to gain access to EU institutions and influence EU policies. Framing is often referred to as spinning – that is, the strategic way of presenting information or portraying a situation in order to highlight those aspects that are functional to the pursuit of the interest group's demands and preferences (see Entman 1993; Klüver *et al.* 2015; Eising *et al.* 2015).

A notable exception in this literature is offered by Woll (2008), who provides a constructivist interpretation of business–government relations in the context of service trade. By resting on Granovetter's (1985) concept of 'embeddedness', she shows that the political and regulatory context in which corporate actors are embedded shapes the content of firms' rationality, perceptions and preferences. Importantly, she demonstrates that ideas play a constitutive role: 'New identities and beliefs shaped *how* firms redefined their economic interests, while strategic changes explain *when* and *why* they abandoned their traditional demands' (Woll 2008: 151, emphasis in the original). The change in the preferences of economic actors was not the result of the update of information or the reordering of previously held preferences, but came about thanks to social interactions leading to the adoption of new goals. Constructivist insights have also shaped some of the work on NSAs in international relations, convincingly demonstrating the capacity of NSAs to create new norms at the international level as well as the relevance of ideational factors and rule-following behaviours to understand changes in international politics (Finnemore and Sikkink 1998; Keck and Sikkink 1998; O'Neill *et al.* 2004; Joachim 2003). For example, Keck and Sikkink (1998) demonstrate the relevance of norms, principles and ideas in their study on transnational advocacy coalitions, while Joachim (2003) introduces constructivist insights to explain how NGOs managed to influence the UN's agenda on women's rights. Nevertheless, the predominant trend in the literature on NSAs adopts a rationalist perspective, thus missing a part of the story about NSA lobbying: the social embeddedness of actors and the fact that knowledge travels and gets developed through socially thick interactions.

Telling the story of lobbying in EU foreign policy

The existing literature thus focuses either on constructivism and EU foreign policy – but not on NSAs – or on interest groups, but almost exclusively from a rationalist perspective and not in the field of EU foreign policy. This book therefore aims to combine the elements of these different sets of literature and explore how we can form a complete picture of lobbying in the EU's foreign policy-making process, with special emphasis on the Israeli–Palestinian conflict.

While most scholars expect to see limited or null lobbying in EU foreign policy due to its remarkably intergovernmental features (cf. Coen and Richardson 2009), this book demonstrates that NSAs are not only very active, but are also able to influence EU foreign policy-making. Moreover, this book shows that the ideas of socially thick interactions and embeddedness, which are borrowed from constructivism, are crucial for our understanding of how actors behave and create knowledge. Metaphorically, this aspect can be visualised through the image of the 'stage'. Like in the performance of a play, each actor needs other actors to develop the plot and 'make sense' of the story. In the same way, NSAs and decision-makers are intertwined: NSAs' advocacy on EU foreign policy makes sense because of the existence of the EU and, concomitantly, EU decision-makers rely on NSAs to perform their institutional tasks and legitimise their actions.

In addition, particular relevance will be given to the role of ideational factors and to the social construction of knowledge.[5] Following a constructivist understanding, knowledge develops and emerges from social interactions among actors. Information and knowledge become the object of discussion, dialogue and reinterpretation by the parties. By arguing and deliberating, NSAs and EU actors build a new understanding of the situation at hand, which in turn affects EU policies. Thus, bargaining is seen as a much less effective form of interaction, based on a strategic exchange between the parties.

On the basis of these premises, this book develops an analytical framework around three crucial factors: roles, frames and levels. First, the social interactions taking place between NSAs and the EU are encapsulated in the concept of 'roles'. Like the characters in a play, the ways in which actors interact with each other reflect the 'rules of the game' in a specific context. In other words, roles tell us the nature of the 'story' that actors are playing. On the basis of the modes of social interactions, three types of roles are identified: the dialogue-builder, the voice-articulator and the opponent. These roles are the basis on which 'frames', the second element of the framework, travel and get developed. To paraphrase Gamson (1975), framing defines a rim and the boundaries of an activity, and provides the lens through which reality is understood and analysed. Therefore, frames represent the perspective from which actors make sense of the world. Three types of frames are used in the analysis: technical, mixed and political. The third element of the analytical framework is the level of action. Given the EU's multi-level system, NSAs can play at the national level, the EU level or both. While the two levels are part of the same system, namely the EU foreign policy system, we still need to investigate how these arenas are connected when lobbying actions are taken into account.

Playing the role of dialogue-builder in EU foreign policy-making

The roles played by NSAs are the first analytical factor that is necessary to investigate in order to understand how NSAs contribute to the EU's foreign policy-making process. This way, it is also possible to have a complete picture of the functioning of the EU's political system and of the actors involved. Roles are defined here on the basis of the different forms of social interaction that characterise them and, given this socially thick understanding, provide the basis on which frames are constructed and travel. As will be elaborated below, three types of roles have been identified: the dialogue-builder, the voice-articulator and the opponent. This distinction will highlight that different roles are likely to be played at the EU and national levels. Moreover, depending on the role they play, NSAs will have a different impact on EU foreign policy.

The concept of role has been used by Aggestam (2006) and Elgström and Smith (2006) to analyse EU foreign policy. Drawing on sociological role theory and on the analogy of the theatre proposed by Goffmann (1971), this concept provides the link between agent and structure, as a role requires an action but also a structure within which it is performed. Roles become a lens through which actors look at the world and the framework within which their goals are defined, which still leaves some room for strategic behaviour (Aggestam 1999, 2000).[6] By using a metaphor, it can be argued that actors, as in a theatrical play, behave on the basis of a 'script' of norms and values without following it word-by-word. Roles thus provide actors with guidance, as they consist of what other actors expect from them (role expectation), the subjective view of the actor in terms of right/wrong (role conception) and the concrete actions undertaken (role performance). From a sociological perspective, roles are the result of social interactions and processes of socialisation and learning (Aggestam 2004, 2006). In other words, 'actors perform certain roles through symbolic and dramaturgic action' (Sedelmeier 2003: 4). This also means that roles are not simply attributed by others; we choose the role to play by giving our actions certain meaning and sticking to some general 'script'.

By focusing on the forms of social interaction, the concept of role offers interesting insights for a conceptualisation of NSAs in EU foreign policy. First, it highlights the importance of rules and expected behaviour in identifying a set of features that orient actors. Second, actors' performances – that is, their actions and interactions – define the elements that shape their reciprocal behaviours. In the case of the relationships between the EU and NSAs, these forms of social interaction are defined on the basis of the level of contention existing between them. In contentious politics, which is a concept widely used in the literature on social movements (McAdam *et al.* 2001; Tilly and Tarrow 2007), social interactions between two sides vary in terms of confrontation between the claim-makers and the claim-bearers, and the outside/inside position that NSAs have in relation to the state. The dialectical relationship between the two parties and the nature of these social dynamics shape how actors define themselves in relation to their counterpart.

This idea can be linked to the different lobbying strategies discussed in the literature on interest groups. The three main forms of interest representation, namely access, voice and litigation (Beyers 2004; Bouwen and McCown 2007), can be reinterpreted by highlighting the nature and the degree of contestation in the interactions between the EU and NSAs. To start with, access is a form of inside lobbying,[7] through which NSAs approach policy-makers directly and in informal settings (behind the scenes), so that interactions occur outside the reach of public scrutiny. The parties of the interaction recognise each other as partners, so that interactions are mainly consensual and cooperative (Beyers 2004). In contrast, voice is a form of representation based on conveying information and knowledge in public spheres, where the interactions between policy-makers and

NSAs are visible to a larger audience. This approach can take two forms: 'information politics' and 'protest politics' (Beyers 2004). On the one hand, information politics consists in the organisation of public events such as seminars, workshops, etc. or in the publication of articles in newspapers, on websites, etc. as ways to transmit information at strategic decision points. It might reach the public at large, but is mainly aimed at specialised audiences or key policymakers. On the other hand, protest politics aims at attracting attention and expanding the conflict (Beyers 2004; Coen 1998). It can be equated with constituency-building strategies, as it is a way to target politicians indirectly, by 'gaining support of individual voters and citizens, who, in turn, express their policy preferences to political decision makers' (Hillman and Hitt 1999: 834).[8] Examples of protest politics are letter-campaigns, demonstrations, etc. to express dissent with regard to certain policies and decisions. While information politics can lead to cooperation, especially when it is in the form of workshops and seminars, protest politics reflects an adversarial stance that openly criticises the EU. Finally, litigation, which is widely used in the USA, is a form of interest representation based on judicial means. NSAs file cases to courts, make use of the *amicus curiae* briefs to express their views on certain issues and show the consequences of potential outcomes, and push courts in order to have rulings that favour their objectives (see de Figueiredo and de Figueiredo 2002; Alter and Vargas 2000; Rubin *et al.* 2001). In the EU multi-level system, two types of court are available: national courts and the European Court of Justice (ECJ). Generally, 'private parties' disputes are brought to the Court through the preliminary reference mechanism of Article 234 of the treaties' (Bouwen and McCown 2007: 426), now article 267 of the Treaty on the Functioning of the European Union. This article provides for the ECJ to give preliminary rulings on the interpretation of the treaties and on the validity and interpretation of acts of EU institutions, bodies and agencies. National tribunals may (or in certain cases are obliged to) refer to the ECJ, if they have a question concerning the aforementioned points. Litigation is therefore a 'strategy for targeting EU policy that begins at the national level, by bringing a case in a national court, based on a point of EU law' (ibid.). Not only can the ECJ's decisions remove national legislation, they can also shape the form future legislation will take.[9] National courts can also be used to file cases concerning purely national aspects, so that there are no or limited repercussions at the EU level.

Moreover, the political system itself shapes the type of interaction. Mahoney (2007b, 2008) and Woll (2012) show that the EU is a context where interactions tend to be more consensual and cooperative than in the USA due to the political opportunity structure in which NSAs act. The EU is a consensus-oriented system, which favours a cooperative approach ('the soft-spoken') (ibid.). In a similar vein, and recalling the debate in International Relations, two communicative interaction modes define how interest groups interact with governmental institutions, namely bargaining and arguing (Beyers 2008). The former is based on the promises and costs incurred if a particular exchange of resources does not take place. The latter describes an interaction in which the parties are open to change their minds and try to persuade each other on the basis of the better argument. Risse (2000: 7) convincingly maintains that arguing consists in a process of persuasion of the normative validity of one's argument and the attempt to achieve a communicative consensus on the situation. Similarly, Riddervold (2011: 568) demonstrates that deliberation has an effect on actors' preferences through 'argument-based learning', namely the acceptance by an actor of the validity of another actor's argument which leads to an action. According to this view, it is the better argument that prevails in a process of deliberation and persuasion.

By linking strategies, forms of interaction and the level of contention, I propose three types of role to analyse EU–NSAs relationships: the dialogue-builder, the voice-articulator and the opponent. These roles are then used as basis on which frames, the second analytical factor, travel and get developed, given that the form of social interaction used is also linked to the degree of shared understanding and the construction of meaning reached by NSAs and the EU.

As shown in Table 1.1, the role of dialogue-builder is characterised by the access approach, which allows for cooperative social interactions. NSAs might disagree with the policies implemented by the EU, but they cooperate and establish a dialogue with EU officials and politicians to identify alternative perspectives and ways to deal with the issues at stake. Interactions are based on arguing and deliberation with a view to reaching mutual and shared

Table 1.1 Categories of NSA roles

	The dialogue-builder	*The voice-articulator*	*The opponent*
Approach	Access	Information politics	Protest politics and litigation
Form of social interaction	Cooperative and dialogical	Mixed between cooperative and contentious	Confrontational and contentious
Style	Arguing and persuasion	Challenging, a mix of bargaining and arguing	Contestation, no room for consensual interactions
Target audience	Officials and policy-makers	Public, but specifically officials, policy-makers and the informed public	General public
Means	Informal meetings and private communications	Workshops, seminars, editorial/newspaper articles	Judicial means, demonstrations, letter campaigns
Results in	Cooperation and shared understanding/ meaning (argumentation)	Partial cooperation/ partial challenge; shared meaning possible	Conflict and no compromise on a shared meaning/ understanding

Source: Author's own compilation.

understandings. By doing so, they also legitimise EU policies, as they do not challenge their existence per se. The second type of role, called the voice-articulator, is based on information politics, whereby social interactions take a less consensual form. NSAs operate in the public sphere by organising work-shops, seminars or writing op-eds or articles in order to 'give voice' to and amplify their concerns and requests. Given that the targeted audience is generally limited (politicians, officials, informed public), there is some room for the construction and negotiation of meaning. Finally, the role of the opponent implies confrontational and contentious forms of social interaction based on protest poli-tics and litigation. The parties mutually delegitimise each other and define them-selves by opposing and challenging the other.

Therefore, the more NSAs play the role of dialogue-builder, the more likely it is that they influence EU foreign policy, because the EU is 'a system that relies on consensus-building' (Woll 2012: 195) and is aimed at accommodating as many interests as possible (Mahoney 2008).[10] Those that play the role of oppo-nent are generally not succeeding at the EU level, as they do not play according to the rules of the game (H. Müller 2004; Woll 2012). In contrast, NSAs lobbying at the national level tend to play the role of opponent, given the nature of the system, which is a more polarised and politicised context.

Framing EU foreign policy

The 'currency of lobbying in the EU is information' (Chalmers 2013: 39), an aspect over which there is widespread consensus in the literature (e.g., Bouwen 2004b; Chalmers 2011; Broscheid and Coen 2003; Zippel 2004). Material resources are considered as the basis for carrying out lobbying activities, but they do not represent an exchange good as they do in the USA (e.g., funding of elec-toral campaigns). Despite recognising the importance of informational lobbying, most of the literature does not distinguish between information and knowledge, two concepts that, however, differ. Information is refined or relevant data that reduce uncertainty and ambiguity, where data represent the 'raw material' obtained from observation (Majone 1989: 48; Huber 1991: 89). It can take vari-ous forms, such as having a technical nature (e.g., the number of settlements in the West Bank) or giving details concerning the discontent of constituencies. It can be conceived as a good provided by NSAs involved in lobbying, although the relevance of information to policy-makers might change (Klüver 2013a). In contrast, knowledge is a more sophisticated concept, which is linked to the process of framing. Knowledge relates to cognitive frames and the interpretation of information in order to define 'cause–effect' relationships and attribute mean-ing to the surrounding reality (Huber 1991; Bicchi 2014). More specifically, framing consists in the 'process of selecting and emphasising aspects of an issue according to an overriding evaluative or analytical criterion. Policy frames iden-tify what is at stake in an issue' (Daviter 2011: 2). Frames 'promote a particular problem definition, causal interpretation, moral evaluation and/or treatment recommendation' (Entman 1993: 52). By simplifying the world, frames offer roadmaps and give inputs to policy-makers in terms of the possible policies and actions to take. Framing is therefore linked to problem definition, namely the organisation of facts and perceptions and how people understand and think about the reality and the situations around them (Dery 2000), which shapes the nature of the solutions adopted (Bardwell 1991). While framing has increasingly become an issue of attention for scholars of interest groups in the EU, the strategic use of frames and the idea of spinning remain the predominant understanding (e.g., Klüver *et al.* 2015; Eising *et al.* 2015).

This discussion about information and knowledge is part of a broader debate on the role of ideational factors in public policy (see Béland and Cox 2011a; Fischer and Forester 1993; Braun and Busch 1999). While rationalist scholars privilege interest-based explanations and use ideational factors as a residual explanation (cf. Goldstein and Keohane 1993), constructivists give a central role to the explanatory power of ideational variables. From a rationalist perspective, frames are used strategically and with manipulative aims in order to shift preferences in favour of one side or actor (Payne 2001; Riker 1986; Daviter 2007, 2011; Princen 2007, 2011; Baumgartner and Jones 1993; Trommer 2011) or/and to mobilise certain biases in the policy process and define the scope of the conflict between alternatives (Schattschneider 1960; Bachrach and Baratz 1962). Cognitive processes occur at the individual level, as there is no social interaction leading to a common definition of meaning or to the establishment of shared knowledge. Ideational factors are thus considered in the same way as material ones – that is, they can be used strategically to pursue interests (Klüver 2012; Augustin 2008; Sell and Prakash 2004; Zippel 2004). In contrast, constructivist approaches maintain that

> [i]deas are constantly in flux, being reconsidered and redefined as actors communicate and debate with one another. Political action is motivated by ideas, but the goals people articulate and the strategies they develop have feedback effects that further shape their original ideas.
>
> (Béland and Cox 2011b: 5)

While there are different positions within the constructivist camp, they all stress how belief systems and cognitive frameworks are the result of the social embeddedness of individuals and of the collective production of meaning (Braun 1999).[11] This opening to constructivist analyses on the role of ideas is observable in International Relations literature, with the works by, among others, Finnemore and Sikkink (1998), Keck and Sikkink (1998), Legro (2000) and O'Neill *et al.* (2004). Studies of social movements, which have long been characterised by rationalist approaches based on the concepts of resource mobilisation and political opportunity structure, have increasingly opened to constructivist insights and focused on framing as 'an active, creative, constitutive process' (McAdam *et al.* 2001: 16; see also Khagram *et al.* 2002; McClurg Mueller 1992).[12]

As Snow (2004: 384) argues when discussing social movements, 'meanings do not automatically or naturally attach themselves to objects, events or experiences we encounter, but often arise, instead, through interactively based interpretative processes'. Framing is therefore an interaction involving the producer, the receiver and the object of framing (Williams 2004). In the field of EU public policy Radaelli (1999) explains how actors use what he calls 'narratives' to make problems amenable to action and to attribute meaning to what happens around them. He further argues that 'once accepted as a set of shared beliefs about policy, a dominant narrative "frames" policy choices and reorients preferences' (ibid.: 98). This is the result of 'the dialectic relationship between agency (the narrative as resource) and structure (the narrative as cognitive structure within which action is embedded). ... ideas provide the elements *with* which actors work and also a set of structured elements *from* which the actors work' (ibid.: 112, emphasis in the original).[13]

Therefore, arguing and deliberation become the main modes of interaction through which ideas, discourse, norms, etc. spread around and are diffused (Risse 2000; Niemann 2004; H. Müller 2004), as frames are the result of processes of dialogical interaction through which the parties discuss and aim to persuade each other in an attempt to convince the other side of the validity of an argument, and the perceptions of the actors involved change due to this interaction. The more social interactions are characterised by contestation, the less likely it is that frames can smoothly travel and a common understanding will be developed.

On the basis of the features displayed, three types of frames, namely political, technical and mixed frames, can be identified in the case of EU foreign policy. Frames can be distinguished in terms of their content and central argument, namely what is the main focus of the frame (e.g., technical, evoking shared goals, economic impact, etc.) (cf. Mahoney 2008). Moreover, frames can have prognostic and/or diagnostic elements – that is, they identify a problem and its causes and/or provide possible solutions to overcome the situation (Benford and Snow 2000; Kaplan 2008; Dery 2000; Bardwell 1991). Resonance of frames is also an important element in their effectiveness. Snow and Benford (1992) determine the resonance of a frame in terms of its empirical credibility (evidence and empirical support for a claim), experiential commensurability (the extent to which actors are directly affected) and ideational centrality (striking a responsive chord of already existing beliefs and myths).[14] Therefore, there is a 'fit between frames and audiences' previous beliefs, worldviews and life experiences' (Williams 2004: 105) as well as between frames and the experiences and the empirical context of the targeted audience (Joachim 2003). Williams (2004) also adds the credibility of the claim-maker as a precondition for interacting with policy-makers. Furthermore, the salience and hence the resonance of a frame can increase when a focusing event (e.g., a crisis, a disaster or something that focuses the attention of the public on a specific issue or problem) occurs (Mahoney 2008).[15]

As shown in Table 1.2, technical frames are defined as frames that contain arguments that focus on technical, scientific, economic and legal arguments. They highlight, for example, the breach of legal commitments and legislation, the economic impact of EU policies (or lack of action), the feasibility of certain actions.

Table 1.2 Categories of frames used by NSAs

Technical frame	Mixed frame	Political frame
– Focus on technical, scientific, economic and legal arguments (e.g., law violation, economic impact, feasibility) – Empirical credibility – Abundant evidence in the form of legal references, figures, economic impact analyses, etc. – Reference to principles or interests of the EU – Prognostic/diagnostic elements present: nature of a problem identified and solutions proposed – Solutions often provide alternatives to the mainstream approaches	– Arguments mix political claims with some technical and legal references – Empirical evidence provided, especially in terms of facts and events – Mainly references to normative values and the rhetoric–practice gap in EU policies – Prognostic/diagnostic elements are present, but reflect the mainstream view and do not offer alternatives	– Arguments are purely political and refer to discrimination, values, public opinion, etc. – Little empirical credibility (no or limited evidence provided) – Ideational centrality is key (historical events, political sphere) – Emotional component/leverage on beliefs and preconceptions of people and politicians – No prognostic/diagnostic elements

Source: Author's own compilation.

They have a solid empirical credibility, which is achieved thanks to abundant evidence provided in terms of legal references, figures, analyses and well-constructed and solid argumentations. These frames identify the problem in EU foreign policy, but also provide a solution which is generally an alternative view to the mainstream analysis of the EU's foreign policy. Instead of focusing on dichotomies on good/bad, winner/loser, they highlight the legal, economic and technical dimensions of EU policies. The criticisms of the existing status of a policy and its problems are usually counterbalanced with the offer of solutions and alternatives. The proposal/request is presented as a win–win case, in which both the EU and the third party benefit from it. For example, the MATTIN Group, a Ramallah-based NGO, framed EU policy towards Israel as an issue involving the violation of EU legislation and EU obligations under international law. The proposed solution did not call for the suspension of EU–Israeli agreements, but for the redrafting of these agreements to ensure that their implementation by Israel does not endanger EU legal obligations under international law.

In contrast, political frames appeal to values and rest on what Snow and Benford (1992) call ideational centrality: the fact that they evoke an already present belief or myth. Given that these frames make leverage on emotional aspects, beliefs and preconceptions, the argument presented in political frames does not need to be supported by strong evidence. The predominant themes highlight the discriminatory nature of a policy, refer to contentment/discontent of the public opinion or constituencies with a policy, evoke shared goals due to cultural commonalities, call upon historical responsibilities or show the suffering of people. Moreover, the language used and the ideas expressed often evoke the dichotomies of winner/loser and good/bad. By doing (or not doing) something, EU policies unjustly 'punish' someone or make someone 'suffer'. For example, on the occasion of the 2006 World Cup (football) the European Coalition for Israel (EC4I), a group of Christians promoting European–Israel cooperation, launched a campaign in which a comparison was drawn between Hitler's opening of the 1936 Olympic Games and the participation of the Iranian President Mahmoud Ahmadinejad. The EC4I claimed that it was 'history repeating itself' and that allowing Ahmadinejad to go to Germany was a 'bad' and 'morally wrong' action, thereby striking a very sensitive chord in Europe and especially among Germans.[16]

Between these two extremes, there are mixed frames. These propose a mix of political claims with some technical and legal references. There is usually empirical evidence brought in support of these claims. Mainly, the references are to normative values of the EU and the rhetoric–practice gap in EU policies. These frames often invoke the idea of good/bad and/or of moral responsibility. By doing so, they identify a problem, but they do not propose any alternative view of the issue at stake, nor do they offer alternative solutions to the mainstream views based on a 'power game' and on the benefit/drawback leverage (Interviewee 1). For instance, a network of NGOs published a report in 2010 entitled *Dashed Hopes: Continuation of the Gaza Blockade* in which it appealed to the international community to ensure the end of the blockade in Gaza. While the report is rich in details, figures and references to international law, the final recommendations contain a strong normative component, such as 'the international community *must* do its part to ensure that its repeated appeals to end the blockade are finally heeded' (International Federation for Human Rights 2010: 9, emphasis added).

Following the argument advanced in the case of roles, technical frames give NSAs higher possibilities of engagement with EU officials and of influence on EU policies. These frames are more likely to lead to a reframing of EU policies and positions, as the EU system has a rather technocratic or regulatory nature (Majone 1994) and is often in need of information and knowledge to formulate and implement policies (Gornitzka and Sverdrup 2011). While the definition of technocracy or regulatory state might not describe the whole range of EU policies, it is undoubtedly true that the level of politicisation and political contestation in the EU is inferior to that in the member states and a more consensus-building policy mode is predominant (Radaelli 1999; Follesdal and Hix 2006). However, it is likely that the preferred type of frame differs between the Commission/ European External Action Service (EEAS) and the European Parliament (EP). The Commission and the EEAS are predominantly technocratic institutions, the guardians of the treaties, whose primary task is to implement EU policies and foster EU integration. In contrast, the EP is more politicised, being comprised of politicians with an electoral mandate. They are thus more receptive to frames that contain political elements which they can use as leverage on their constituencies in their electoral campaigns. In light of this, we can expect that the EP is also open to mixed frames, which combine a mix of technical and political arguments that suit the more political nature of the Parliament while being apt to the EU machinery as well. The Council of the European Union, given that it is composed of the representatives of member states, is viewed here as a case of lobbying of national governments. In particular, in the case of foreign policy, national representatives take instructions from their capitals due to the sensitivity of this policy area. Unlike the EU level, lobbying at the national level is mainly based on political frames due to the more prominent politicisation of foreign policy issues and the electorate mandate of national politicians.

The level of lobbying and the Europeanisation of NSAs

The EU's foreign policy system is a multi-level system, so that the EU and the national levels are interconnected and mutually dependent on each other (White 2001). Moreover, member states still play a central role in EU foreign policy, which remains a mainly intergovernmental policy field. While NSAs are active at the EU level, as explained above, lobbying at the national level is also expected to take place, given the role that member states play in this policy field. It is therefore important to understand whether – and, if so, how – the national level is used in lobbying activities related to EU foreign policy. Not only is it useful to identify the loci of lobbying and how the national and EU levels are connected when it comes to lobbying, it is also worth comparing the roles and frames used by NSAs at different levels. This will make it possible to assess the level of cohesiveness and integration of the EU foreign policy system: whether NSAs consider it important to lobby at both levels and how different contexts affect lobbying activities.

The argument advanced in the book is that lobbying at the national level is based on the roles of opponents and relies on political frames. This is the result of the different context of national politics, where polarisation and politicisation are more evident than at the EU level. The two levels, despite the creation of umbrella organisations at the EU level and the activities of some actors at both levels, tend to be disentangled and not strongly connected. This means that lobbying at the national level, although there are some exceptions, is focused on national policies and problems, without reaching a strong European dimension. In what follows, I will contextualise my argument in the literature on interest groups to show the relevance of investigating this factor when studying lobbying activities.

The multi-level features of the EU's system are normally discussed in relation to the ideas of venue-shopping and Europeanisation. The former refers to the political opportunity structure of the EU and how the existence of different levels as well as different actors offers numerous possibilities for NSAs. These can indeed choose where to act to promote and reach their goals, an activity that is called 'venue-shopping' (Pralle 2003; Princen and Kerremans 2008). In the EU's multi-level system, venue-shopping occurs both horizontally (i.e., the institution that is targeted) and vertically (i.e., the level – national or EU – at which NSAs decide to act). The choice of the national level implies that NSAs lobby their governments and parliaments in member states to indirectly influence EU policies. National politicians are then supposed to upload NSAs' preferences at the EU level (Mazey and Richardson 2006). It is possible to have a broad conception of the 'national level', extending beyond the strictly geographical borders of a state to include the Permanent Representations (PermReps). PermReps, especially when it comes to foreign policy, are in close contact with their capitals when decisions need to be taken and are staffed with national officials. Targeting any of the PermReps means aiming at persuading and influencing the position of one member state, which will then upload this preference to the EU level (Haynes-Renshaw 2009; Saurugger 2009). Table 1.3 summarises the EU and national channels that NSAs can use in their lobbying.

As for the Europeanisation of interest representation, different aspects have been raised. To start with, Europeanisation can be defined as 'the reorientation of a (sub)national actor's *champ d'activité* towards supranational institutions, politics and/or policy-making' (McCauley 2011: 1020), 'the result of a process whereby the scope of the niche in which domestic interest groups are traditionally active – or *niche width* – expands beyond national borders' (Beyers and Kerremans 2007: 461, emphasis in the original) and the 'exten[sion of] their lobbying activities to the European level' (Klüver 2010: 176). Scholars such as Green Cowles (2001) and Schmidt (1999) have investigated the impact of the EU on the patterns of national interest intermediation with a view to identifying areas of convergence/divergence among different national systems. This top-down research line has shown how differences among national systems (statist, corporatist and pluralist) lead to different trajectories in terms of the changes in lobbying strategies of NSAs based in member states (e.g., Schmidt 1999; Eising 2009; Green Cowles 2001). This refers to the top-down Europeanisation identified by Börzel and Risse (2007), namely the process of transformation of domestic politics and institutions due to the impact exerted by the EU. In contrast, others have considered both the top-down and bottom-up dimensions of Europeanisation, namely the impact of European integration on member states as well as the

Table 1.3 The levels of lobbying

EU LEVEL
- Commission
- EEAS
- Parliament
- ECJ
- EU delegations

NATIONAL LEVEL
- Capitals of member states (government, parliament, national courts)
- Council in its different formations
- Permanent representations
- Embassies on the ground

Source: Author's own compilation.

establishment of distinct structures at the EU level as a consequence of the EU integration (Saurugger 2005: 395–6). This process of uploading, combined with the process of downloading, conceives Europeanisation as encompassing the two dimensions and stressing the circularity and mutual adaptation between the national and EU levels.[17]

Following this latter approach, Balme *et al.* (2002) propose three processes that reflect the modes of Europeanisation of interest groups (cf. Saurugger 2005). The first one, internalisation, is the top-down/downloading movement, according to which local and national actors mobilise and lobby around EU issues at the national level as a result of the increasing importance of EU policies. The second process is externalisation, the direct representation of NSAs' interests at the EU level, while the third is supranationalisation, the establishment of umbrella groups (e.g., federations of associations) at the EU level. This implies that NSAs' lobbying can range from a complete disregard of and disinterest in EU policy to the integration of EU topics in lobbying activities. While in the former case national NSAs just lobby their member states on issues related to national foreign policies, in the latter situation there are various degrees to which NSAs can take the EU dimension into consideration. While it is clear that lobbying at the EU level takes place and this can be equated with forms of uploading, it is also worth comparing the activities at the EU and national levels to identify whether lobbying activities at the domestic level incorporate EU issues (internalisation), as well as the form that externalisation and supranationalisation take. These three patterns are compatible; that is to say, national NSAs can use all these options instead of opting for just one of them, as the more channels they use, the greater the chances of success (e.g., Greenwood 1997, 2003).[18] It is important to note that the form or forms chosen have implications for the EU's foreign policy system per se. For example, if supranationalisation is not combined with internalisation, the integration between levels is quite limited. At the same time, if NSAs active in member states only focus on national foreign policies, and leave lobbying on EU issues to NSAs based in Brussels (or umbrella organisations), the link between EU and national foreign policies is weak and, again, the levels are poorly integrated.

Besides investigating the links and interconnections between levels, it is also worth comparing the EU and national levels to investigate the forms that lobbying takes in these two contexts. As mentioned above, NSAs active at the national level are expected to be playing the role of opponent as well as to use political frames. National arenas are indeed the place where different parties compete on the basis of different political programmes, with the aim of being elected and receiving power. Therefore, there is a higher degree of politicisation than at the EU level, making confrontational stances more likely to be taken. Moreover, strong references to emotional and ideological aspects are more likely to resonate with national public opinions, as political leaders have to appeal to their constituencies.

To summarise, investigating the level of action (national and/or EU) is a key element in the multi-level EU foreign policy system. It gives us the possibility of understanding which patterns NSAs follow to pursue their objectives and of assessing the level of integration in the EU foreign policy system. The more the lobbying activities at the two levels are linked, the more integrated the system is. Conversely, limited actions or inertia at the national level as far as EU foreign policy is concerned show a lower degree of integration. The analysis carried out at the national level is therefore fundamental to understanding the broader framework of lobbying on EU foreign policy towards the Israeli–Palestinian conflict, of which the national level is clearly an aspect. The scope here is limited to understanding how lobbying is conducted at both levels and what types of link exist between the two. It does not consider whether lobbying on national foreign policies has indirect repercussions on EU foreign policy.

Researching EU foreign policy and NSAs

This section aims at providing a short overview of the methodology adopted in this research, with a specific focus on how to address the issue of influence/impact of NSAs and on the case selection and generalisability of the findings. While discussing these aspects, mentions of the methods used will be made to explain how data were collected and analysed.

Understanding how NSAs influence EU policy is one of the thorniest issues in political science and finding direct measures of it is difficult, if not impossible. As Lowery (2013: 19) argues, influence 'is very complex and hard to observe. At best, our research designs capture only brief snapshots – however important – of influence in democratic systems'. Several problems confront the scholars who intend to grasp how much influence NSAs have, starting from the same definition of influence. Discussing what influence means leads to a minefield, where the concepts of power and its three faces (Dür 2008a; Lukes 1974) come to the front. To a great extent the literature on lobbying looks at influence of NSAs in terms of the first face of power (i.e., the ability to shape political decisions in line with their preferences), with the idea that the target of lobbying would have not acted in this way if not coerced, persuaded and/or convinced by the actions of the lobbyist. While some readers might be disappointed, this book adopts a different stance, namely it takes a more nuanced view on the influence or impact of NSAs. More specifically, influence is understood in a constructivist way, according to which the focus is on the relational dimension, namely on how NSAs interact with policy-makers, participate in and contribute to the policy-making process. The book indeed looks at the ideational (framing) processes that lead to the construction or adaptation of frames, thus shaping the cognitive framework on which decisions are then taken. The focus is not so much on the exchange of resources between policy-makers and NSAs, but rather on the social interactions that give rise to new frames for action. The main idea, as expressed above, is that EU and national officials engage with NSAs in a process of framing. The frames that come out of these interactions are, in line with a constructivist thinking, the outcome of a social process, which is not attributable to one single actor, but is the result of the social construction of knowledge. Influence is indeed not unidirectional, but circular in the form of a relation.[19] NSAs' frames are not simply copy-pasted by policy-makers, but the final policy outcome is the result of the contribution of NSAs and all the other actors that are involved in the policy-making process and take part in the framing processes.

To understand the impact of NSAs, we then need to investigate how NSAs participate in the policy-making process and how the interactions between policy-makers and NSAs lead to the creation of new frames. This makes it of utmost importance to investigate lobbying through the lenses of roles, frames and levels, as this focus will allow us to identify the pathways through which NSAs try to lobby the EU (Dür 2008b) and to highlight when these processes of interactions are more successful in translating some of the elements suggested by NSAs into EU policies. Counterfactuals can help us to identify what would have happened in the absence of lobbying. We can indeed argue that NSAs provide important information to policy-makers to which they would probably never have access; they are the reality check that politicians need to see whether their policies are working, and bring in new elements that can be translated into a new frame driving EU foreign policy. Whenever possible, counterfactuals are used in the conclusions of this book and in the concluding sections of the empirical sections, with a view to reflecting on whether the EU would have taken different decisions in the absence of lobbying.

It has also to be kept in mind that the book does not claim that NSAs are all powerful or that all decisions are shaped by them. What it is argued is that these actors are part and parcel of the policy-making process and as such, they play a role in the framing processes which lead to EU decisions. The extent to which their involvement is valued and translates into EU policies depends, as explained above, on the role played, the type of frame used and the levels at which lobbying is conducted. Yet, this clarification does not exclude a second problem, namely the need to show causality and clearly determine that certain factors led to the specific outcome of interest. To deal with this issue, process tracing has been used as one of the primary methods of this research, as it is useful for tracing the process and highlighting the causal chain between causes and effects (cf. Beach and Pedersen 2013; Bennett and Checkel 2014). In line with the constructivist angle of this research,

> [process tracing] is used to identify and study complex ... agent-structure relations [and to provide] a way of studying not only the proposed theoretical concepts and of testing research hypotheses, but also of studying ideational factors, the evolution of social phenomena, and the influence of these phenomena on actors' behaviour.
>
> (Lupovici 2009: 202)

Although Dür (2008b) argues that this method suffers from several weaknesses, including the fact that it relies too heavily on interviews (which in his view are not sufficiently reliable) and does not allow for an assessment of the degree of influence due to the lack of a specific yardstick, it still represents the most suitable approach to answer the questions of this book as well as to investigate social interactions and framing processes from a constructivist angle. In addition, a large number of interviews (see below) were conducted and information was cross-checked across actors and with other primary and secondary sources. Furthermore, the aim of the book is to see how NSAs contributed to the policy-making process, without quantifying it towards a yardstick (but more in relation to each other's efforts). In order to discuss the degree of influence, the preference attainment method is probably more suitable, as there is a comparison between the initial ideal preferences of the actors involved in the policy-making process (both institutions and interest groups) and the final outcome of the decision-making process. Here the researcher checks how preferences have moved along a continuum and towards which interest group the final policy has moved. For example, Klüver (2013a) adopts quantitative text analysis to measure this impact, using consultation documents to assess how the initial proposal of the Commission changed after the consultation procedure. While this method can offer some insights when measuring influence, it completely obscures the process, which is actually the focus and interest of this book.

Having discussed how influence and impact are treated in the book, the second issue that deserves attention relates to the generalisability of the findings of this research. As mentioned in the introduction (and further developed in the conclusions of this book), this research aims to provide an exploratory analysis of the role of NSAs in EU foreign policy. In particular, the focus on EU foreign policy towards the Israeli–Palestinian conflict is determined by the importance that this intractable conflict has on the EU's agenda. Since the 1970s the EU has been vocal on the Israeli–Palestinian conflict and, within the frameworks of the Euro-Mediterranean Partnership/Union for the Mediterranean (EMP/UfM) and the European Neighbourhood Policy (ENP), has developed strong bilateral relations with both Israel and Palestine. While being a very sensitive issue over which member states are often divided, it is also one where convergence of views has been reached. The EU has nowadays a well-defined position towards the Israeli–Palestinian conflict, which is based on two pillars: the two-state solution and respect for international law, international humanitarian law and human rights (Tocci 2009). These two elements define the space of disagreement: member states might differ on how to approach an issue, which policies to implement and how to diplomatically react to events on the ground, but they do so within the overarching framework of the two pillars. Furthermore, EU policy towards the Israeli–Palestinian conflict is an instance of EU foreign policy in the field of conflict resolution in its southern and eastern neighbourhood. Conflict resolution is indeed one of the EU's objectives and over the years the EU has developed a wide range of instruments and policies to promote peace (cf. Tocci 2007).

Within the broader realm of EU–Israel/Palestine relations, the book focuses on three specific cases, which provide a sufficiently broad coverage of the different policies that the EU implements towards its neighbours. In particular, the issue of the rules of origin related to the EU–Israel Association Agreement (Chapter 4), the EU's policy towards the Goldstone Report (UN report) following Operation

Cast Lead in Gaza between December 2008 and January 2009 (Chapter 5) and the case of the EU–Israel Agreement on Conformity Assessment and Acceptance (ACAA) of industrial products (Chapter 6) offer variation in terms of the policy areas covered (trade policy, human rights policy, regulatory policy), the competences of the different institutions involved (e.g., different role of the EP) and the level of salience of these issues (e.g., the Goldstone Report received a lot of media coverage compared to the more technical issue of the rules of origin). Not only do they represent significant instances of the types of policies and instruments that the EU has at its disposal in dealing with its southern neighbourhood, but also these issues are all cases of active NSAs' lobbying. In line with Mahoney (2008), the topics that were mentioned more frequently by NSAs and where lobbying activities were evident were selected for further investigation. Clearly, this approach leaves out the non-decisions and those issues that go unnoticed (Bachrach and Baratz 1962), but it was necessary to limit the investigation to those cases that were traceable.[20]

An analysis of the national level has also been necessary due to the relevance of member states in EU foreign policy and the potential channel the national level represents in lobbying activities. Because it was not possible to investigate all 27 member states, three states were selected: the United Kingdom, Germany and France. These member states are particularly relevant in EU foreign policy-making and, more specifically, in the context of the Israeli–Palestinian conflict. Importantly, they are the three largest member states, displaying strong administrative capabilities and significant economic power, which they can use to influence the policy-making process (P. Müller 2012; Musu 2010). Despite some similarities, they differ with regard to other relevant dimensions: the type of political system, the prevailing form of interest intermediation and the cultural legacies of their past policies. To start with, these states have different political systems which in turn shape the form of interest intermediation as well as the general approach towards NSAs. As explained in Chapter 7, the United Kingdom is an example of a pluralist system, France of a statist model and Germany of a consensual setting. Therefore, it is likely that national political actors respond differently to the pressure and requests coming from NSAs (Eising 2009). Moreover, their historical involvement with the Israeli–Palestinian case has differently shaped their current stance towards the conflict and the parties involved. Given their importance within the EU and the variation on several dimensions, they represent suitable cases to generate a better understanding of the dynamics taking place at the national level and the interaction with the EU level as far as lobbying is concerned.

Empirical evidence has been gathered as follows. Primary sources were used whenever possible, but, given the secretiveness that surrounds both matters of EU foreign policy and lobbying activities, access to information was not always easy. In order to minimise these obstacles, I triangulated different methods and relied on a variety of primary and secondary sources.[21] The literature on EU foreign policy towards the Israeli–Palestinian conflict has provided important inputs to understand the key trends and policy areas that characterise EU policies at both the multilateral and bilateral levels, as well as how the issues analysed fit into the broader picture. Primary and secondary sources have also been used to create an original dataset that contains over 300 NSAs which lobby (or have the potential interest in doing so) on Israel/Palestine (see Chapter 3). Interviews were used to collect further information and to expand the database through the 'snowball effect' method (Corbetta 2003). Between February 2010 and June 2013 I conducted 109 semi-structured interviews with EU and national policy-makers, NSAs and experts in Brussels, London, Paris, Berlin and Israel. Given the guarantee of anonymity to all interviewees, I will not be able to quote their names, although these interviewees will be referred to in the following chapters.[22]

For each case study I have employed process tracing and frame analysis. The former has been used to both reconstruct the 'story' behind the events and, by identifying the critical junctures in the policy process, to reconstruct the temporal sequence of events and the ways in which the EU–NSA relationship has developed (Beach and Pedersen 2013; Bennett and Checkel 2014; George and Bennett 2005). Frame analysis has been used in its interpretative form (Boräng *et al.* 2014; David *et al.* 2011; Goffman 1975; Koenig 2005)[23] in order to identify the prevailing conceptualisations employed by NSAs in written documents (when available) and interviews.[24]

In conclusion, this exploratory research on lobbying in the case of EU foreign policy towards the Israeli–Palestinian conflict allows us to identify broader patterns of interactions between EU/national institutional actors and NSAs. The framework presented in the previous sections is indeed applicable to cases of lobbying in EU foreign policy in the neighbourhood, where the institutional context and the instruments at EU disposal are similar. Moreover, in line with a constructivist approach, this research reaches contingent generalisations – that is, their applicability is limited to a subset of cases and within specific limitations (time, context, culture). This book will therefore highlight patterns of interaction, but their scope and form does not take the form of law-like generalisations that are universally applicable to all cases of EU foreign policy (cf. George and Bennett 2005; Lupovici 2009; Mahoney and Goertz 2006). The concluding chapter will offer further reflections on the applicability and extension of the findings of this research to other instances of EU foreign policy and to the conceptualisation of the interactions between the EU and interest groups.

Conclusions

The main purpose of this book is to investigate lobbying activities in EU foreign policy, with particular focus on the Israeli–Palestinian conflict, to understand who is involved in this process and how NSAs influence EU foreign policy. The central argument is that a complete and thorough understanding of EU foreign policy-making needs to take NSAs into account, as they are not only very active on certain issues, but they are also able to have an impact on EU policies. To show how NSAs participate in the policy-making process, I have developed an analytical framework characterised by three dimensions: roles, frames and levels. These features allow us to identify who these actors are and how they interact with policy-makers (roles), which tools they use in the lobbying activities (frames) and whom they target (levels).

First, the concept of role helps us better capture the social interactions and the embeddedness that characterise lobbying activities in the EU. Roles offer a way to define the actions and reactions of actors, as well as the rules and expected behaviours, and provide the basis on which frames travel and get developed. On the basis of the forms of social interactions and the degree of contention that develops between the EU and NSAs, I have identified three types of role: dialogue-builder, voice-articulator and opponent. The role of dialogue-builder is characterised by an access approach based on direct and behind-closed-doors contacts between the EU and NSAs. There is the development of mutual trust among the parties, who interact in consensual and dialogical ways. In contrast, the role of the opponent is based on a confrontational approach: NSAs rely on protest politics and litigation to challenge EU policies. NSAs do not aim to develop cooperative relations to find a common understanding of the events and how to overcome certain issues. In the middle there is the voice-articulator: NSAs playing this role rely on information politics – that is, they use the public arena to express their claims – but their main targets are policy-makers and the informed public. Although the room for a shared construction of meaning and knowledge is more limited than in the case of NSAs playing the role of dialogue-builder, occasions such as workshops and conferences can still provide the context for an exchange of views and be seen as an attempt to negotiate understanding of the facts and events.

Second, frames tell us how NSAs act – that is, what tools they use in their lobbying. Frames define how actors perceive the world and the basis on which they act. By offering relationships of cause–effect or right–wrong, frames orient and steer action. They are the result of social construction, as meaning and knowledge derive from the social interactions between the producer, the receiver and the object of the framing process. NSAs present certain frames to policy-makers; these frames are then discussed and shaped by the social interactions that define NSA–EU relations. I have suggested three types of frames, namely political, technical and mixed. Political frames are not based on strong evidence in support of the argument proposed, making leverage on emotional aspects linked, for example, to discriminatory aspects, historical memories and moral ideas of good/bad. In contrast, technical frames present well-structured arguments which are based on sound evidence in the form of figures, data, detailed analyses, legal arguments, etc. These frames propose an alternative approach to deal with policy issues and are anchored on key principles and interests of the EU. Finally, mixed frames are based on sound empirical work which relies on some legal and technical references. However, there is always a political element that underpins these narratives, generally the idea of an opposition between good/bad or right/wrong.

Finally, an analysis of lobbying in EU foreign policy needs to consider the level where lobby takes place. NSAs can indeed decide at which level to lobby (national/EU) to influence EU foreign policy. For example, they could use the national channel as a way to exert indirect influence on the EU, or decide to directly target EU institutions. At the same time, it could happen that some actors are active at the EU level, while those working only in member states do not take into account the European dimension and remain focused on national policies. This issue is linked to the question of Europeanisation of lobbying and what patterns it takes, namely internalisation (inclusion of the EU dimension in national lobbying), externalisation (use of the Brussels venue) and supranationalisation (creation of umbrella organisations). Whether Europeanisation takes place and how is an empirical question which will be discussed in the following chapters.

Empirical evidence shows that NSAs carry out significant lobbying activities in the field of EU foreign policy towards the Israeli–Palestinian conflict. This evidence refutes the idea that this policy domain (high politics) is an area where NSAs are comparatively less important and EU policy-makers are more autonomous in taking decisions. Moreover, the claim that the Israeli lobby is powerful and able to steer the course of EU foreign policy (Cronin 2011) does not find supporting evidence in the empirical chapters of this book, which instead offer a more nuanced picture of EU foreign policy-making. NSAs adopting a pro-Israel position do not dictate EU foreign policy, nor do pro-Palestinian NSAs.[25] The picture that emerges shows that different actors participate in the policy-making process and different ideas contribute to policy formulation in a way that goes beyond the 'zero-sum game' that often characterises rationalist perspectives.

A final point, which will be elaborated on in the conclusions of the book, relates to the reasons why NSAs at the EU level take (or are moving towards) a more consensual approach and tend to use technical arguments, while the reverse holds true at the national level. Rationalist arguments would suggest that the roles played and the frames used (as well as any change in this regard) are the result of a strategic choice on the part of NSAs, which aim to increase their chances of success. However, an alternative explanation is that NSAs are socialised according to the context and the 'rules of the game' where they lobby. As defined by Checkel (2005), socialisation is the process of internalisation of the norms and rules of a community. On the basis of constructivist insights, it is plausible to suggest that social interactions lead to the socialisation of NSAs. In this case, NSAs active at the EU level are socialised to the consensual policy-making of EU institutions and their more technocratic and regulatory nature. In contrast, NSAs based in member states interiorise the norms and rules of the national political system, where the degree of politicisation and contestation is higher. This possible explanation will be useful in the conclusions of the book, when the findings of this research will be summed up and assessed.

To summarise, by analysing the roles played by NSAs, the frames and the level where lobbying activities are carried out, this book will explain lobbying in EU foreign policy-making by stressing the social interactions between the EU and NSAs and how social interactions are the basis on which frames travel and develop. As said, lobbying can be likened to performing on a stage, where the performance is not the result of what one actor does on the basis of a rational calculation, but also depends on where, how and with whom this actor acts. In the end, this framework will also provide insights in terms of the degree of influence that NSAs have on EU foreign policy, showing how certain roles and frames are more conducive to the participation of NSAs in the EU policy process.

Borrowing insights from constructivism, this book aims to see how far this approach carries the analysis, without testing it against a rationalist stance. Given the limited amount of work on EU foreign policy and lobbying, it is an exploratory and critical analysis, which intends to open up a new research line as well as to combine two sets of literature that have rarely spoken to each other.

Notes

1 There are different ways of categorising constructivists (see Checkel 2007 and Adler 2002). The main distinction rests on differences in epistemology and philosophy of science.
2 For some exceptions, see Dembinski and Joachim (2008); Anders (2003); Voltolini (2012).
3 For example, see the INTEREURO project, which aims 'to get a more comprehensive theoretical and empirical understanding of the role that interest groups play in the European polity' (www.intereuro.eu, last accessed 20 December 2014). See also 'Special Issue: Methodological Issues of Large-N Research on Interest Representation, Interest Groups and Advocacy', 3 (2), 2014, available at: http://www.palgrave-journals. com/iga/journal/v3/n2/index.html (last accessed 20 December 2014).
4 Unlike the US context, material resources such as financial incentives and support for electoral campaigns are not relevant in EU lobbying due to the non-elective character of Commission officials and the less relevant role of EU parliamentary elections.
5 On this aspect, see also the constructivist and social-psychological literature on social movements (e.g., McClurg Mueller 1992).
6 Similarly, Bradbury *et al.* (1972) highlight that actors' actions are not entirely dictated by the structure, but there is an interaction between structure and agents. See also Saurugger (2010).
7 On the distinction between inside and outside lobbying, see Kollmann (1998).
8 Hillman and Hitt's description of constituency-building strategy resembles that of 'voice strategy' given by Beyers when it comes to activities and tactics. According to the former, the resource exchanged is 'constituent support' and is channelled indirectly 'by gaining support of individual voters and citizens, who, in turn, express their policy preferences to political decision makers' (Hillman and Hitt 1999: 834). For Beyers (2004), voice strategies are used to convey information through public voicing of policy positions. The focus is less on the support provided by the electors and more on the form in which information is communicated.
9 On the role of the ECJ, see also Stone Sweet *et al.* (2001) and McCown (2009).
10 This predominance of consensual policy-making has also been identified for the European Parliament (cf. Settembri 2006; Hix and Hoyland 2011) and the Council (Lewis 2008).
11 Ideational elements are variously described as frames (Crespy 2010), narratives (Radaelli 1999) and discursive practices (Schmidt 2011; Schmidt and Radaelli 2004; Holzscheiter 2005).
12 Closer to constructivists for their strong emphasis on the role of norms, symbols and ideas are the rationalist approaches used by Edelman (1964) on the symbolic uses of politics and by Schimmelfennig (2001) on rhetorical action/entrapment.

13 Recently, Bicchi (2014) investigated knowledge in EU foreign policy-making. By using a definition of knowledge akin to framing, she focuses on the communities of practice formed by European diplomats. Her attention is more on the practices that develop among actors and lead to knowledge construction. This book shares the constructivist perspective on framing, but remains anchored in the traditional constructivist discussion on the role of knowledge – in other words, the impact that framing has on social interactions.

14 On ideational centrality, see also Gamson (2004), who claims that frames become stronger when they resonate with cultural narrations and the cultural heritage of a group.

15 When discussing framing in relation to social movements, Gerhards (1995) describes the dimensions of an ideal type of frame. This includes not only the issue and its interpretation as a social problem, but also the identification of causal agents for the problem, the interpretation of goals and chances of success, the addressee for the protest and the legitimisation of the actors themselves. These dimensions are, however, more relevant to social movements than NSAs as interpreted here, and to the mobilisation phase, which is not investigated in this thesis.

16 This is the content of their campaign, as published on their website: '70 years ago, in 1936, Adolf Hitler marched into Berlin's newly built Olympiastadion to open the XI Summer Olympic games. He made no secret of his ambition to wipe out the Jewish people and in less than nine short years, 6 million Jews were dead. This summer Iranian President Mahmoud Ahmadinejad – a man who has openly stated his intention to 'wipe Israel off the map' – wants to come to the World Cup in Germany: a sporting contest that culminates in the exact same stadium. Some see just a game. We see history repeating itself' (European Coalition for Israel 2013).

17 Saurugger's view is akin to the third approach to Europeanisation presented by Börzel and Risse (2007), who, however, argue that only downloading Europeanisation (i.e., the impact on the domestic level) is useful and deserves investigation.

18 For the reasons why NSAs Europeanise (or not) their activities, see Beyers and Kerremans (2012) and Beyers (2002) for the link between Europeanisation and access at the national level; Klüver (2010) and Beyers and Kerremans (2007) for resources; McCauley (2011) for the distinction between EU opportunities as 'out of reach' (because of the lack of resources, access, etc.) or 'out of focus' (conscious distancing from them).

19 Cf. Lowery (2013) on the symmetrical feedback.

20 Other topics (such as the issue of the Palestinian statehood in the United Nations, the problem of labelling of goods, etc.) that can also be used as instances of lobbying will be mentioned in the book, but will not constitute the bulk of the analysis.

21 On triangulation, see Davies (2001); Bryman (2004).

22 For the list of interviews, see Appendix 2.

23 This approach can be criticised, given the potential arbitrariness in the identification of frames. To limit this potential bias, the criteria used have been specified (see section on frames). Moreover, the empirical chapters will highlight the evidence referring to the various elements of the frames, so that the reader has the possibility of following the procedure applied in the analysis.

24 Interviews were not recorded, given previous experiences in which respondents refused to be recorded or did not feel at ease knowing that the interview was recorded. Moreover, the topic investigated is quite sensitive: Israel/Palestine has always been a delicate issue and lobbying is also covered by some secrecy. Notes were taken during the interview and typed up after each interview. Direct quotations will therefore not be used.

25 On these definitions, see Chapter 3.

References

Abelson, Donald E. 2002. *Do Think Tanks Matter? Assessing the Impact of Public Policy Institutes*. Montreal: McGill-Queen's University Press.

Adler, Emanuel. 2002. 'Constructivism and International Relations'. In *Handbook of International Relations*, edited by Walter Carlsnaes, Thomas Risse and Beth A. Simmons. London: SAGE. 95–118.

Aggestam, Lisbeth. 1999. *Role Conceptions and the Politics of Identity in Foreign Policy*. WP 99/8. ARENA Working Papers. Oslo: Arena.

———. 2000. 'A Common Foreign and Security Policy: Role Conceptions and the Politics of Identity in the EU'. In *Security and Identity in Europe: Exploring the New Agenda*, by Lisbeth Aggestam and Adrian Hyde-Price. London/Basingstoke: Palgrave Macmillan. 86–115.

———. 2004. 'Role-Identity and the Europeanisation of Foreign Policy: A Political-Cultural Approach'. In *Rethinking European Union Foreign Policy*, edited by Ben Tonra and Thomas Christiansen. Manchester: Manchester University Press. 81–98.

———. 2006. 'Role Theory and European Foreign Policy: A Framework of Analysis'. In *The European Union's Roles in International Politics: Concepts and Analysis*, edited by Ole Elgström and Michael Smith. Abingdon/New York: Routledge. 11–29.

Alter, Karen J. and Jeannette Vargas. 2000. 'Explaining Variation in the Use of European Litigation Strategies'. *Comparative Political Studies* 33 (4): 452–82.

Anders, Holger. 2003. *The Role of Non-State Actors in the European Small Arms Regime*. Working Paper 4. Peace Studies Papers, No. 4. Bradford: University of Bradford.

Augustìn, Lise Rolandsen. 2008. 'Civil Society Participation in EU Gender Policy-Making: Framing Strategies and Institutional Constraints'. *Parliamentary Affairs* 61 (3): 505–17.

Bachrach, Peter and Morton Sachs Baratz. 1962. 'Two Faces of Power'. *American Political Science Review* 56 (4): 947–52.

Balme, Richard, Didier Chabanet and Vincent Wright, eds. 2002. *L'action collective en Europe*. Paris: Presses de Sciences Po.

Bardwell, Lisa V. 1991. 'Problem-Framing: A Perspective on Environmental Problem-Solving'. *Environmental Management* 15 (5): 603–12.

Baumgartner, Frank and Bryan D. Jones. 1993. *Agendas and Instability in American Politics*. Chicago: University of Chicago Press.

Baumgartner, Frank and Christine Mahoney. 2008. 'The Two Faces of Framing'. *European Union Politics* 9 (3): 435–49.

Baumgartner, Frank R., Jeffrey M. Berry, Marie Hojnacji, David C. Kimball and Beth L. Leech. 2009. *Lobbying and Policy Change*. Chicago: University of Chicago Press.

Baumgartner, Frank R. and Beth L. Leech. 1998. *Basic Interests: The Importance of Groups in Politics and Political Science*. Princeton, NJ: Princeton University Press.

Beach, Derek and Rasmus Brun Pedersen. 2013. *Process-Tracing Methods*. Michigan: University of Michigan.

Béland, Daniel and Robert Henry Cox, eds. 2011a. *Ideas and Politics in Social Science Research*. New York: Oxford University Press.

———. 2011b. 'Introduction: Ideas and Politics'. In *Ideas and Politics in Social Science Research*, edited by Daniel Béland and Robert Henry Cox. New York: Oxford University Press. 3–20.

Benford, Robert D. and David A. Snow. 2000. 'Framing Processes and Social Movements: An Overview and Assessment'. *Annual Review of Sociology* 26: 611–39.

Bennett, Andrew and Jeffrey T. Checkel. 2014. *Process Tracing From Metaphor to Analytic Tool*. London: Cambridge University Press.

Berger, Peter L. and Thomas Luckmann. 1966. *The Social Construction of Reality: A Treatise in the Sociology of Knowledge*. London: Penguin.

Beyers, Jan. 2002. 'Gaining and Seeking Access: The European Adaptation of Domestic Interest Associations'. *European Journal of Political Research* 41 (5): 585–612.

———. 2004. 'Voice and Access: Political Practices of European Interest Associations'. *European Union Politics* 5 (2): 211–40.

———. 2008. 'Policy Issues, Organisational Format and the Political Strategies of Interest Organisations'. *West European Politics* 31 (6): 1188–211.

Beyers, Jan and Bart Kerremans. 2007. 'Critical Resource Dependencies and the Europeanization of Domestic Interest Groups'. *Journal of European Public Policy* 14 (3): 460–81.

———. 2012. 'Domestic Embeddedness and the Dynamics of Multilevel Venue Shopping in Four EU Member States'. *Governance* 25 (2): 263–90.

Beyers, Jan, Rainer Eising and William Maloney. 2008. 'Researching Interest Group Politics in Europe and Elsewhere: Much We Study, Little We Know?' *West European Politics* 31 (6): 1103–28.

———, eds. 2010. *Interest Group Politics in Europe*. London/New York: Routledge.

Bicchi, Federica. 2007. *European Foreign Policy Making towards the Mediterranean*. New York: Palgrave Macmillan.

———. 2010. 'Dilemmas of Implementation: EU Democracy Assistance in the Mediterranean'. *Democratization* 17 (5): 976–96.

———. 2011. 'The EU as a Community of Practice: Foreign Policy Communications in the COREU Network'. *Journal of European Public Policy* 18 (8): 1115–32.

———. 2014. 'Information Exchanges, Diplomatic Networks and the Construction of European Knowledge in EU Foreign Policy'. *Cooperation and Conflict* 49 (2): 239–59.

Boräng, Frida, Rainer Eising, Heike Klüver, Christine Mahoney, Daniel Naurin, Daniel Rasch and Patrycja Rozbicka. 2014. 'Identifying Frames: A Comparison of Research Methods'. *Interest Groups & Advocacy* 3 (2): 188–201.

Börzel, Tanja and Thomas Risse. 2007. 'Europeanization: The Domestic Impact of the European Union Politics'. In *Handbook of European Union Politics*, edited by Knud Erik Jørgensen, Mark A. Pollack and Ben Rosamond. London: SAGE. 483–504.

Bouris, Dimitris. 2012. 'The European Union's Role in the Palestinian Territories: State-Building through Security Sector Reform?' *European Security* 21 (2): 257–71.

Bouwen, Pieter. 2002a. 'Corporate Lobbying in the European Union: The Logic of Access'. *Journal of European Public Policy* 9 (3): 365–90.

———. 2002b. 'A Comparative Study of Business Lobbying in the European Parliament, the European Commission and the Council of Ministers'. MPIfG Discussion Paper 02/7.

———. 2004a. 'Exchanging Access Goods for Access: A Comparative Study of Business Lobbying in the EU Institutions'. *European Journal of Political Research* 43 (3): 337–69.

———. 2004b. 'The Logic of Access to the European Parliament: Business Lobbying in the Committee on Economic and Monetary Affairs.' *Journal of Common Market Studies* 42 (3): 473–95.

Bouwen, Pieter and Margaret McCown. 2007. 'Lobbying versus Litigation: Political and Legal Strategies of Interest Representation in the European Union'. *Journal of European Public Policy* 14 (3): 422–43.

Bradbury, Malcolm, Bryan Heading and Martin Hollis. 1972. 'The Man and the Mask: A Discussion of Role-Theory'. In *Role*, edited by J. A. Jackson. London: Cambridge University Press. 41–64.

Braun, Dietmar. 1999. 'Interests or Ideas? An Overview of Ideational Concepts in Public Policy Research'. In *Public Policy and Political Ideas*, edited by Dietmar Braun and Andreas Busch. Cheltenham/Northampton: Edward Elgar. 11–29.

Braun, Dietmar and Andreas Busch, eds. 1999. *Public Policy and Political Ideas.* Cheltenham/Northampton: Edward Elgar.

Bretherton, Charlotte and John Vogler. 2006. *The European Union as a Global Actor.* 2nd eds. London/New York: Routledge.

Broscheid, Andreas and David Coen. 2003. 'Insider and Outsider Lobbying of the European Commission: An Informational Model of Forum Politics'. *European Union Politics* 4 (2): 165–89.

Bryman, Alan. 2004. 'Interviewing in Qualitative Research'. In *Social Research Methods*, by Alan Bryman, 2nd edn. Oxford: Oxford University Press.

Bugdahn, Sonja. 2008. 'Travelling to Brussels via Aarhus: Can Transnational NGO Networks Impact on EU Policy?' *Journal of European Public Policy* 15 (4): 588–606.

Bull, Hedley. 1982. 'Civilian Power Europe: A Contradiction in Terms?' *JCMS: Journal of Common Market Studies* 21 (2): 149–70.

Bunea, Adriana. 2013. 'Issues, Preferences and Ties: Determinants of Interest Groups' Preference Attainment in the EU Environmental Policy'. *Journal of European Public Policy* 20 (4): 552–70.

Carlsnaes, Walter. 2007. 'European Foreign Policy'. In *Handbook of European Union Politics*, edited by Knud Erik Jørgensen, Mark A. Pollack and Ben Rosamond. London: SAGE. 545–60.

Chalmers, Adam William. 2011. 'Interests, Influence and Information: Comparing the Influence of Interest Groups in the European Union'. *Journal of European Integration* 33 (4): 471–86.

———. 2013. 'Trading Information for Access: Informational Lobbying Strategies and Interest Group Access to the European Union'. *Journal of European Public Policy* 20 (1): 39–58.

Checkel, Jeffrey T. 2001. 'Why Comply? Social Learning and European Identity Change'. *International Organization* 55 (3): 553–88.

———. 2005. 'International Institutions and Socialization in Europe: Introduction and Framework'. *International Organization* 59 (4): 801–26.

———. 2007. 'Constructivism and EU Politics'. In *Handbook of European Union Politics*, edited by Knud Erik Jørgensen, Mark A. Pollack and Ben Rosamond. London: SAGE. 57–76.

Checkel, Jeffrey T. and Andrew Moravcsik. 2001. 'A Constructivist Research Program in EU Studies?' *European Union Politics* 2 (2): 219–49.

Coen, David. 1998. 'The European Business Interest and the Nation-State: Large-Firm Lobbying in the European Union and Member States'. *Journal of Public Policy* 18 (1): 75–100.

———. 2007. 'Empirical and Theoretical Studies in EU Lobbying'. *Journal of European Public Policy* 14 (3): 333–45.

Coen, David and Jeremy Richardson, eds. 2009. *Lobbying the European Union: Institutions, Actors and Issues*. Oxford: Oxford University Press.

Corbetta, Piergiorgio. 2003. *Social Research: Theory, Methods and Techniques*. London: SAGE.

Crespy, Amandine. 2010. *Legitimizing Resistance to EU Integration: Social Europe as a Europeanized Normative Frame in the Conflict over the Bolkenstein Directive*. 3. Le Cahiers européens de Sciences Po. Paris: Centre d' études européennesat Sciences Po.

Cronin, David. 2011 *Europe's Alliance with Israel*. London: Pluto Press.

da Conceição-Heldt, Eugénia and Sophie Meunier. 2014. 'Speaking with a Single Voice: Internal Cohesiveness and External Effectiveness of the EU in Global Governance'. *Journal of European Public Policy* 21 (7): 961–79.

Damro, Chad. 2012. 'Market Power Europe'. *Journal of European Public Policy* 19 (5): 682–99.

David, Clarissa C., Jenna Mae Atun, Erika Fille and Christopher Monterola. 2011. 'Finding Frames: Comparing Two Methods of Frame Analysis'. *Communication Methods and Measures* 5 (4): 329–51.

Davies, P. H. J., 2001. 'Spies as Informants: Triangulation and the Interpretation of Elite Interview Data in the Study of the Intelligence and Security Service'. *Politics* 21 (1): 73–83.

Davis Cross, Mai'a K. 2010. *Cooperation by Committee: The EU Military Committee and the Committee for Civilian Crisis Management*.82. Occasional Paper. Paris: EU ISS.

———. 2013. 'Rethinking Epistemic Communities Twenty Years Later'. *Review of International Studies* 39 (1): 137–60.

Daviter, Falk. 2007. 'Policy Framing in the European Union'. *Journal of European Public Policy* 14 (4): 654–66.

———. 2011. *Policy Framing in the European Union*. Basingstoke: Palgrave Macmillan.

De Bièvre, Dirk and Jappe Eckhardt. 2011. 'Interest Groups and EU Anti-Dumping Policy'. *Journal of European Public Policy* 18 (3): 339–60.

de Figueiredo, John M. and Rui de Figueiredo. 2002. *The Allocation of Resources by Interest Groups: Lobbying, Litigation and Administrative Regulation*. Working Paper 8981. National Bureau of Economic Research.

Dembinski, Matthias and Jutta Joachim. 2008. 'Von Der Zusammenarbeit Europäischer Regierungen Zum Europäischen Regieren? Nichtregierungesorganisationen in Der EU-Außenpolitik.' *Forschungsjournal NSB* 21 (2): 42–51.

Dery, David. 2000. 'Agenda Setting and Problem Definition'. *Policy Studies* 21 (1): 37–47.

Dûchene, François. 1973. 'The European Community and the Uncertainties of Interdependence'. In *A Nation Writ Large? Foreign Policy Problems before the European Community*, edited by Max Kohnstamm and Wolfgang Hager. London: Macmillan. 1–21.

Dür, Andreas. 2008a. 'Measuring Interest Group Influence in the EU: A Note on Methodology'. *European Union Politics* 9 (4): 559–76.

———. 2008b. 'Interest Groups in the European Union: How Powerful Are They?' *West European Politics* 31 (6): 1212–30.

Dür, Andreas and Dirk De Bièvre. 2007a. 'Inclusion without Influence? NGOs in European Trade Policy'. *Journal of Public Policy* 27 (1): 79–101.

———. 2007b. 'The Question of Interest Group Influence'. *Journal of Public Policy* 27 (1): 1–12.

Dür, Andreas and Gemma Mateo. 2010. 'Irish Associations and Lobbying on EU Legislation: Resources, Access Points, and Strategies'. *Irish Political Studies* 25 (1): 107.

————. 2012. 'Who Lobbies the European Union? National Interest Groups in a Multilevel Polity'. *Journal of European Public Policy* 19 (7): 969–87.

Edelman, Murray. 1964. *The Symbolic Uses of Politics*. Urbana: University of Illinois.

Eising, Rainer. 2008. 'Interest Groups in EU Policy-Making'. *Living Reviews in European Governance* 3 (4).

————. 2009. *The Political Economy of State-Business Relations in Europe*. Abingdon/ New York: Routledge.

Eising, Rainer, Daniel Rasch and Patrycja Rozbicka. 2015. 'Institutions, Policies, and Arguments: Context and Strategy in EU Policy Framing'. *Journal of European Public Policy* 22 (4): 516–33.

Elgström, Ole. 2000. 'Norm Negotiations: The Construction of New Norms Regarding Gender and Development in EU Foreign Aid Policy'. *Journal of European Public Policy* 7 (3): 457–76.

Elgström, Ole and Michael Smith, eds. 2006. *The European Union's Roles in International Politics: Concepts and Analysis*. Abingdon/New York: Routledge.

Entman, Robert M. 1993. 'Framing: Toward Clarification of a Fractured Paradigm'. *Journal of Communication* 43 (4): 51–8.

European Coalition for Israel. 2013. 'Football World Cup '06: Keep Ahmadinejad Out'. http://www.ec4i.org/index.php?option=com_content&view=article&id=44:football-world-cup-06-keep-ahmadinejad-out&catid=83:campaigns&Itemid=56

Fairbrass, Jenny. 2003. 'The Europeanization of Business Interest Representation: UK and French Firms Compared'. *Comparative European Politics* 1: 313–34.

Faleg, Giovanni. 2012. 'Between Knowledge and Power: Epistemic Communities and the Emergence of Security Sector Reform in the EU Security Architecture'. *European Security* 21 (2): 161–84.

Fearon, Emanuel and Alexander Wendt. 2002. 'Rationalism v. Constructivism: A Skeptical View'. In *Handbook of International Relations*, edited by Walter Carlsnaes, Thomas Risse and Beth A. Simmons. London: SAGE. 52–71.

Finnemore, Martha and Kathryn Sikkink. 1998. 'International Norm Dynamics and Political Change'. *International Organization* 52 (4): 887–917.

Fischer, Frank and John Forester, eds. 1993. *The Argumentative Turn in Policy Analysis and Planning*. Durham, NC/London: Duke University Press.

Follesdal, Andreas and Simon Hix. 2006. 'Why There is a Democratic Deficit in the EU: A Response to Majone and Moravcsik'. *Journal of Common Market Studies* 44 (3): 533–62.

Gamson, William A. 1975. 'Frame Analysis: An Essay on the Organization of Experience'. *Contemporary Sociology* 4 (6): 603–7.

————. 2004. 'Bystanders, Public Opinion, and the Media'. In *The Blackwell Companion to Social Movements*, edited by David A. Snow, Sarah A. Soule and Hanspeter Kriesi. Oxford: Blackwell. 242–61.

George, Alexander L. and Andrew Bennett. 2005. *Case Studies and Theory Development in the Social Sciences*. Cambridge: BCSIA.

Gerhards, Juergen. 1995. 'Framing Dimensions and Framing Strategies: Contrasting Ideal- and Real-Type Frames'. *Social Science Information* 34 (2): 225–48.

Gerlach, Carina. 2006. 'Does Business Really Run EU Trade Policy? Observations about EU Trade Policy Lobbying.' *Politics* 26 (3): 176–83.

Giddens, Anthony. 1979. *Central Problem in Social Theory: Action, Structure and Contradiction in Social Analysis*. London/Basingstoke: Palgrave Macmillan.

————. 1984. *The Constitution of Society*. Cambridge: Polity Press.

Ginsberg, Roy H. 1999. 'Conceptualizing the European Union as an International Actor: Narrowing the Theoretical.' *Journal of Common Market Studies* 37 (3): 429.

Goffman, Erving. 1971. *The Presentation of Self in Everyday Life*. Harmondsworth: Penguin.

———. 1975. *Frame Analysis: An Essay on the Organization of Experience*. Peregrine Books. Harmondsworth: Penguin.

Goldberg, David Howard. 1990. *Foreign Policy and Ethnic Interest Groups: American and Canadian Jews Lobby for Israel*. New York/London: Greenwood Press.

Goldstein, Judith and Robert Keohane, eds. 1993. *Ideas and Foreign Policy: Beliefs, Institutions and Political Change*. Ithaca: Cornell University Press.

Gornitzka, Åse and Ulf Sverdrup. 2011. 'Access of Experts: Information and EU Decision-Making'. *West European Politics* 34 (1): 48–70.

Granovetter, Mark. 1985. 'Economic Action and Social Structure: The Problem of Embeddedness'. *American Journal of Sociology* 91: 481–510.

Green Cowles, Maria. 2001. 'The Transatlantic Business Dialogue and Domestic Business-Government Relations'. In *Transforming Europe: Europeanization and Domestic Change*, edited by James Caporaso, Thomas Risse and Maria Green Cowles. Ithaca: Cornell University Press. 159–79.

Greenwood, Justin. 1997. *Representing Interests in the European Union*. London: Palgrave Macmillan.

———. 2003. *Interest Representation in the European Union*. Basingstoke: Palgrave Macmillan.

Grossman, Emiliano and Sabine Saurugger. 2006. *Les Groupes D'interet. Action Collective et Strategies de Representation*. Paris: Armand Colin.

Gullberg, Anne Therese. 2008. 'Lobbying Friends and Foes in Climate Policy: The Case of Business and Environmental Interest Groups in the European Union'. *Energy Policy* 36: 2964–72.

Hägel, Peter and Pauline Peretz. 2005. 'States and Transnational Actors: Who's Influencing Whom? A Case Study in Jewish Diaspora Politics during the Cold War'. *European Journal of International Relations* 11 (4): 467–93.

Haney, Patrick J. and Walt Vanderbush. 1999. 'The Role of Ethnic Interest Groups in US Foreign Policy: The Case of the Cuban American National Foundation'. *International Studies Quarterly* 43 (2): 341–61.

Haynes-Renshaw, F. 2009. 'Least Accessible But Not Inaccessible: Lobbying the Council and the European Council'. In *Lobbying the European Union: Institutions, Actors and Issues*, edited by David Coen and Jeremy Richardson. Oxford: Oxford University Press. 3–15.

Hill, Christopher. 2003. *The Changing Politics of Foreign Policy*. New York: Palgrave Macmillan.

Hillman, Amy and Michael Hitt. 1999. 'Corporate Political Strategy Formulation: A Model of Approach, Participation, and Strategy Decisions'. *The Academy of Management Review* 24 (4): 825–42.

Hix, Simon and Bjorn Hoyland. 2011. *The Political System of the European Union*. London: Palgrave Macmillan.

Hoffmann, Stanley. 2000. 'Towards a Common European Foreign and Security Policy?' *Journal of Common Market Studies* 38 (2): 189–98.

Hojnacji, Marie, David C. Kimball, Frank R. Baumgartner, Jeffrey M. Berry and Beth L. Leech. 2012. 'Studying Organizational Advocacy and Influence: Reexamining Interest Group Research'. *Annual Review of Political Science* 15: 379–99.

Holzscheiter, Anna. 2005. 'Discourse as Capability: Non-State Actors' Capital in Global Governance'. *Millennium: Journal of International Studies* 33 (3): 723–46.

Hrebenar, Ronald J. and Thomas Clive. 1995. 'The Japanese Lobby in Washington: How Different Is It?' In *Interest Group Politics*, edited by Allan J. Cliger and Burdette Loomis. Washington, DC: CQ Press. 349–67.

Huber, George P. 1991. 'Organizational Learning: The Contributing Processes and the Literatures'. *Organization Science* 2 (1): 88–115.

Hudson, Valerie M. 2007. *Foreign Policy Analysis: Classic and Contemporary Theory.* New York: Rowman and Littlefield.

Hyde-Price, Adrian. 2006. '"Normative" Power Europe: A Realist Critique'. *Journal of European Public Policy* 13 (2): 217–34.

———. 2008. 'A "Tragic Actor"? A Realist Perspective on "Ethical Power Europe"'. *International Affairs* 84 (1): 29–44.

International Federation for Human Rights. 2010. *Dashed Hopes: Continuation of the Gaza Blockade.* http://www.unhcr.org/refworld/docid/4cf62f9e2e8.html

Joachim, Jutta. 2003. 'Framing Issues and Seizing Opportunities: The UN, NGOs, and Women's Rights'. *International Studies Quarterly* 47: 247–74.

Jørgensen, Knud Erik. 2004. 'European Foreign Policy: Conceptualising the Domain'. In *Contemporary European Foreign Policy*, edited by Walter Carlsnaes, Helene Sjursen and Brian White. London: SAGE. 32–56.

Jünemann, Annette. 2002. 'From the Bottom to the Top: Civil Society and Transnational Non-Governmental Organizations in the Euro-Mediterranean Partnership'. *Democratization* 9 (1): 87–105.

Kaplan, Sarah. 2008. 'Framing Contests: Strategy Making under Uncertainty'. *Organization Science* 19 (5): 729–52.

Keck, Margaret E. and Kathryn Sikkink. 1998. *Activists beyond Borders: Advocacy Networks in International Politics.* Ithaca, NY: Cornell University Press.

Khagram, Sanjeev, James Riker and Kathryn Sikkink, eds. 2002. *Restructuring World Politics. Transnational Social Movements, Networks, and Norms.* Minneapolis: University of Minnesota Press.

Klüver, Heike. 2009. 'Measuring Interest Group Influence Using Quantitative Text Analysis'. *European Union Politics* 10 (4): 535–49.

———. 2010. 'Europeanization of Lobbying Activities: When National Interest Groups Spill Over to the European Level'. *Journal of European Integration* 32 (2): 175–91.

———. 2012. 'Informational Lobbying in the European Union: The Effect of Organisational Characteristics'. *West European Politics* 35 (3): 491–510.

———. 2013a. *Lobbying in the European Union Interest Groups, Lobbying Coalitions, and Policy Change.* Oxford: Oxford University Press.

———. 2013b. 'Lobbying as a Collective Enterprise: Winners and Losers of Policy Formulation in the European Union'. *Journal of European Public Policy* 20 (1): 59–76.

Klüver, Heike and Sabine Saurugger. 2013. 'Opening the Black Box: The Professionalization of Interest Groups in the European Union'. *Interest Groups & Advocacy* 2 (2): 185–205.

Klüver, Heike, Christine Mahoney and Marc Opper. 2015. 'Framing in Context: How Interest Groups Employ Framing to Lobby the European Commission'. *Journal of European Public Policy* 22 (4): 481–98.

Knodt, Michele and Sebastiaan Princen, eds. 2003. *Understanding the European Union's External Relations.* Abingdon/New York: Routledge.

Koenig, Thomas. 2005. 'Concepts for Frame Analyses'. http://www.ccsr.ac.uk/methods/publications/frameanalysis/ (web address no longer live)

Kollman, Ken. 1998. *Outside Lobbying: Public Opinion and Interest Group Strategies.* Princeton, NJ: Princeton University Press.

Legro, Jeffrey W. 2000. 'The Transformation of Policy Ideas'. *American Journal of Political Science* 44 (3): 419–32.

Lewis, Jeffrey. 2008. 'Strategic Bargaining, Norms, and Deliberation: Modes of Action in the Council of the Euro Pean Union'. In *Unveiling the Council: Games Governments Play in Brussels*, edited by Daniel Naurin and Helen Wallace. Basingstoke: Palgrave Macmillan. 165–84.

Lowery, David. 2013. 'Lobbying Influence: Meaning, Measurement and Missing'. *Interest Groups & Advocacy* 2 (1): 1–26.

Lucarelli, Sonia and Ian Manners, eds. 2006. *Values and Principles in European Union Foreign Policy.* lst edn. Routledge Advances in European Politics 37. New York: Routledge.

Lukes, S. 1974. *Power: A Radical View.* Basingstoke: Macmillan.

Lupovici, Amir. 2009. 'Constructivist Methods: A Plea and Manifesto for Pluralism'. *Review of International Studies* 35 (1): 195–218.

Mahoney, Christine. 2007a. 'Networking vs Allying: The Decision of Interest Groups to Join Coalitions in the US and the EU'. *Journal of European Public Policy* 14 (3): 441–66.

———. 2007b. 'Lobbying Success in the United States and the European Union'. *Journal of Public Policy* 27 (1): 35.

———. 2008. *Brussels versus the Beltway: Advocacy in the United States and the European Union.* Washington, DC: Georgetown University Press.

Mahoney, James and Gary Goertz. 2006. 'A Tale of Two Cultures: Contrasting Quantitative and Qualitative Research'. *Political Analysis* 14 (3): 227–49.

Majone, Giandomenico. 1989. *Evidence, Argument, and Persuasion in the Policy Process.* New Haven: Yale University Press.

———. 1994. 'The Rise of the Regulatory State in Europe'. *West European Politics* 17 (3): 77–101.

Manners, Ian. 2002. 'Normative Power Europe: A Contradiction in Terms?' *Journal of Common Market Studies* 40 (2): 235–58.

March, James G. and Johan P. Olsen. 1998. 'The Institutional Dynamics of International Political Orders'. *International Organization* 52 (4): 943–69.

Mazey, Sonia and Jeremy Richardson. 2006. 'Interest Groups and EU Policy-Making: Organizational Logic and Venue Shopping'. In *European Union: Power and Policy-Making*, by Jeremy Richardson. London/New York: Routledge. 247–68.

McAdam, Doug, Sidney Tarrow and Charles Tilly. 2001. *Dynamics of Contention.* New York: Cambridge University Press.

McCauley, Darren. 2011. 'Bottom-Up Europeanization Exposed: Social Movement Theory and Non-State Actors in France'. *Journal of Common Market Studies* 49 (5): 1019–42.

McClurg Mueller, Carol. 1992. 'Building Social Movement Theory'. In *Frontiers in Social Movements Theory*, edited by Carol McClurg Mueller and Aldon D. Morris. New Haven: Yale University Press. 3–25.

McCormick, James M. 1998. 'Interest Groups and the Media in Post-Cold War US Foreign Policy'. In *After the End: Making US Foreign Policy in the Post-Cold War World*, edited by James M. Scott. Durham, NC/London: Duke University Press. 170–98.

McCown, Margaret. 2009. 'Interest Groups and the European Court of Justice'. In *Lobbying the European Union: Institutions, Actors and Issues*, edited by David Coen and Jeremy Richardson. Oxford: Oxford University Press. 89–104.

Mearsheimer, John J. and Stephen M. Walt. 2006. 'The Israel Lobby and US Foreign Policy'. *London Review of Books* 28 (6): 3–12.

———. 2007. *The Israel Lobby and US Foreign Policy*. London: Allen Lane.

———. 2009. 'Is It Love or the Lobby? Explaining America's Special Relationship with Israel'. *Security Studies* 18: 58–78.

Miller, Aaron David. 2008. *The Much Too Promised Land: America's Elusive Search for Arab-Israeli Peace*. New York: Bantam Books.

Moravcsik, Andrew. 1998. *The Choice for Europe: Social Purpose and State Power from Messina to Maastricht*. Cornell Studies in Political Economy. Ithaca, NY: Cornell University Press.

Müller, Harald. 2004. 'Arguing, Bargaining and All That: Communicative Action, Rationalist Theory and the Logic of Appropriateness in International Relations'. *European Journal of International Relations* 10 (3): 395–435.

Müller, Harald and Thomas Risse-Kappen. 1993. 'From the Outside In and from the Inside Out'. In *The Limits of State Autonomy: Societal Groups and Foreign Policy Formation*, edited by D. Skidmore and Valerie M. Hudson. Boulder, CO/Oxford: Westview Press.

Müller, Patrick. 2012. *EU Foreign Policymaking and the Middle East Conflict: The Europeanization of National Foreign Policy*. CSS Studies in Security and International Relations. London: Routledge.

Musu, Costanza. 2010. *European Union Policy towards the Arab–Israeli Peace Process: The Quicksands of Politics*. Basingstoke: Palgrave Macmillan.

Niemann, Arne. 2004. 'Between Communicative Action and Strategic Action: The Article 113 Committee and the Negotiations on the WTO Basic Telecommunications Services Agreement'. *Journal of European Public Policy* 11 (3): 379–407.

Niemann, Arne and Charlotte Bretherton. 2013. 'EU External Policy at the Crossroads: The Challenge of Actorness and Effectiveness'. *International Relations* 27 (3): 261–75.

Nuttall, Simon. 2000. *European Foreign Policy*. Oxford: Oxford University Press.

O'Neill, Kate, Jörg Balsiger and Stacy D. VanDeveer. 2004. 'Actors, Norms, and Impacts: Recent International Cooperation Theory and the Influence of the Agent-Structure Debate'. *Annual Review of Political Science* 7 (1): 149–75.

Organski, Abramo F. K. 1990. *The 36 Billion [Dollar]Bargain: Strategy and Politics in US Assistance to Israel*. New York: Columbia University Press.

Pappi, Franz U. and Christian H. Henning. 1999. 'The Organisation of Influence on the EC's Common Agricultural Policy: A Network Approach'. *European Journal of Political Research* 36: 257–81.

Parmar, Inderjeet. 2004. *Think Tanks and Power in Foreign Policy: A Comparative Study of the Role and Influence of the Council on Foreign Relations and the Royal Institute of International Affairs, 1939–1945*. Basingstoke: Palgrave Macmillan.

Paul, David M. and Rachel Anderson Paul. 2009. *Ethnic Lobbies and US Foreign Policy*. London: Lynne Rienner.

Payne, Rodger A. 2001. 'Persuasion, Frames and Norm Construction'. *European Journal of International Relations* 7 (1): 37–61.

Pollack, Mark. 2007. 'Rational Choice and EU Politics'. In *The SAGE Handbook of European Union Politics*, edited by Knud Erik Jørgensen, Mark A. Pollack and Ben Rosamond. London: SAGE. 31–56.

Pralle, Sarah B. 2003. 'Venue Shopping, Political Strategy, and Policy Change: The Internationalization of Canadian Forest Advocacy'. *Journal of Public Policy* 23 (3): 233–60.

Princen, Sebastiaan. 2007. 'Agenda-Setting in the European Union: A Theoretical Exploration and Agenda for Research'. *Journal of European Public Policy* 14 (1): 21–38.
———. 2011. 'Agenda-Setting Strategies in EU Policy Processes'. *Journal of European Public Policy* 18 (7): 927–43.
Princen, Sebastiaan and Bart Kerremans. 2008. 'Opportunity Structures in the EU Multi-Level System'. *West European Politics* 31 (6): 1129–46.
Radaelli, Claudio M. 1999. 'The Power of Policy Narratives in the European Union: The Case of Tax Policy'. In *Public Policy and Political Ideas*, edited by Dietmar Braun and Andreas Busch. Cheltenham/Northampton: Edward Elgar. 98–115.
Rein, Martin and Donald Schön. 1993. 'Reframing Policy Discourse'. In *The Argumentative Turn in Policy Analysis and Planning*, edited by Frank Fischer and John Forester. Durham, NC/London: Duke University Press. 145–66.
Richards, John P. and Jack Heard. 2005. 'European Environmental NGOs: Issues, Resources and Strategies in Marine Campaigns'. *Environmental Politics* 14 (1): 23–41.
Riddervold, Marianne. 2011. 'From Reason-Giving to Collective Action: Argument-Based Learning and European Integration'. *Cooperation and Conflict* 46 (4): 563–80.
Riker, William H. 1986. *The Art of Political Manipulation*. New Haven: Yale University Press.
Risse, Thomas. 2000. '"Let's Argue!": Communicative Action in World Politics'. *International Organization* 54 (1): 1–39.
Rogers, Elizabeth. 1993. 'The Conflicting Roles of American Ethnic and Business Interests in the US Economic Sanctions Policy'. In *The Limits of State Autonomy. Societal Groups and Foreign Policy Formulation*, edited by David Skidmore and Valerie M. Hudson. Boulder, CO/Oxford: Westview Press. 185–204.
Rubin, Paul H., Christopher Curran and John F. Curran. 2001. 'Litigation versus Legislation: Forum Shopping by Rent Seekers'. *Public Choice* 107: 295–310.
Saurugger, Sabine. 2002. 'L'expertise comme mode de participation des groupes d'intérêt au processus décisionnel communautaire.' *Revue Française de Science Politique* 52 (4): 375–401.
———. 2005. 'Europeanization as a Methodological Challenge: The Case of Interest Groups'. *Journal of Comparative Policy Analysis* 7 (4): 239–78.
———. 2009. 'COREPER and National Governments'. In *Lobbying the European Union*, by David Coen and Jeremy Richardson. Oxford: Oxford University Press. 105–27.
———. 2010. 'The Social Construction of the Participatory Turn: The Emergence of a Norm in the European Union'. *European Journal of Political Research* 49 (4): 471–95.
Schattschneider, E. E. (Elmer Eric). 1960. *The Semisovereign People: A Realist's View of Democracy in America*. New York/London: Holt, Rinehart and Winston.
Schimmelfennig, Frank. 2001. 'The Community Trap: Liberal Norms, Rhetorical Action, and the Eastern Enlargement of the European Union'. *International Organization* 55 (1): 47–80.
Schimmelfennig, Frank and Ulrich Sedelmeier. 2005. 'The Politics of EU Enlargement'. In *The Politics of European Union Enlargement*, edited by Frank Schimmelfennig and Ulrich Sedelmeier. Abingdon/New York: Routledge. 3–32.
Schmidt, Vivien. 1999. 'National Patterns of Governance under Siege: The Impact of European Integration'. In *The Transformation of Governance in the European Union*, edited by Beate Kohler-Koch and Rainer Eising. London: Routledge. 155–72.
———. 2011. 'Reconciling Ideas and Institutions through Discursive Institutionalism'. In *Ideas and Politics in Social Science Research*, edited by Daniel Béland and Robert Henry Cox. New York: Oxford University Press. 47–64.
Schmidt, Vivien and Claudio Radaelli. 2004. 'Policy Change and Discourse in Europe: Conceptual and Methodological Issues'. *West European Politics* 27 (2): 183–210.

Sedelmeier, Ulrich. 2003. *EU Enlargement, Identity and the Analysis of European Foreign Policy: Identity Formation Through Policy Practice*. European Forum Series RSC No. 2003/13. EUI Working Paper RSCAS. Badia Fiesolana, San Domenico di Fiesole: EUI.

————. 2005. 'Eastern Enlargement: Risk, Rationality and Role-Compliance'. In *The Politics of European Union Enlargement*, edited by Frank Schimmelfennig and Ulrich Sedelmeier. Abingdon/New York: Routledge. 120–41.

Sell, Susan K. and Aseem Prakash. 2004. 'Using Ideas Strategically: The Contest between Business and NGO Networks in Intellectual Property Rights'. *International Studies Quarterly* 48 (1): 143–75.

Settembri, Pierpaolo. 2006. 'Is the European Parliament Competitive or Consensual ... "and Why Bother"?' In *The European Parliament and the European Political Space*. London. http://www.fedtrust.co.uk/filepool/FedT_workshop_Settembri.pdf

Sjursen, Helene. 2006. 'Values or Rights? Alternative Conceptions of the EU's "Normative" Role'. In *The European Union's Roles in International Politics: Concepts and Analysis*, edited by Ole Elgstrom and Michael Smith. Abingdon/New York: Routledge. 85–100.

Skidmore, David and Valerie M. Hudson. 1993. *The Limits of State Autonomy: Societal Groups and Foreign Policy Formulation*. Boulder, CO: Westview Press.

Slater, Jerome. 2009. 'The Two Books of Mearsheimer and Walt'. *Security Studies* 18 (1): 4–57.

Smith, Karen E. 2005. 'Beyond the Civilian Power Debate'. *Politique Européenne* 1 (17): 63–82.

Smith, Michael E. 2004a. 'Institutionalization, Policy Adaptation and European Foreign Policy Cooperation'. *European Journal of International Relations* 10 (1): 95–136.

————. 2004b. 'Toward a Theory of EU Foreign Policymaking: Multi-Level Governance, Domestic Politics, and National Adaptation to Europe's Common Foreign and Security Policy'. *Journal of European Public Policy* 11 (4): 740–58.

Smith, Richard. 1995. 'Interest Group Influence in the US Congress'. *Legislative Studies Quarterly* 20 (1): 89–139.

Smith, Steve. 2000. 'International Theory and European Integration'. In *International Relations Theory and the Politics of European Integration: Power, Security and Community*, edited by Morten Kelstrup and Michael Charles Williams. London: Routledge. 33–56.

Smith, Tony. 2000. *Foreign Attachments: The Power of Ethnic Groups in the Making of American Foreign Policy*. Cambridge, MA: Harvard University Press.

Snow, David A. 2004. 'Framing Processes, Ideology, and Discursive Field'. In *The Blackwell Companion to Social Movements*, edited by David A. Snow, Sarah A. Soule and Hanspeter Kriesi. Oxford: Blackwell. 380–412.

Snow, David A. and Robert D. Benford. 1992. 'Master Frames and Cycles of Protest'. In *Frontiers in Social Movements Theory*, edited by Carol McClurg Mueller and Aldon D. Morris. New Haven: Yale University Press. 133–55.

Spiegel, Steven L. 1987. 'Ethnic Politics and the Formulation of US Policy towards the Arab–Israeli Dispute'. In *Ethnic Groups and US Foreign Policy*, edited by Mohammed E. Ahrari. Westport, CT: Greenwood Press.

Stoddard, Abby. 2006. *Humanitarian Alert: NGO Information and Its Impact on US Foreign Policy*. Bloomfield: Kumarian Press.

Stone, Diana. 2000. 'Think Tank Transnationalisation and the International Market for Non Profit Analysis, Advice and Advocacy'. *Global Society* 14 (2): 153–72.

Stone Sweet, Alec, W. Sandholz and N. Fligstein. 2001. *The Institutionalization of Europe*. Oxford: Oxford University Press.

Tilly, Charles and Sidney Tarrow. 2007. *Contentious Politics*. Boulder, CO: Paradigm.

Tocci, Nathalie, 2007. *The EU and Conflict Resolution: Promoting Peace in the Backyard*. Abingdon/New York: Routledge.

———. ed. 2008. *Who is a Normative Foreign Policy Actor? The European Union and its Global Partners*. Brussels: CEPS.

———. 2009. 'Firm in Rhetoric, Compromising in Reality: The EU in the Israeli–Palestinian Conflict'. *Ethnopolitics* 8 (3): 387–401.

———. 2011. *The European Union, Civil Society and Conflict*. Abingdon/New York: Routledge.

Tonra, Ben. 2003. 'Constructing the Common Foreign and Security Policy: The Utility of a Cognitive Approach'. *Journal of Common Market Studies* 41 (4): 731–56.

Tonra, Ben and Thomas Christiansen, eds. 2004. *Rethinking European Union Foreign Policy*. Manchester: Manchester University Press.

Trice, Robert H. 1976. *Interest Groups and the Foreign Policy Process: US Policy in the Middle East*. Beverly Hills: SAGE.

Trommer, Silke. 2011. 'Activists beyond Brussels: Transnational NGO Strategies on EU–West African Trade Negotiations'. *Globalizations* 8 (1): 113–26.

Uslaner, Eric M. 1995. 'All Politics are Global: Interest Groups and the Making of Foreign Policy'. In *Interest Group Politics*, edited by Allan J. Cliger and Burdette Loomis. Washington: CQ Press. 369–91.

Vanhoonacker, Sophie and Karolina Pomorska. 2013. 'The European External Action Service and Agenda-Setting in European Foreign Policy'. *Journal of European Public Policy* 20 (9): 1316–31.

Voltolini, Benedetta. 2012. *The Role of Non-State Actors in EU Policies towards the Israeli–Palestinian Conflict*. Occasional Paper 99. Paris: EU ISS.

Wendt, Alexander. 1987. 'The Agent-Structure Problem in International Relations Theory'. *International Organization* 41 (3): 335–70.

———. 1998. 'On Constitution and Causation in International Relations'. *Review of International Studies* 24 (5): 101–18.

———. 1999. *Social Theory of International Politics*. New York: Cambridge University Press.

White, Brian. 2001. *Understanding European Foreign Policy*. Basingstoke: Palgrave.

Williams, Rhys H. 2004. 'The Cultural Contexts of Collective Action: Constraints, Opportunities, and the Symbolic Life of Social Movements'. In *The Blackwell Companion to Social Movements*, edited by David A. Snow, Sarah A. Soule and Hanspeter Kriesi. Oxford: Blackwell. 91–115.

Woll, Cornelia. 2007. 'Leading the Dance? Power and Political Resources of Business Lobbyists'. *Journal of Public Policy* 27 (1): 57–78.

———. 2008. *Firm Interests: How Governments Shape Business Lobbying on Global Trade*. Ithaca/London: Cornell University Press.

———. 2012. 'The Brash and the Soft-Spoken: Lobbying Styles in a Transatlantic Comparison'. *Interest Groups & Advocacy* 1 (2): 193–214.

Youngs, Richard. 2004. 'Normative Dynamics and Strategic Interests in the EU's External Identity'. *Journal of Common Market Studies* 42 (2): 415–35.

Zippel, Kathrin. 2004. 'Transnational Advocacy Networks and Policy Cycles in the European Union: The Case of Sexual Harassment'. *Social Politics: International Studies in Gender, State & Society* 11 (1): 57–85.

2 The EU and the Israeli–Palestinian conflict

An overview of declarations, policies and actors

The European involvement in the Middle East dates back to the beginning of the twentieth century, when the United Kingdom and France were given a mandate by the League of Nations to control the territories of the former Ottoman Empire. Today's Israel, the West Bank and the Gaza Strip were under the British mandate, which lasted until May 1948, when the British withdrew from the territories in light of the intractable situation of the region.[1] Immediately afterwards, the state of Israel was proclaimed, leading to the outbreak of the first of a series of Arab–Israeli wars that have characterised the following decades. While historical ties and the sense of guilt of Western powers towards the Jews, who were persecuted by the Nazi regime, have played a clear role in defining the European stance towards the Middle East, geostrategic and economic reasons have also influenced European decisions and policies over the years. Energy dependency, on which the oil crisis of 1973 turned the spotlight, migration pressures, fear of terrorism and radicalisation as well as a broader concern for the stability of the region have significantly shaped European reactions to the events in the area (cf. Hollis 2010). Moreover, the European Council (2003) has recognised how the Israeli–Palestinian conflict has continuously affected the dynamics and stability in the region, and it has thus been a priority on the EU's agenda.

This chapter provides an overview of the EU's involvement in the Israeli–Palestinian conflict by analysing EU diplomatic initiatives, policies and actions on the ground as well as the institutional actors participating in the policy-making process.[2] In doing so, it highlights two main features that define EU foreign policy towards Israel and Palestine. On the one hand, the positions of member states have become more similar over the decades, leading to a well-developed and established EU position towards the conflict which rests on two pillars: the two-state solution and respect for human rights, international law and international humanitarian law (Tocci 2009). On the other hand, the instruments and policies at the EU's disposal have progressively expanded, moving from a declaratory level to a wider engagement through a variety of policies.[3] In parallel, this has been matched by an increase in the number of institutional actors involved in the policy-making process.

By delineating the historical and institutional framework of EU foreign policy towards the Israeli–Palestinian conflict, this chapter contributes to contextualising NSAs' lobbying activities. It indeed identifies the policy field in which NSAs perform their actions and which actors they interact with. This is in no way an exhaustive or detailed history of the relations between the EU and Israel/ Palestine, but merely serves to equip the reader with some background on EU foreign policy towards the conflict, so that the activities of NSAs presented in the following chapters can be understood within the broader picture of EU foreign policy.[4] The first section will discuss the progressive crystallisation of the EU's position around key and shared views. This will be followed by an explanation of the relevant actors involved in the policy process. Before turning to the conclusions, the chapter will also offer a snapshot of the main issues on the agenda and the most recent events.

A smaller distance between 'converging parallels'

Since the first steps of European political cooperation, the Middle East has been an experimental field of EU foreign policy. Member states have tested new forms of cooperation and new policy instruments on the Arab–Israeli conflict, which has been on the EU's agenda since the Six-Day War of 1967, when Israel defeated Egypt, Jordan and Syria and incorporated the territories of the West Bank, Gaza Strip, Golan Heights and the Sinai Peninsula.[5] On that occasion the then members of the European Community did not manage to formulate a single statement, due to the division between France – which wanted to take the lead on the issue – and the rest of the EU (Miller 2011). The event was, however, a trigger that favoured a deeper reflection at the European level. Since then, the Arab– Israeli conflict, and the Israeli–Palestinian conflict more specifically, has been on the EU's agenda and EU member states have progressively narrowed their divergences on how to deal with it. The distance between what Musu (2010) called 'converging parallels' has decreased over the years and the positions of member states, although not yet forming a single and unified voice, have converged on some key points. There is now a solid and well-established position based on the two-state solution and respect for international law, human rights and humanitarian law, and it is in accordance with this position that the EU formulates its policies and declarations.

In the early stages of the European integration, foreign policy was left in the hands of member states. The main goal was, paraphrasing Milward (1992), to 'rescue the nation-state' and economic cooperation was the inevitable step to foster the growth of national economies and to contain the risk of another war. However, the building of a common commercial policy and pressing external events, among which the Six-Day War in 1967 was an important one, were triggers that favoured reflection about the need to match the EU's economic power with a comparable political stance. Following the Hague Summit in 1969 and the Davignon Report, member states agreed to meet at least twice a year and consult each other on important foreign policy matters. Palestine became a central issue in the discussion, although disunity on the subject was still manifest (Miller 2011). In 1970, as part of the newly established European Political Cooperation (EPC), foreign ministers held consultations on the Middle East, 'a topic which was to remain on the agenda' (Dosenrode and Stubkjaer 2002: 5).

On 13 May 1971 EU member states formulated a joint paper on the Middle East, the so-called Schuman Paper (Miller 2011: 21). Although the document was never officially published and there were different views concerning its status (for France it represented the official position of the EU, while for Germany and the Netherlands it was only a working document), this was the first sign of convergence among member states' positions, especially if compared to the uncoordinated reactions to the 1967 war (Dosenrode and Stubkjaer 2002). The content of this document, which was later revealed by the German press group Springer, revolved around six principles that were consistent with UN Resolution 242. These principles provided for the establishment of demilitarised zones, the internationalisation of Jerusalem, the overall withdrawal of Israel from the Occupied Territories with minor border adjustments, a choice for Arab refugees to decide where to live, postponement of the issue of sovereignty of East Jerusalem and approval of the UN Jarring Mission (Greilsammer and Weiler 1984: 133).

Following the Yom Kippur War in 1973, EU member states called on the parties to respect UN Resolutions 242 and 338 and maintained that the 'legitimate rights of the Palestinians' must be respected in any peace solution. This change in rhetoric is significant, as the Palestinians moved from being only considered as refugees to a 'political issue' that needed to be treated accordingly (Pardo and Peters 2012: 106–7). Moreover, the EU also called for Israel 'to end territorial occupation' (Miller 2011: 33). A few years later, at the European Council in London in 1977, EU member states referred to the 'legitimate right of the Palestinian people to give effective expression to its national identity' and the 'need for a homeland for the Palestinian people' (European Council 1977).[6]

Towards the end of the 1970s, strong activism for the Palestinian issue was also shown by small states such as Belgium and Ireland, whose actions were directed against the efforts of the Carter administration within the 1979 Camp David Agreement between Israel and Egypt. Following this approach and building on its previous declarations, the European Council conclusions in 1980, also known as the Venice Declaration, became the landmark of the EU's efforts in the Middle East Peace Process, defining all subsequent EU moves. The member states clearly declared that the Palestinian people should be allowed to exercise their right to self-determination, the Palestinian Liberation Organisation (PLO) was to be associated in future negotiations and Israel, while having the right to exist, had to stop the occupation. Moreover, they stated that they would not recognise unilateral moves that would change the status of Jerusalem and that settlements were illegal under international law (European Council 1980). By issuing this declaration the EU showed its 'pioneering' and visionary policy, a forerunner of what would then become the shared view of the international community. Although the Venice Declaration did not lead to a single European foreign policy or to a proactive policy, it paved the way for the development of the EU's common position towards the Israeli–Palestinian conflict that informs all its current policies (Musu 2010).

Despite some attempts to take a more active role in the Middle East Peace Process (MEPP), in the 1980s and 1990s the EU was diplomatically dormant. The USA was leading the dance and the Europeans were playing second fiddle. While being one of the main advocates for an international peace conference,[7] Europe was excluded from the political negotiations in the 1991 Madrid Conference co-promoted by the USA and Russia. The EU was marginalised to the multilateral track discussions and technical issues, being relegated to the roles of chair of the working group on Regional Economic Development and co-sponsor of the working groups on water, environment and refugees. The signing of the Oslo Accords in 1993 did not really change the EU's position in the MEPP, mainly transforming the EU into the main payer of the peace process through its financial support to the newly established Palestinian Authority (PA). Although it did not manage to increase its diplomatic stance in the multilateral efforts led by the USA, the EU started a new regional initiative in the Mediterranean, which led to the creation of the Euro-Mediterranean Partnership (EMP) in 1995 (see Bicchi 2007). From a European perspective, the EMP was supposed to be complementary to the MEPP by creating a multilateral context in which the relationships between the EU and the Mediterranean countries, as well as among these countries, could prosper. Included in the EMP, both Israel and the Palestinians (through the PLO) signed an Association Agreement with the EU, bilateral agreements that defined the legal framework of policies towards them. By embedding the EU's policy of conflict resolution into the broader multilateral framework of the EMP, the EU also aimed to bolster its political power through the use of its economic strength. This hope was, however, dashed quite soon, as the division between the MEPP and the EMP was too artificial to work (Müller 2012).

Despite its political marginalisation, the EU proved once again that it could be a key player in the MEPP. It indeed provided new political impetus with its 1999 Berlin European Council Conclusions. Drawing on the Venice Declaration, EU member states restated their support for the Palestinians and declared their readiness to recognise 'a Palestinian state in due course' (European Council 1999). In an attempt to avoid the unilateral declaration of statehood by the PLO in May 1999,[8] the EU reaffirmed the Palestinian rights to self-determination, 'including the option of a state' whenever conditions would be ripe. This declaration basically beefed up the EU's previous declarations and definitively forged its position towards the Israeli–Palestinian conflict, constituting the first element of a two-pillar approach (Tocci 2009). The two-state solution with Israelis and Palestinians living side-by-side in a peaceful way is the first pillar. In the EU's view, the Palestinian state, established along the pre-1967 war borders, should be a sovereign, independent, democratic and viable state. While this implies the withdrawal of Israel from the territories it occupied in 1967, this is conceived by the EU as being to Israel's advantage, as it would ensure Israel's long-term security. As a second pillar of its approach, the EU views respect for international law, international humanitarian law and human rights as a fundamental element in the peace process. This is reflected in the constant references to UN resolutions as well as to the obligations under the Fourth Geneva Convention relative to the Protection of Civilian Persons in Time of War and the broader corpus of international humanitarian law.

With the eruption of the Second Intifada in 2000 and Operation Defensive Shield in 2002, during which Israel invaded the areas of the West Bank that were handed over to the PA during the Oslo years, the EU made clear diplomatic efforts to bring violence to an end and push the parties to resume talks. In particular, the EU significantly contributed to the work done by the international community, especially providing new ideas and ways to deal with the conflict. Although the Quartet – the multilateral forum established in 2002 and formed by the USA, the United Nations, Russia and the EU – is dominated by the Americans (De Soto 2007; Müller 2014), the EU has contributed to the ideational dimension of the work of the Quartet by designing the Roadmap which was launched in 2003. This plan to solve the conflict was heavily based on proposals advanced by the Europeans, namely the Fischer seven-point plan (named after the author, the German foreign minister Joschka Fischer) and the inputs provided by the rotating Danish presidency of the Council (Tocci 2011; De Soto 2007).

While its ideational role has thus been important in shaping the position of the international community, events have once again shown the lack of political clout at critical junctures. For example, on the occasion of the Palestinian parliamentary elections in 2006, which the EU observation mission defined as fair and appropriate, the Quartet, led by the USA, decided to impose three conditions (the renunciation of violence, the recognition of Israel and the acceptance of all previously signed agreements) before recognising Hamas as the legitimate government (Middle East Quartet 2006). Given Hamas's refusal to comply with these conditions, the EU decided not to recognise the new government and to suspend financial support to the PA and all operational partnerships such as the EUPOL COPPS, the police support mission launched in 2006.[9] While the attempts to establish a national unity government thanks to the Saudi mediation in March 2007 opened up the possibility of engagement between the EU and Hamas, the takeover of the Gaza Strip by Hamas in June 2007 definitively closed any window of opportunity. The Quartet adopted the 'West Bank First' approach – that is, complete support for the Fatah-led government based in Ramallah and the exclusion of the Hamas-governed territories (Gunning 2010). These decisions were always phrased within the two-pillar approach that characterises EU policies, although the implementation of this approach on the ground can be seen as ambiguous and incomplete, to say the least.

Significant divergences among member states emerged between December 2008 and January 2009, when Israel launched Operation Cast Lead in Gaza as a way to retaliate against the launch of missiles from the Strip. As shown in Table 2.1, member states' reactions to the events varied greatly, with some criticising Israel for its violations of human rights and humanitarian law, others openly supporting Israeli actions as a form of legitimate defence against the firing of rockets from Gaza and still others trying to maintain a more balanced position

Table 2.1 EU member states' positions/votes on key issues

Issue	MSs supportive	MSs against	Balanced/abstaining MSs
Criticisms of Israel's Gaza offensive 2008–9[*]	Ireland, Belgium, Sweden, Luxembourg, Cyprus, Finland, Malta (focus on human rights and humanitarian law)	Germany, Italy, the Czech Republic, the Netherlands, Denmark, Romania	United Kingdom, France and Spain (criticise Israeli disproportionate use of force, Hamas considered responsible for the conflict)
Swedish draft declaration December 2009[**]	United Kingdom, Ireland, Belgium, Luxembourg, Portugal, Finland, Sweden, Malta	France, Italy, Germany, the Netherlands, the Czech Republic, Romania, Poland, Spain, Hungary, Slovenia, Slovakia	Cyprus, Austria, Bulgaria, Latvia, Lithuania, Estonia, Denmark, Greece (not mentioned in the newspapers, no disclosed records of the meeting of the Council)
UN vote on Palestinian statehood (non-Member Observer State) November 2012 – UNGA A/67/L.28[***]	Austria, Belgium, Cyprus, Denmark, Finland, France, Greece, Luxembourg, Malta, Portugal, Sweden, Italy, Ireland, Spain	The Czech Republic	Germany, Hungary, the Netherlands, Poland, Romania, Bulgaria, United Kingdom, Slovenia, Slovakia, Estonia, Latvia, Lithuania

Sources:
[*] Euro-Mediterranean Human Rights Network (2009);
[**] Media, own compilation: Barber (2009); Beesley (2009); Elgot (2009a, 2009b); EUbusiness (2009a, 2009b); EurActiv (2009); Financial Times (2009); Haaretz (2009); ICEJ (2009); Jerusalem Post (2009); MAE (2009); Rettman (2009a, 2009b); The Local (2009); World Jewish Congress (2009);
[***] UNGA (2012).

which criticised both sides of the conflict (Euro-Mediterranean Human Rights Network 2009). After Operation Cast Lead, however, member states' positions towards the conflict changed: this episode was the point when 'the penny dropped' (Interviewees 4, 91). The Council, which had agreed to grant Israel an advanced status in June 2008, opted to freeze the upgrade process until the situation on the ground improved, as expressed on the occasion of the EU–Israel Association Council in June 2009 (Pardo and Peters 2012: 491–501).[10] This trend was strengthened by the Council Conclusions in December 2009, in which the EU set out the parameters, principles and issues for the resolution of the conflict. Not only did the EU express its support for the two-state solution, it also stressed that settlements were illegal under international law, that the closure of Gaza was a serious problem, that Jerusalem was supposed to be the capital of both states

(Israel and Palestine) and that negotiations should be resumed soon (ibid.: 503–6). This document was the result of difficult negotiations among member states on the wording of the text and a more watered-down version of what the Swedish presidency had proposed (see Table 2.1).[11]

While the EU's commitment to the two-state solution is not disputed, member states do not agree on how to reach this goal. This was particularly clear in the case of the Palestinian bid for statehood in 2011 and 2012. The Palestinian President Abbas made a formal request to the UN Security Council for full membership in the UN in 2011. This request was, however, rejected due to the Security Council's inability to make a unanimous recommendation to the Assembly (and the threat of a veto by the USA). In 2012 the Palestinians there-fore changed strategy and asked to be recognised as a 'non-Member Observer State', a position that only requires simple majority in the General Assembly.[12] Eventually, in November 2012, the UN General Assembly granted Palestine the status of non-Member Observer State (UNGA 2012).[13] On that occasion, EU member states were not able to vote as a unified bloc: while only the Czech Republic voted against the resolution, the others were split into those abstaining from the vote or those casting their vote in favour of the resolution (see Table 2.1). Divisions within the UN are not new, and are also frequent in the Human Rights Council (Smith 2011). For example, in the ECFR Review on Human Rights 2011, Gowan and Brantner (2011) highlighted that in the preceding three years Israeli–Palestinian issues had caused the majority of divisions among member states in the Human Rights Council. However, 'the EU's members still regularly vote together in favour of UN resolutions defending the Palestinians' basic rights. In February 2011, all European members of the Council backed a Security Council resolution – vetoed by the US – attacking Israel's settlement programme' (ibid.: 8). In essence, there are divisions, but the EU's commitment to the two-state solution and respect for human rights, international law and inter-national humanitarian law is repeated in all Council Conclusions on the Middle East (Council of the European Union 2009, 2010, 2011, 2012a, 2012b) and has not been challenged. While the EU is in favour of a Palestinian state, member states are not united when it comes to the ways in which this should be estab-lished (via international recognition or in the context of the peace agreement).[14]

This period of intense diplomatic activity was also accompanied by further developments concerning the key principles and parameters of the EU's two-pillar approach. In May 2011, following the reconciliation between Hamas and Fatah, the EU declared its readiness to recognise and support a Palestinian government headed by Abbas, as long as it would comply with the conditions imposed by the Quartet (Council of the European Union 2011). A year later, the EU reiterated the two pillars of its policy and highlighted the problems related to settlement construction, the trade of settlement goods, Area C in the West Bank and the closure of Gaza. In the EU's view, these issues had to be addressed in order to find a peaceful solution to the conflict (Council of the European Union 2012a). In December 2012 the EU further stressed these points and inserted a new element in its declaration, namely the reference to the territorial scope of its agreements with Israel, which are limited to the internationally recognised borders of Israel – that is, the Green Line (Council of the European Union 2012b). This type of reference had previously been made with regard to the Europol Agreement in the EU–Israel Association Council Conclusions, but the December Conclusions extended it to all agreements (European Union 2011; Council of the European Union 2012b).

This short overview shows that EU member states do not agree on all aspects that relate to the Israeli–Palestinian conflict, as they have different interests and priorities in their foreign policy due to a variety of factors ranging from geostrategic and economic calculations to historical legacies and the importance accorded to transatlantic relations. Declarations and decisions are thus the result of long negotiations and careful wording. Member states keep their bilateral relationships with Israel and the Palestinians, often making official declarations alongside the EU's framework and interpreting facts, events and policies differently (see also Chapter 7). Musu (2010: 83) convincingly points out that the EU's policy towards the Arab–Israeli conflict is a policy of 'converging parallels': member states agree on collective action, but 'the enduring reality of distinctly different national approaches to the issue, conflicting priorities and diverse and sometimes diverging interests' remains. Despite these differences, these parallels are today much closer than in the past. Divergences are indeed confined within the established boundaries of a two-state solution and respect for international law, which seem to be immovable and have not been affected by the successive rounds of enlargement (Kolaraska Bobinska and Mughrabi 2008; Müller 2012).

The expansion of EU policies

While the EU's stance has remained basically untouched during the past few decades, its policies and tools have significantly expanded. Its diplomatic position has been progressively supported by a series of economic, financial and technical policies and instruments, which make the EU one of the most important partners for both Israel and the Palestinians.[15] Given the evident disparities between the two countries, the EU has developed a more advanced relationship with Israel – which is involved in many EU programmes and with which cooperation is significant – while it has become the main payer for the Palestinians through its aid policies and state-building support. This section will offer a brief overview of the main aspects that define the EU's relations with Israel and the Palestinians, so that the policy field in which NSAs lobby acquires more precise contours.

In 1995 the EU launched a regional initiative for the entire Mediterranean area, known as the Barcelona process or the EMP. Importantly, by linking the region through political, economic and social ties, the EU aimed at increasing the prosperity of the area and fostering its political and economic development. Built on three interrelated pillars (political, economic and socio-cultural), the EMP established the foundations for the Association Agreements that the EU signed with its Mediterranean partners, including Israel and the PLO. The idea of bringing together Israel and the Arab states in a multilateral context was also meant to have positive repercussions on the peace process (Bicchi 2007; Volpi 2004; Del Sarto and Schumacher 2005). In the mid-2000s this regional framework was complemented by the European Neighbourhood Policy (ENP). This policy is based on bilateral agreements between the EU and the third country and allows for a differentiated approach that takes into account the needs of the partner state and its development. The extent to which the different ENP countries benefit from it depends on their economic and political conditions, as areas of cooperation are defined by the EU in accord with its partner country in the so-called Action Plans (Del Sarto and Schumacher 2005; Whitman and Wolff 2010; Herman 2006). Without offering the prospect of membership, the ENP has favoured a progressive integration into the EU's internal market and its various policies and programmes.

The EMP/ENP framework has therefore offered the EU a vast array of means and tools to foster its relations with the parties. In particular, bilateral contractual tools can exert significant leverage, as the EU is the stronger actor in these bilateral relationships and could use conditionality in order to push Israel and Palestine to make progress in the MEPP. While this possibility is present, it generally remains on paper, as the EU often refrains from making a clear use of these instruments and linking its bilateral relations to significant advance in the peace process (Tocci 2007, 2010).

This is especially evident in the case of Israel, which has seen a strengthening of its bilateral relations with the EU, despite the lack of substantial progress on the peace process. At the Essen European Council in 1994 the heads of state and government of the member states declared that Israel 'should enjoy special status in its relations with the European Union' (European Council 1994). While this approach could potentially reinforce the EU's aim to solve the Israeli–Palestinian conflict, the EU has barely relied on conditionality to convince Israel to make concessions and move on in terms of the peace process (Tocci 2010). In contrast, Israel has often benefited from a special relationship with the EU and has been capable of keeping the MEPP separate from its economic and technical relations with the EU. The areas of cooperation have significantly expanded from the initial trade and commercial relations. As the EU–Israel ENP Action Plan makes clear, the objective is to 'gradually integrate the country into European policies and programmes' (European Commission 2005). Today, Israel is indeed one of the most integrated neighbouring countries, participating in a number of programmes and policies as associate country (e.g., participation in the multi-annual research framework programme), and has signed numerous agreements, such as an Agreement on Agriculture and Fishery in 2009 and the Agreement on Conformity Assessment and Acceptance of Industrial Products in 2012.

In the case of the Palestinians the relationship is strongly asymmetrical, with the EU being the main donor and a crucial actor in supporting the process of state- and institution-building in Palestine. Since the Oslo Agreements of the early/mid-1990s, the EU has been the biggest donor to the PA. The peak of this inflow of millions into the PA's coffers was reached in 2011 with 524.9 million

(European Union 2013).[16] Moreover, the support ranges from financial assistance in the form of payment of the salary of the public administration to the implementation of programmes aimed at providing the know-how and the necessary training to run the state.[17] A substantial amount of money has also been used to support state-building initiatives, including the two CSDP missions EUPOL COPPS and EUBAM Rafah. While the former is aimed at building the police capacities of the Palestinians, the latter, a border-control mission, was intended to support the parties to the conflict to implement the Agreement on Movement and Access. The EU was in charge of controlling the crossing of Rafah between the Gaza Strip and Egypt, and training the Palestinians to perform this task. However, the mission has always suffered from the limitations imposed by Israel, which was preventing the EU from carrying out its job (Gisha and Physicians for Human Rights 2009). Despite the attempts of the EU, these missions as well as the training programmes implemented by the EU have not succeeded in ensuring accountability and civilian oversight. Instead of granting internal security for the Palestinians, security is often for Israel (Bouris 2012, 2014). When promoting democracy, the EU's main concerns for state-building and security have often trumped democracy, which is always interpreted through the lens of the conflict (Pogodda 2012; Voltolini and Bicchi 2015).

The policies and instruments that the EU can use to cajole or pressure Israel and the Palestinians have enormously increased over the decades. EU diplomacy has moved from the initial declarations, when member states cooperated in the loose form of the EPC, to a structured framework that defines the relations of the EU with the two countries. The EMP/ENP frameworks offer a wide range of tools as well as the option of using conditionality to implement EU objectives in terms of conflict resolution. However, this opportunity has often been left unexploited, as the EU has preferred a positive engagement and dialogue with the parties, instead of resorting to conditionality.

Actors involved in EU foreign policy-making towards Israel and Palestine

The increase in the number of policies and tools at the EU's disposal also implies a consequent increase in the number of actors involved in the policy-making process. Member states remain key actors in EU foreign policy, but the Commission, the European Parliament and the European Court of Justice have progressively influenced EU foreign policy through their decisions and actions. While this is in part due to the fact that some areas fall under the exclusive competences of the EU (e.g., trade), the entry into force of the Lisbon Treaty has also expanded the powers of the EU in external matters (Eeckhout 2011).

Cooperation at the EU level has not supplanted national foreign policies towards Israel and the Palestinians, but it has imposed some limits to the scope of national policies, as all member states comply with the common position based on the two pillars. The complex relationship between EU and member states' foreign policies is nicely captured by Müller (2012), who offers an in-depth analysis of the Europeanisation of the national foreign policies of France, the United Kingdom and Germany. Importantly, these states have been influenced by EU foreign policy, adapting their policies accordingly, but they have also managed to upload some of their preferences to the EU level, shaping the content of EU positions. The importance of member states has also been stressed in interviews with NSA representatives, who argue that it is crucial to have member states (especially the big three) on their side (e.g., Interviewees 2, 4, 60).

In addition to conducting bilateral relations with Israel and the Palestinians (which will not be the focus of this book), member states define common positions and policies at the EU level, more specifically in the Council of the European Union where all of them are represented. The Council meets in different configurations, depending on the topic discussed. In the case of external relations, the Foreign Affairs Council (FAC) is crucial, as it is here that many decisions about the course of EU foreign policy towards the Middle East are taken. For example, many declarations that will be referred to in the rest of the book are from the FAC, providing guidance to the European External Action Service (EEAS) and the Commission in relation to the implementation of policies or the development of bilateral relations.[18] However, the broad policy framework which defines the relations between the EU and Israel and/or Palestine is not confined to the FAC. Depending on the issue at hand, Israel/Palestine can be discussed in other policy domains (e.g., agriculture), thus implying the involvement of sector-specific ministers (e.g., ministers of agriculture) who decide on specific agreements and policies.

In the course of the 1990s two key positions were added in the field of foreign policy, with the aim of assisting the Council in the performance of its tasks: the High Representative for the Common Foreign and Security Policy and the Special Representatives. These last, nominated by the Council, are generally appointed in troubled areas with the aim of strengthening the voice of the EU in the promotion of stability, peace and the rule of law. Given the centrality of the Middle East on the agenda, in 1996 Miguel Angel Moratinos was appointed as EU Special Representative to the Middle East with a view to coordinating member states' policies and positions. This position was then taken over by Marc Otte (2003–11) and Andreas Reinicke (2012–14). As for the position of High Representative, Javier Solana was appointed in 1999, being in charge of Directorate-General (DG) E of the General Secretariat of the Council. During his mandate, the Middle East was a key issue on the agenda and Solana was active in trying to make the EU's presence more visible and effective. With the entry into force of the Lisbon Treaty in 2009, the role of the High Representative has seen an increase in powers. The new position, first filled by Catherine Ashton (2009–14) and currently by Federica Mogherini, is a double-hatted role combining the former position of High Representative for the Common Foreign and Security Policy with that of Vice-President of the Commission in charge of external relations.

Member states are not only present, usually via their ministers, in the high-level meetings of the Council. They are indeed represented in the various working groups, preparatory bodies and groups within the Council that have to prepare and work on EU policies and where ambassadors, counsellors or junior diplomats meet regularly. Each member state has a Permanent Representation (PermRep) in Brussels, which is staffed with diplomatic personnel in charge of the various policy areas decided at the EU level. PermReps are therefore an important institutional element in the EU foreign policy system, as they have first-hand information on EU policies and work as *trait d'union* between the EU and the national capitals, thus uploading member states' positions and downloading information and EU policies to their capitals.

Given the crucial role of the Council in the policy-making process, member states can be a central target of lobbying. The national route (Mazey and Richardson 2006) – that is, the use of the national channel to influence EU policies – has two forms. On the one hand, NSAs can decide to lobby in the capitals, and ask their governments to upload their preferences to the EU's forums. On the other hand, they can approach member states in Brussels by targeting the staff of the PermReps (which means targeting also the people involved in the various bodies and groups the Council is made of) (Haynes-Renshaw 2009; Saurugger 2009). While it is argued in the literature that national diplomats seconded to Brussels are in a different environment from the national capitals and can be subject to socialisation effects (Lewis 2005), this is not so pronounced on a sensitive issue such as the Israel–Palestine dossier, which does not leave much space for independent decisions by diplomats in Brussels. They are generally requested to report back to their Foreign Ministry, which then decides on the action to be taken within the EU (Interviewee 72).

In addition to member states, both the Commission and the Parliament are involved in various aspects of the Israeli–Palestinian conflict. Since the Lisbon Treaty, the EEAS – which incorporates the former DG E dealing with foreign and military affairs of the General Secretariat of the Council and DG RELEX (External Relations) of the Commission – is the service coordinating the EU's international activities. Moreover, the newly introduced position of High Representative of the Union for Foreign Affairs and Security Policy, who is also the Vice-President of the European Commission, coordinates all activities concerning EU external action, thus having a compound role (Missiroli 2010). The Israeli–Palestinian dossier is split among three desks: Desk Israel, Desk Occupied Palestinian Territories and Desk Middle East Peace Process. Those officials in charge are tasked with the preparation of material and documents for the formulation and implementation of EU foreign policy and with liaising with the parties on a frequent basis. They deal with the political side of EU policy, are involved in all the aspects related to the ENP and provide the umbrella framework for all the programmes and policies implemented by the Commission or by the Delegations on the ground.

Although the more political dimension of external relations is now under the supervision of the EEAS, the Commission still plays an important role when it comes to other policy areas. The EU's relations with Israel and the Palestinians cover a wide range of policies, thus implying the involvement of sector-specific competences and expertise. For example, DG Trade is in charge of drafting trade agreements with both Israel and the PA; DG DEVCO (International Cooperation and Development) is responsible for the management and implementation of many EU programmes and policies, such as the European Instrument for Democracy and Human Rights, and for the provision of funds under the ENP Instrument; DG Enterprise and DG SANCO (Health and Consumers) were involved in the case of the Agreement on Conformity Assessment and Acceptance of Industrial Products signed between the EU and Israel, given the focus on pharmaceutical products and certification procedures; similarly, DG AGRI (Agriculture and Rural Development) deals with agreements concerning agricultural matters, etc. While the political direction comes from the EEAS and the High Representative, the definition of agreements and the implementation of policies are often done by the sector-specific DGs. Moreover, the monetary and budgetary aspects of all programmes and policies are still in the hands of the Commission.[19]

The European Parliament's competences have also been expanded in many areas since December 2009. According to Articles 207 and 218 of the Treaty on the Functioning of the European Union (TFEU), the European Parliament is invested with the power of giving its consent when certain types of agreements (e.g., association agreements, policy areas in which the ordinary procedure applies) are decided upon. Although the Commission remains in charge of the negotiation process on the basis of a Council's decision, the entry into force of the agreement can only occur when both the Council and the Parliament have given their consent. This increases the power of the Parliament on EU external policies (see also Chapter 6). While this clearly opens new opportunities for NSAs when lobbying the EU, the Parliament has always been a target of lobbying. The Parliament has always been vocal on international matters: the Israeli–Palestinian conflict, given its saliency, has often been the subject of parliamentary resolutions. While these resolutions do not have the same diplomatic impact as the Council Conclusions, they represent one of the voices of the EU and they can matter a lot for NSAs. For example, the Friends of the Earth Middle East used the resolution of the European Parliament on the Lower Jordan River, issued on 9 September 2010, to lobby the governments of Israel, Jordan and the PA to take action to protect the river (Interviewee 45; Voltolini 2012). Moreover, the European Parliament also plays a role in keeping the other institutions accountable through the use of oral and written questions. Members of the European Parliament (MEPs) can ask the Commission or the Council to explain or justify certain policies, issues or positions of the EU. They often point to incoherence in EU foreign policy due to the clash between EU rhetoric about human rights and democracy and the actual pursuit of geopolitical and economic interests. This argument on the inconsistency of EU foreign policy has been frequently used in the case of Israel, with various MEPs denouncing Israeli violations of human rights and the permissive stance of the EU.[20]

Last, but not least, the EU has also numerous Delegations around the world, including in Israel (headquartered in Tel Aviv) and Palestine (headquartered in East Jerusalem). By working on the ground, these offices act as intermediaries between the local actors (NSAs as well) and the EU. They can channel information and communications between Brussels and Israel/Palestine and contribute to EU foreign policy-making (Interviewees 23, 88). For example, the EU Delegation to the West Bank and Gaza Strip usually participates in the drafting of the Heads of Mission Reports (Bicchi 2014). Both EU Delegations and member states' consulates/embassies are thus key actors in the policy-making process and can become the target of local NSAs, who might not be able to go to Brussels to carry out their lobbying activities.

EU policies towards the conflict: what is on the agenda now?

From a declaratory perspective, not much has changed over the past few years. The two-pillar policy remains the cornerstone of EU foreign policy towards the Israeli–Palestinian conflict and shapes its decisions and policies. However, some issues deserve further attention for their importance on the EU's agenda and the international repercussions that they can generate. First, the issue of Palestinian statehood remains an open chapter, with an increasing number of EU member states offering bilateral recognition. Second, the situation of Gaza has deteriorated exponentially, especially with the recent war in the summer of 2014. Third, some changes have occurred in EU–Israel relations, with some relevant steps being taken by the EU in terms of the implementation of its policies.

In July 2013 the USA sponsored the resumption of the peace talks between Israel and the Palestinians. The initiative was supposed to last nine months during which the parties would be able to negotiate and solve the main points of contention. The initial step aimed at establishing a framework for negotiations, which had to be followed by the permanent-status agreement. Not only did the EU support the peace talks, it even promised a Special Privileged Partnership to both partners, should the peace talks be successful (Council of the European Union 2013a, 2013b). Despite numerous talks and attempts, the peace talks failed and no concrete steps were reached by April 2014. The talks were flawed from the beginning, and neither Israel nor the Palestinians were truly engaged in them. On the one hand, the Palestinians trusted neither the Americans nor the Israelis. On the other hand, Israel wanted the recognition of Israel as a Jewish state before discussing anything else and it did not stop the construction of settlements in the Occupied Territories during the talks. Moreover, the announcement of a Fatah–Hamas unity government was rejected by Israel, which also used it to suspend the negotiations (Black and Beaumont 2014). Hopes for a resumption of the negotiations as well as support for the recent reconciliation between Hamas and Fatah were reiterated in May 2014 by the Council, stressing the readiness of the EU to assist the process by offering this privileged partnership to the parties (Council of the European Union 2014).

Tensions between Israel and the Palestinians deteriorated in the summer of 2014, when another conflict between Gaza and Israel broke out. Operation Protective Edge, which Israel started at the beginning of July, ended after around seven weeks of conflict leading to the destruction of Gaza and the killing and wounding of many people.[21] The events of the summer reopened a long-lasting problem, namely the dire situation of the Gaza Strip, which has been sealed off from the external world since 2007, after the coup that brought Hamas to power. This issue has also been the target of lobbying, with numerous NGOs calling on the international community for some action aimed at alleviating the situation of the people in Gaza and at removing the blockade which has been starving the population and damaging any possible economic development (e.g., Oxfam GB 2008; Oxfam International 2009; International Federation for Human Rights 2010).

While the issue of Gaza is still lingering on, the question of Palestinian statehood has again gained attention. Formally recognised by Sweden in October 2014, symbolic votes on the recognition have been held in the United Kingdom, in Ireland, in Spain and in France, while the European Parliament expressed its recognition in principle of Palestinian statehood (Rettman 2014; Youngs 2014; European Parliament 2014). At the time of writing (December 2014), it remains unclear what the PA will do with its bid in the UN, especially in light of the American opposition to any move in this sense. The EU is also divided on how to proceed in this regard, although the newly appointed High Representative Federica Mogherini made it clear in her statement at the European Parliament plenary assembly at the end of November 2014 that the EU has to show a united position on the issue of recognition to become a fundamental actor in the peace process (Mogherini 2014).

Over the past few years there has also been an important shift in EU–Israeli relations. While the general framework has not substantially changed, as the EU maintains its position based on two pillars and continues to support peace talks between Israel and Palestine as the best way for reaching a common solution to the conflict, it has modified the way in which it implements its bilateral agreements with Israel. More specifically, in July 2013 the EU published the 'Guidelines on the eligibility of Israeli entities and their activities in the territories occupied by Israel since June 1967 for grants, prizes and financial instruments funded by the EU from 2014 onwards', in which it is stated that Israeli settlements or activities conducted in the occupied territories (unless the protected persons under the terms of international humanitarian law who live in these territories benefit from these activities and/or they aim at promoting the MEPP in line with EU policy) will not be funded by the EU under the new EU budget 2014–20.[22] In a nutshell, this document explains how the Commission executes the budget and how it implements EU policies. While the legal intricacies of the Guidelines are not the focus of this book, the important point is that the EU has made clear that its agreements and policies will only be applied to the territory of the state of Israel as internationally recognised. The Guidelines ensure the respecting of EU commitments and obligations under its own legislation, international law and humanitarian law. Moreover, they offer a solution that is horizontally applicable across all EU programmes and funds and 'effective in terms of providing legal certainty and financial security by establishing clear mechanisms of implementation and enforcement' (Nikolov 2014: 176).[23]

Conclusions

Characterised by a logic of diversity (Hoffmann 1966), the EU's approach towards the Israeli–Palestinian conflict has been described as a policy of converging parallels – that is, lines that tend towards the same direction, but never cross (Musu 2010). Divergences clearly persist among member states, due to different geopolitical and economic interests as well as different historical legacies. Yet, the EU has reached a well-established and widely shared position based on two pillars, namely the two-state solution and respect for human rights, international law and international humanitarian law (Tocci 2009). Differences among member states are confined by the boundaries created by these two pillars, which are not questioned. Metaphorically, the distance between the converging parallels has significantly diminished over the years.

The EU has often been a forerunner in its diplomatic stance, paving the way for decisions that the international community would then subscribe to. Not only did the EU envision the two-state solution already with the Venice Declaration of 1980, but EU actors were also instrumental in providing the bases for the Roadmap proposed by the Quartet in 2003. EU diplomacy has also been accompanied by an expansion of the policies and instruments that the EU can use to play a role in the Israeli–Palestinian conflict. The establishment of the EMP and the ENP has created a framework with numerous opportunities for engagement with Israel and the Palestinians in both multilateral and bilateral forms. More specifically, the EU's bilateral contractual relations with Israel and the PA give the EU strong leverage on the parties and the possibility of linking these policies to its broader conflict resolution policy.

The expansion of policies and instruments has also led to an increase in the number of actors involved, which in turn implies more potential targets for NSAs. The EEAS (and before it DG RELEX in the Commission and DG E in the Council Secretariat) is a key target, given that it deals with and coordinates the various aspects of EU relations with Israel/Palestine and the MEPP. DGs in the Commission and the Council (in its different formations and related working groups, etc.) are also lobbied on the basis of the specific policy areas they deal with (e.g., DG DEVCO in the Commission deals with aid policies, DG AGRI with agricultural agreements, etc.). The European Parliament, especially due to the increase in its competences and powers following the entry into force of the Lisbon Treaty, has also become an important target of NSA lobbying.

This chapter has presented the policy field in which NSAs' actions take place and the actors they interact with when lobbying on EU foreign policy towards the Israeli–Palestinian conflict. But who are these NSAs and what do they do? The next chapter will answer these questions by highlighting the key features and trends of the NSA population in the case of EU foreign policy towards the Israeli–Palestinian conflict.

Notes

1 For detailed accounts of this period, see, for example, Tessler (1994); Milton-Edwards (2009); Fraser (2004).
2 The term 'European Union' (EU) refers in this book to all stages of the integration process. A more precise use would require a distinction between the different names

that have been used over the decades. For example, I should refer to the European Community when speaking of certain policy areas before the entry into force of the Treaty of Lisbon in 2009. However, for simplicity, in most cases I refer to the EU.

3 For an overview of the instruments/policies, see Musu (2010). For an analysis of the EU's cross-pillar policy-making, see Stetter (2007).

4 For more detailed accounts of EU foreign policy towards the Israeli–Palestinian conflict, see Musu (2010); Müller (2012); Persson (2014); Özgür-Kaya (2013); Pardo and Peters (2010).

5 For a map showing Israeli conquests of 1967, see Gilbert (2012). The Sinai was returned to Egypt after the Israel–Egypt Peace Treaty of 1979.

6 For a detailed account of the years following the Yom Kippur War, see Miller (2011), Chapter 4.

7 For example, in 1987 the EU called for a UN-sponsored international conference (cf. Miller 2011: 113).

8 In May 1999 Arafat announced that he would declare the State of Palestine on 4 May, as the agreement between Israel and the PLO within the Oslo framework had indicated May 1999 as the deadline for a final agreement.

9 For further information about EU missions in the Palestinian Territories, see Bouris (2014) and the following links: http://www.eubam-rafah.eu/ and http://eupolcopps.eu/

10 The European Parliament had already expressed its contrariety to any strengthening of the bilateral relations with Israel in December 2008, when it postponed the vote on the participation of Israel in Community programmes, arguing that Israeli policies in the Occupied Territories had not changed in the last years and Israel did not deserve to receive additional benefits from the EU (European Parliament 2008; Morgantini 2008).

11 The original text referred to East Jerusalem as the capital of the Palestinian state (*Haaretz* 2009; Bicchi 2014). This move gave rise to strong opposition by many member states, not to mention Israel, so that the final version was a compromise referring to the EU's usual position of Jerusalem as the capital of two states.

12 For an overview of the process, see BBC (2012).

13 http://www.un.org/News/Press/docs/2012/ga11317.doc.htm (accessed 20 March 2013).

14 In this regard, it is also interesting that some member states (e.g., Sweden) recognised the Palestinian state in 2014, following a stalemate in the peace negotiations. Similarly, in December 2014 the European Parliament voted on a resolution stating that it recognises, in principle, Palestinian statehood and that this should be parallel to the advancement of peace talks.

15 More details can be found on the websites of the EU delegation to Israel (http://eeas.europa.eu/delegations/israel/index_en.htm) and the EU delegation to the West Bank and Gaza Strip (http://www.eeas.europa.eu/delegations/westbank/index_en.htm).

16 This amount includes the money channelled through the European Neighbourhood Policy Instrument (ENPI), other thematic lines and humanitarian aid.

17 On state-building, see Bouris (2014).

18 In the past this formation of the Council was merged with the General Affairs Council and ministers divided the agenda between general and foreign affairs. Now there are two separate council formations, so that the division of labour is clearer.

19 The European Neighbourhood Policy is in the portfolio of the same Commissioner dealing with enlargement, who is supposed to work together with the HR. While the enlargement policy has its own DG within the Commission, the ENP is dealt with in the EEAS. Given that the EEAS does not have a budget per se, it relies on the Commission for the implementation of its policies and programmes. Please note that there was a partial reorganisation of the DGs in November 2014.

20 Oral and written questions are available on the European Parliament's website: http://www.europarl.europa.eu/aboutparliament/en/003a6f9886/Access-to-documents.html

21 Details can be found on the OCHA website and in this report: http://www.ochaopt.org/documents/gaza_crisis_appeal_9_september.pdf (accessed 1 December 2014).

22 http://eeas.europa.eu/delegations/israel/documents/related-links/20130719_guidelines_on_eligibility_of_israeli_entities_en.pdf (accessed 1 December 2014).
23 Nikolov (2014) provides a detailed and precise reconstruction of the establishment of the Guidelines.

References

Barber, Tony. 2009. 'Protests Force EU to Drop Jerusalem Plan'. *Financial Times*, 8 December. http://www.ft.com/intl/cms/s/0/340e81a6-e408-11de-b2a9-00144feab49a. html#axzz2RZxmuoTS

BBC. 2012. 'Q&A: Palestinians' Upgraded UN Status'. 30 November. http://www.bbc. co.uk/news/world-middle-east-13701636

Beesley, Arthur. 2009. 'EU Rowing Back on Palestinian Stance'. *Irish Times*, 8 December. www.irishtimes.com

Bicchi, Federica. 2007. *European Foreign Policy Making towards the Mediterranean*. New York: Palgrave Macmillan.

———. 2014. 'Information Exchanges, Diplomatic Networks and the Construction of European Knowledge in EU Foreign Policy'. *Cooperation and Conflict* 49 (2): 239–59.

Black, Ian and Peter Beaumont. 2014. 'Israel Suspends Peace Talks with Palestinians after Fatah-Hamas Deal'. *Guardian*, 24 April, World News section. http://www.theguardian. com/world/2014/apr/24/middle-east-israel-halts-peace-talks-palestinians

Bouris, Dimitris. 2012. 'The European Union's Role in the Palestinian Territories: State-Building through Security Sector Reform?' *European Security* 21 (2): 257–71.

———. 2014. *The European Union and Occupied Palestinian Territories: State-Building without a State*. Oxford: Routledge.

Council of the European Union. 2009. 'Council Conclusions on the Middle East Peace Process – 2985th FOREIGN AFFAIRS Council Meeting'. http://www.consilium. europa.eu/uedocs/cms_data/docs/pressdata/EN/foraff/111829.pdf

———. 2010. 'Council Conclusions on the Middle East Peace Process – 3058th FOREIGN AFFAIRS Council Meeting'. http://www.consilium.europa.eu/uedocs/ cmsUpload/118448.pdf

———. 2011. 'Council Conclusions on the Middle East Peace Process – 3091st FOREIGN AFFAIRS Council Meeting'. http://eeas.europa.eu/delegations/israel/ documents/press_corner/20110523_01_en.pdf

———. 2012a. 'Council Conclusions on the Middle East Peace Process – 3166th FOREIGN AFFAIRS Council Meeting'. http://www.consilium.europa.eu/uedocs/cms_ Data/docs/pressdata/EN/foraff/130195.pdf

———. 2012b. 'Council Conclusions on the Middle East Peace Process – 3209th FOREIGN AFFAIRS Council Meeting'. http://www.consilium.europa.eu/uedocs/cms_ data/docs/pressdata/EN/foraff/134140.pdf

———. 2013a. 'Council Conclusions on the Middle East Peace Process. FOREIGN AFFAIRS Council Meeting Brussels, 22 July 2013'. Brussels: European Union. http:// www.consilium.europa.eu/uedocs/cms_data/docs/pressdata/EN/foraff/138293.pdf

———. 2013b. 'Council Conclusions on the Middle East Peace Process. FOREIGN AFFAIRS Council Meeting Brussels, 16 December 2013'. Brussels: European Union. http://www.consilium.europa.eu/uedocs/cms_data/docs/pressdata/EN/foraff/140097.pdf

———. 2014. 'Council Conclusions on the Middle East Peace Process. FOREIGN AFFAIRS Council Meeting Brussels, 12 May 2014'. Brussels: European Union. http:// www.consilium.europa.eu/uedocs/cms_data/docs/pressdata/EN/foraff/142555.pdf

Del Sarto, Raffaella and Tobias Schumacher. 2005. 'From EMP to ENP: What's at Stake with the European Neighbourhood Policy towards the Southern Mediterranean?' *European Foreign Affairs Review* 10 (1): 17–38.

De Soto, Alvaro. 2007. *End of Mission Report*. United Nations. http://image.guardian. co.uk/sys-files/Guardian/documents/2007/06/12/DeSotoReport.pdf

Dosenrode, Sören and Anders Stubkjaer. 2002. *The European Union and the Middle East*. London/New York: Sheffield Academic Press.

Eeckhout, Piet. 2011. *EU External Relations Law*. Oxford: Oxford University Press.

Elgot, Jessica. 2009a. 'France Unlikely to Back EU Plan to Split Jerusalem'. 3 December. http://www.thejc.com/news/world-news/24560/france-unlikely-back-eu-plan-split-jerusalem

———. 2009b. 'EU: Jerusalem Must Be Capital of Israel and Palestine'. 9 December. http://www.thejc.com/news/israel-news/24690/eu-jerusalem-must-be-capital-israel-and-palestine

EUbusiness. 2009a. 'Controversy over EU Stance on East Jerusalem–European Business, Finance and EU Political News from EUbusiness – EUbusiness.com'. *EUbusiness*, 7 December.http://www.eubusiness.com/news-eu/mideast-diplomacy.1tm/

———. 2009b. 'EU Ministers Seek Joint Stance on Jerusalem's Future'. *EUbusiness*, 8 December.

EurActiv. 2009. 'EU Says Jerusalem Should Be Capital of Two States'. *EurActiv.com*, 9 December. http://www.euractiv.com/global-europe/eu-jerusalem-capital-states-news-223181

Euro-Mediterranean Human Rights Network. 2009. *Active But Acquiescent: The EU's Response to the Israeli Military Offensive in the Gaza Strip*.

European Commission. 2005. 'EU–Israel Action Plan'. Brussels.

European Council. 1977. 'Presidency Conclusions, London, 29–30 June 1977'. London. http://www.european-council.europa.eu/media/854634/london_june_1977__eng_.pdf

———. 1980. 'Presidency Conclusions, Venice, 12–13 June 1980'. Venice. http://www. european-council.europa.eu/media/854488/venice_june_1980__eng_.pdf

———. 1994. 'Presidency Conclusions, Essen, 9–10 December 1994'. Essen: European Union.

———. 1999. 'Presidency Conclusions, Berlin, 24–25 March 1999'. Berlin: European Union. http://www.consilium.europa.eu/uedocs/cms_data/docs/pressdata/en/ec/ACFB2.html

———. 2003. 'A Secure Europe in a Better World: European Security Strategy'. Brussels: European Union.

European Parliament. 2008. 'Debate: Israel's Participation in Community Programmes'. http://www.europarl.europa.eu/sides/getDoc.do?pubRef=-//EP//TEXT+CRE+20081203+ITEM-015+DOC+XML+V0//EN

———. 2014. 'European Parliament resolution of 17 December 2014 on Recognition of Palestine Statehood' Strasbourg.

European Union. 2011. 'Tenth Meeting of the EU–Israel Association Council Statement of the European Union'. http://eeas.europa.eu/delegations/israel/press_corner/all_news/news/2011/20110222_01_en.htm

———. 2013. *The European Union and the Palestinians. Real Partners Make a Real Difference*. Jerusalem: European Union Delegation to the West Bank and the Gaza Strip. http://eeas.europa.eu/delegations/westbank/documents/news/2013_generalbrochure_en.pdf

Financial Times. 2009. 'Israel's Revealing Fury towards EU'. *Financial Times*, 13 December. http://www.ft.com/intl/cms/s/0/ba991878-e811-11de-8a02-00144feab49a. html#axzz2RZxmuoTS

Fraser, Thomas G. 2004. *The Arab-Israeli Conflict*. 2nd edn. London/Basingstoke: Palgrave Macmillan.

Gilbert, Martin. 2012. *The Routledge Atlas of the Arab-Israeli Conflict*. 10th edn. Abingdon/New York: Routledge.

Gisha and Physicians for Human Rights. 2009. *Rafah Crossing: Who Holds the Keys?* Israel: Gisha/Physicians for Human Rights.

Gowan, Richard and Franziska Brantner. 2011. *The EU and Human Rights at the UN: 2011 Review*. Policy Memo. European Council on Foreign Relations. http://ecfr.eu/ content/entry/the_eu_and_human_rights_at_the_un_2011_review

Greilsammer, Ilan and Joseph Weiler. 1984. 'European Political Cooperation and the Palestinian–Israeli Conflict: An Israeli Perspective'. In *European Foreign Policy-Making and the Arab–Israeli Conflict*, edited by David Allen and Alfred Pijpers. The Hague: Martinus Nijhoff. 121–60.

Gunning, Jeroen. 2010. 'The Conflict and the Question of Engaging with Hamas'. In *European Involvement in the Arab–Israeli Conflict*, edited by Esra Bulut Aymat. Chaillot Paper 124. Paris: EU ISS. 97–108.

Haaretz. 2009. '*Haaretz* Exclusive: EU Draft Document on Division of Jerusalem'. *Haaretz.com*, 1 December. http://www.haaretz.com/news/haaretz-exclusive-eu-draft-document-on-division-of-jerusalem-1.3029

Haynes-Renshaw, F. 2009. 'Least Accessible But Not Inaccessible: Lobbying the Council and the European Council'. In *Lobbying the European Union: Institutions, Actors and Issues*, edited by David Coen and Jeremy Richardson. Oxford: Oxford University Press. 3–15.

Herman, Lior. 2006. 'An Action Plan or a Plan for Action? Israel and the European Neighbourhood Policy'. *Mediterranean Politics* 11 (3): 371.

Hoffmann, Stanley. 1966. 'Obstinate or Obsolete? The Fate of the Nation-State and the Case of Western Europe'. *Daedalus* 95 (3): 862–915.

Hollis, Rosemary. 2010. 'The Basic Stakes and Strategy of the EU and Member States'. In *European Involvement in the Arab-Israeli Conflict*, edited by Esra Bulut Aymat. Chaillot Paper 124. Paris: EU ISS. 31–42.

ICEJ, International Christian Embassy Jerusalem. 2009. 'France Rejects Swedish Plan to Declare Palestinian Capital in Jerusalem | ICEJ International'. 3 December. http://int.icej. org/news/headlines/france-rejects-swedish-plan-declare-palestinian-capital-jerusalem

International Federation for Human Rights. 2010. *Dashed Hopes: Continuation of the Gaza Blockade*. http://www.unhcr.org/refworld/docid/4cf62f9e2e8.html

Jerusalem Post. 2009. 'Analysis: Israel Dodges EU Bullet'. *www.JPost.com*, 9 December. http://www.jpost.com/Israel/Analysis-Israel-dodges-EU-bullet

Kolaraska Bobinska, Lena and S. Mughrabi. 2008. *New EU Member States' Policy towards the Israeli-Palestinian Conflict: The Case of Poland*. 69. EuroMesco Paper. EuroMesco.

Lewis, Jeffrey. 2005. 'The Janus Face of Brussels: Socialization and Everyday Decision Making in the European Union'. *International Organization* 59 (4): 937–71.

MAE, Ministero Affari Esteri. 2009. 'Le Conclusioni Del Cagre (Bruxelles 7–8 Dicembre). Appello dell'Ue a Riprendere I Negoziati Israelo–Palestinesi'. http://www. esteri.it/MAE/IT/Sala_Stampa/ArchivioNotizie/Approfondimenti/2009/12/20091209_ conclusioniCagre.htm?LANG=IT

Mazey, Sonia and Jeremy Richardson. 2006. 'Interest Groups and EU Policy-Making: Organizational Logic and Venue Shopping'. In *European Union: Power and Policy-Making*, by Jeremy Richardson. London/New York: Routledge. 247–68.

Middle East Quartet. 2006. 'Statement by the Middle East Quartet'. http://unispal.un.org/ unispal.nsf/fdc5376a7a0587a4852570d000708f4b/354568cce5e38e5585257106007a0834? OpenDocument

Miller, Rory. 2011. *Inglorious Disarray: Europe, Israel and the Palestinians Since 1967*. London: C Hurst & Co.

Milton-Edwards, Beverley. 2009. *The Israeli–Palestinian Conflict: A People's War*. Abingdon/New York: Routledge.

Milward, Alan S. 1992. *The European Rescue of the Nation-State*. London: Routledge.

Missiroli, A. 2010. 'The New EU "Foreign Policy" System after Lisbon: A Work in Progress'. *European Foreign Affairs Review* 15 (4): 427–52.

Mogherini, Federica. 2014. *Statement by HR/VP Mogherini on Recognition of Palestine Statehood at the EP Plenary*. Strasbourg: European Union. http://eeas.europa.eu/top_ stories/2014/271114_post-ep-plenary_en.htm

Morgantini, Luisa. 2008. 'Israele Non È Al Di Sopra Delle Leggi'. 12 April. http:// luisamorgantini.net/node/713

Müller, Patrick. 2012. *EU Foreign Policymaking and the Middle East Conflict: The Europeanization of National Foreign Policy*. CSS Studies in Security and International Relations. London: Routledge.

———. 2014. 'Informal Security Governance and the Middle East Quartet: Survival of the Unfittest?' *International Peacekeeping* 21 (4): 464–80.

Musu, Costanza. 2003. 'European Foreign Policy: A Collective Policy or a Policy of "Converging Parallels"'. *European Foreign Affairs Review* 8: 35–49.

———. 2010. *European Union Policy towards the Arab–Israeli Peace Process: The Quicksands of Politics*. Basingstoke: Palgrave Macmillan.

Nikolov, Krassimir Y. 2014. 'Ashton's Second Hat: The EU Funding Guidelines on Israel as a Post-Lisbon Instrument of European Foreign Policy Making'. *Diplomacy* 11: 168–88.

Oxfam GB. 2008. *The Gaza Strip: A Humanitarian Implosion*. http://policy-practice. oxfam.org.uk/publications/the-gaza-strip-a-humanitarian-implosion-126094

Oxfam International. 2009. *Failing Gaza: No Rebuilding, No Recovery, No More Excuses*. http://www.oxfam.org/policy/failing-gaza-no-rebuilding-no-recovery-no-more-excuses

Özgür-Kaya, Taylan. 2013. *The Middle East Peace Process and the EU: Foreign Policy and Security Strategy in International Politics*. London/New York: I. B.Tauris.

Pardo, Sharon and Joel Peters. 2010. *Uneasy Neighbours: Israel and the European Union*. Lanham, MD: Lexington Books.

———. 2012. *Israel and the European Union : A Documentary History*. Lanham, MD/ Plymouth: Lexington Books.

Persson, Anders. 2014. *The EU and the Israeli–Palestinian Conflict 1971–2013: In Pursuit of a Just Peace*. Lanham, MD: Lexington Books.

Pogodda, Sandra. 2012. 'Inconsistent Interventionism in Palestine: Objectives, Narratives, and Domestic Policy-Making'. *Democratization* 19 (3): 535–52.

Rettman, Andrew. 2009a. 'EU Tries to Breathe Life into Middle East Peace Talks'. *EUobserver*, 8 December. http://euobserver.com/foreign/29118

———. 2009b. 'EU Ministers Face Tough Decision on Israel'. *EUobserver*, 8 December. http://euobserver.com/foreign/29113

———. 2014. 'Danish Parliament to Vote on Palestine Recognition'. *EUobserver*, 24 November. http://euobserver.com/foreign/126641

Saurugger, Sabine. 2009. 'COREPER and National Governments'. In *Lobbying the European Union*, by David Coen and Jeremy Richardson. Oxford: Oxford University Press. 105–27.

Smith, Karen E. 2011. *The European Union and the Review of the Human Rights Council*. Study for the Directorate-General for External Policies of the Union. Brussels: European Parliament.

Stetter, Stephan. 2007. *EU Foreign and Interior Policies: Cross-Pillar Politics and the Social Construction of Sovereignty*. Routledge Advances in European Politics. New York: Routledge.

Tessler, Mark A. 1994. *A History of the Israeli–Palestinian Conflict*. Bloomington: Indiana University Press.

The Local. 2009. 'UK MPs Back Swedish Presidency on Jerusalem – The Local'. 7 December. http://www.thelocal.se/20091207/23692

Tocci, Nathalie. 2007. *The EU and Conflict Resolution: Promoting Peace in the Backyard*. Abingdon/New York: Routledge.

———. 2009. 'Firm in Rhetoric, Compromising in Reality: The EU in the Israeli–Palestinian Conflict'. *Ethnopolitics* 8 (3): 387–401.

———. 2010. 'The Conflict and EU–Israel Relations'. In *European Involvement in the Arab–Israeli Conflict*, edited by Esra Bulut Aymat. Chaillot Paper 124. Paris: EU ISS. 55–64.

———. 2011. *The EU, the Middle East Quartet and (In)effective Multilaterliasm*. Mercury Reports 9.

UNGA, United Nations General Assembly. 2012. 'General Assembly Votes Overwhelmingly to Accord Palestine "Non-Member Observer State" Status in United Nations'. 29 November. http://www.un.org/News/Press/docs/2012/ga11317.doc.htm

Volpi, Frédéric. 2004. 'Regional Community Building and the Transformation of International Relations: The Case of the Euro-Mediterranean Partnership'. *Mediterranean Politics* 9 (2): 145–64.

Voltolini, Benedetta. 2012. *The Role of Non-State Actors in EU Policies towards the Israeli–Palestinian Conflict*. Occasional Paper 99. Paris: EU ISS.

Voltolini, Benedetta and Federica Bicchi. 2015. 'When Security Trumps Democracy: EU Democracy Promotion in Israel and Palestine'. In *The Substance of European Union Democracy Promotion: Conceptual Discussions and Country Comparisons*, edited by Anne Wetzel and Jan Orbie. Basingstoke: Palgrave Macmillan.

Whitman, Richard and Sarah Wolff, eds. 2010. *The European Neighbourhood Policy in Perspective: Context, Implementation and Impact*. Basingstoke: Palgrave Macmillan.

World Jewish Congress. 2009. 'No EU Consensus on Swedish Proposal on Jerusalem'. *San Diego Jewish World*. 8 December. http://www.sdjewishworld.com/2009/12/08/no-eu-consensus-on-swedish-proposal-on-jerusalem/

Youngs, Richard. 2014. 'EU Recognition of Palestinian Statehood Can Only Offer a Partial Solution to the Israel-Palestine Conflict'. *EUROPP*. 27 November. http://blogs.lse.ac.uk/europpblog/2014/11/27/eu-recognition-of-palestinian-statehood-can-only-offer-a-partial-solution-to-the-israel-palestine-conflict/

3 Who's who? Mapping non-state actors in EU policies towards the Israeli–Palestinian conflict

The EU's engagement with NSAs is a crucial part of its policies. While these actors benefit from EU policies and programmes,[1] many of them are also active in trying to shape them. The EU values the involvement of civil society on the input side of the policy cycle, as this allows it to be aware of the needs of stakeholders, thus creating policies that would increase its input legitimacy (Finke 2007; Kohler-Koch and Finke 2007; Saurugger 2008). External policies are no exception to this trend and NSAs lobbying the EU on issues related to its external relations are numerous. Against this background, this chapter provides an analysis of the population of NSAs that lobby, or at least have a potential interest in doing so, the EU on its policies towards Israel and Palestine. Although the NSAs involved are very diverse, they all conceive of the EU as a crucial player that is worth lobbying in order to influence its policies. In mapping the population of NSAs, this chapter complements the previous one, which has identified the policy space in which lobbying takes place, by mapping the NSA population and identifying the main features and trends that define lobby actions. An original dataset that maps the NSA population (potentially) active on Israeli–Palestinian issues is presented in the following pages with the aim of providing the context and the background to understand the dynamics of lobbying in the case of EU foreign policy towards the Israeli–Palestinian conflict. While this chapter gives an overview of NSAs, Chapters 4 to 6 will then zoom in on specific NSAs on the basis of their relevance and involvement in the policy issue discussed as well as on the importance that other NSA representatives and/or EU/national officials have attributed to them.[2]

This chapter is structured as follows. First, it presents the broader issue of NSAs in EU policy-making and the mapping of NSA lobbying on EU foreign policy towards the Israeli–Palestinian conflict, discussing the methodology used to construct the NSA database and the problems encountered. This is followed by a typology of NSAs, in which the different categories of NSAs are presented. Third, the key features and main trends of NSAs are identified and explained. The concluding section summarises the main findings of the chapter.

Mapping NSAs in EU policies towards the Israeli–Palestinian conflict

Lobbying in the EU is a well-known phenomenon. Yet, mapping who these actors are is no mean feat. Due to the lack of a comprehensive census of the interest group population and of a compulsory registry, there are only estimates of the overall NSA population lobbying the EU (Coen and Richardson 2009; Euractiv 2008; Greenwood 2003). Unlike the US system where lobbyists are obliged to register and there is a relatively strict regulation in place (Chari *et al.* 2010; Woll 2012; Greenwood and Dreger 2013), researchers working on the EU lobbying system need to draw on different sources to build their samples.[3] Initially, interest groups were listed in the CONECCS system[4] and between 2006 and 2011 in the Register of Interest Representatives of the Commission. This Register, in which registration was not compulsory, provided only scattered information, as each NSA could decide which information to provide and very limited incentives were put in place to cajole NSAs to voluntarily register.[5] In the case of the European Parliament, there was only a list of people (and their affiliation) in possession of a long-term badge to enter the European Parliament's premises.[6] Following some lobbying scandals,[7] the European Parliament and the Commission decided to take further steps in order to ensure greater transparency of the policy-making process and to better regulate lobbying. In June 2011 the two institutions established a new inter-institutional register, the Transparency Register, and further changes are expected to take place in the course of 2015. The Register still remains voluntary and the only incentive for interest groups to register consists in the possibility of obtaining long-term badges for the European Parliament.

Given this lack of a clear and precise list of interest groups in the EU, scholars have built their own dataset, adopting different definitions of interest groups (Baroni *et al.* 2014), making comparison of results very difficult. Nevertheless, there is a shared understanding that the number of interest groups lobbying the EU has increased over the past decade, but at an irregular pace (Greenwood 2003; Berkhout and Lowery 2010). Moreover, the composition of the interest group population has changed over time. While corporate representation seems to diminish or remain stable, public interest groups have grown in numbers (Berkhout and Lowery 2010).

Constructing the database

The mapping of NSAs lobbying on EU foreign policy towards Israel and Palestine, or potentially interested in doing so, includes actors who have been involved in lobbying actions, those mentioned in interviews and those whose names have been found in reports, books and articles. Even though there has been no visible lobbying for some of them, they all have interests at stake in what the EU does and lobbying cannot therefore be excluded. The task of mapping this population, however, faces the same obstacles highlighted above, namely the lack of a register (with compulsory registration) in which to look for NSAs. Moreover, the previous studies and databases mentioned above were also not apt for the purpose of this research due to their different focus. Four different types of sources have been used to compile the database. First, before 2011 the research relied on the two separate registers of the Commission and the European Parliament. Following the creation of the inter-institutional Transparency Register, the database has been updated taking into account these changes. Second, NGO studies, newspaper articles and books or academic articles dealing with Israel and Palestine, which mentioned the names of certain NSAs, were another key resource (e.g., van Kuppevelt 2009; Cronin 2011; Van Gelder and Kroes 2009; Profundo 2006a, 2006b, 2010; The Coalition of Women for Peace 2010a, 2010b, 2011a, 2011b; Hecker 2005, 2010). A third instrument used has been the internet: the websites of some NSAs contained links to other NSAs or mentioned other actors (especially in the case of NGOs). Finally, interviews with experts, NSAs and officials have been crucial to find additional NSAs that had contacts with EU and national officials.

There are some aspects that need to be clarified in relation to the construction of this dataset. First, the high number of sources consulted and of interviews carried out ensures that the most active NSAs are likely to have been included. It is not possible, however, to rule out the existence of other NSAs whose actions are particularly secretive or that I did not identify. Another potential limit of the database regards the overrepresentation of some categories of NSAs due to the fact that information was not equally available in all cases. Some reports focus on specific actors in certain member states, such as business groups in the United Kingdom or in the Netherlands (e.g., Profundo 2006a; Van Gelder and Kroes 2009); in other instances, language barriers prevented me from getting access to information.[8] To minimise these problems and avoid inflating the number of certain categories, NSA representatives as well as European officials have been asked to suggest the names of other NSAs lobbying on EU foreign policy towards the Israeli–Palestinian case. No geographical restrictions were made when asking this question and, in certain cases, interviewees were explicitly asked for the names of NSAs from the new member states. Finally, the database does not distinguish between the actors that work at the EU, national or both levels. These limitations, however, do not prevent the dataset from providing an overview that contributes to getting a sense of the landscape of NSAs.

The database of NSAs involved in EU foreign policy towards the Israeli–Palestinian conflict contains 325 NSAs as of 22 December 2014.[9] The first important insight that it provides is the significant number of NSAs in a policy area which has long been considered the almost exclusive territory of member states (and, in certain cases, EU institutions). This finding is of utmost importance, as it refutes the widespread idea (and 'null hypothesis' of this research) that there is no or limited lobbying in this policy domain, given its 'high politics' nature. Most accounts on lobbying in the EU tend to assume that interest groups are comparatively less involved and less prominent in this policy area than in other EU policies. In contrast, this database shows a high density of NSAs that are active or potentially interested in lobbying the EU when it comes to its foreign policy towards the Israeli–Palestinian conflict. Second, the database also demonstrates that, despite the rhetoric–practice gap of EU policy towards the Israeli–Palestinian conflict (Tocci 2005), the majority of NSAs view the EU as an important player to be taken into account in their lobbying activities (e.g., Interviewees 1, 2, 60). While the USA is still seen as the dominant actor, NSAs increasingly recognise the EU's potential to exert leverage on the parties to the conflict. Not only is the EU a key trading partner for Israel (European Commission 2012), but the Palestinians also depend heavily on EU financial assistance and contribution to the process of state-building (EU Delegation to the West Bank and Gaza Strip 2013). NSA activism and lobbying has also been confirmed during interviews with EU officials: the Israeli–Palestinian conflict, even when compared to other outstanding issues in the Middle East and North Africa, remains one of the most lobbied policy areas (Interviewee 11).

The NSA population: a typology

In order to provide a better overview of the NSAs included in the database, a typology based on the core activity of NSAs – that is, the main feature that characterises their work – and on some of their structural features has been created. As is the case for all typologies, the categories serve an analytical purpose, which necessarily leads to a simplification of the real world. Many NSAs carry out multiple activities at the same time. Yet, there is always a core activity which singles out one type from another. Dividing NSAs by types is one of the several lenses that can be adopted to study the population of NSAs and it is a criterion widely used in the literature on interest groups.[10] Six categories have been identified in this research, namely business groups, NGOs, solidarity movements, think tanks/foundations, the media and individuals.

In analysing these categories, differences among NSAs in relation to the types of issues on which they lobby, how often they lobby the EU, the channels they use and how they are perceived by EU and national officials are highlighted. If compared along these dimensions, there are significant differences between business groups and other categories in terms of the issues and frequency of lobbying. Solidarity movements also stand out for the type of lobbying they rely on. There is, however, no clear evidence of a link between actor type and the roles/frames used. The choice of the latter seems to be mainly dependent on the nature of the policy system in which NSAs lobby.

As shown in Table 3.1, the majority of NSAs in the database are NGOs (49 per cent), followed by business groups (25 per cent). The remaining categories are smaller: solidarity movements represent 14 per cent of the population of the database, think tanks/foundations 5 per cent, the media 6 per cent and individuals only 1 per cent.

In the following, an overview of all categories is provided in order to build a more complete picture of the landscape of NSAs relevant in the case of EU foreign policy towards the Israeli–Palestinian conflict. The empirical chapters will, however, be predominantly focused on the first three categories, given that

Table 3.1 Frequency of NSAs by type

Type	Frequency	%
Business group	82	25%
NGO	159	49%
Solidarity movement	46	14%
Think tank/foundation	16	5%
Media	19	6%
Individual	3	1%
Total	**325**	**100%**

they are the most numerous actors as well as those mentioned most frequently in interviews. In particular, NGOs have been the category that has been mentioned most often by EU and national officials and policy-makers.

Business groups

The category 'business group' includes NSAs that have profit as their primary concern.[11] They perform economic activities with the aim of increasing their market share or making their business more profitable. They can either be relatively small companies/groups or big multinational corporations. Moreover, NSAs such as trade associations, actors representing the interest of specific business sectors (e.g., BusinessEurope) or bilateral associations like chambers of commerce or similar entities (e.g., the Deutsch-Israelische Wirtschaftsvereinigung) are also included under this category. The sectors of activity vary enormously: some business groups are active in the defence/security sector (e.g., G4S), others work in the pharmaceutical industry (e.g., Teva), some others trade various products (e.g., Brita GmbH) and so on.

Evidence of business group lobbying at the EU level is limited in the case of EU external relations towards Israel and Palestine. They lobby almost exclusively on specific pieces of legislation or on the framework of EU policies that affect their sector of activity (Interviewee 12). On most occasions, business groups tend to be 'silent'. Many EU officials dealing with Israel and Palestine (Interviewees 11, 13, 17, 20, 29, 30) maintain that they rarely meet business groups and have not been subject to their lobbying pressure frequently. When business groups or European business associations (e.g., BusinessEurope) lobby the EU, their activities address general aspects related to EU policies towards the Mediterranean overall, given the market opportunities and potential profits that the area can bring to business actors (Interviewees 19, 26).

From a profit-oriented perspective, the Palestinian economy is not an appealing market. It is extremely small, with fragile institutions and limited opportunities for business actors. However, the limited lobbying from business groups is more puzzling in the case of Israel, as there are significant economic interests and business opportunities at stake in a variety of sectors. Furthermore, many companies conduct business activities in Israel or have trade relations with companies located in Israel. According to some (Interviewees 11, 51), however, Israel is a 'small fish' in terms of market opportunities for EU business groups, which are more interested in the American or Chinese markets. Others argue that business groups do not need to lobby the EU, as the context is already favourable to them (Interviewee 30). Business groups' activities in Israel/Palestine are not subject to EU legislation and there are no significant obstacles in trade relations. Moreover, business actors tend to keep away from political issues and to privilege business-to-business relations when facing some problems or encountering obstacles. For example, the Palestinian International Business Forum, which is 'a private sector organisation bringing together Palestinian, Israeli and Swedish business efforts to create sustainable economic development in Palestine', provides business actors with a favourable context in which they can establish links and explore new business opportunities (Interviewee 28; PIBF 2013). Similarly, in February 2011 the Oxford University's Said Business School organised a one-day conference in which Israeli, Palestinian and British business people were invited to discuss not only the potential contribution of business groups to the peace process, but also the present and future economic opportunities that they had.[12]

Although business groups might not, at first glance, show particular interest towards Israel/Palestine, they also have a variety of formal channels on which they can rely. First, the Commission normally organises public consultations during which business groups can express their views and discuss their concerns (Interviewee 28).[13] For example, the Israeli pharmaceutical company Teva was consulted by the Commission when the Agreement on Conformity Assessment and Acceptance (ACAA) between the EU and Israel was negotiated (Interviewees 55, 63). Another opportunity to express their concerns is the European–Israeli Business Dialogue (EIBD), a forum launched in 2007 by the former Commissioner for Enterprise and Industry Günter Verheugen. The website of DG Enterprise and Industry explains that the business dialogue is:

> a forum where European CEOs meet their Israeli counterparts in order to foster business relationships by taking advantage of the fact that Europe and Israel are sharing similar economic and technological interests. The aim of the business to business dialogue is to strengthen EU–Israel economic relations in areas of mutual interest, by creating a strong, sustainable and expanding dialogue of business leaders of both sides. This direct dialogue between EU business people and companies and Israeli business people and companies, and the recommendations to the government and the EU resulting from this direct dialogue will foster relations and create opportunities to remove barriers of trade and investments and enhance cooperation and joint ventures.[14]

Another channel is offered by the Israeli–EU Chamber of Commerce, which consists of the association of Israel's manufacturers, the federation of Israeli chambers of commerce and the federation of bi-national chambers of commerce. The chairman, Gad Popper, declared that the Chamber 'will actually be the lobbyist of the Israeli business sector in dealing with the EU'.[15] In addition, the market access teams (MATs), local teams that serve as a platform for coordination between the Commission and member states on the one hand, and Israel on the other hand, are another way to lobby. Business groups are involved in the meetings whenever appropriate and can thus express their views (European Commission 2010). Finally, representatives of the business world meet EU officials whenever the Commission goes on a mission to Israel and the Occupied Territories. On those occasions, EU officials organise meetings with all the representatives of civil society in order to have a better picture and understanding of what happens on the ground.

Besides these formal settings for consultations, informal lobbying also takes place. For example, an EU official argued that he was contacted by El Al, the Israeli airline, when the EU and Israel were negotiating the Agreement on Open Sky. El Al was interested in protecting its monopoly in the sector (Interviewee 17). In contrast, a representative of a multinational firm argued that they mainly aim to influence the principles and ideas on which policy frameworks are based more than specific pieces of legislation (Interviewee 12). Even when business groups lobby on specific programmes, legislation, etc., they have to speak about problems and issues that have a European dimension. This means that, for example, different companies across Europe are affected by a certain policy or by the lack thereof, or that the impacts on European consumers are widespread (Interviewee 26).

A final channel for business groups is the use of national governments (Interviewee 30, 65). On the one hand, business groups can push their governments to represent their interests at the EU level. The choice to rely on the government is likely to be determined by the stronger leverage and power that business actors have at the national level. On the other hand, business groups might be interested in strengthening the bilateral economic relations between their country and Israel/Palestine, without any interest for the Brussels level. This clearly emerges when leaders of EU member states go on a mission to Israel, as they are frequently accompanied by representatives of the business community interested in exploring new trade and market opportunities (Interviewee 93).

NGOs

The second category, NGOs, is the most active lobby group on Israel–Palestine. NGOs are the NSAs mentioned most frequently by EU and national officials, who stress their regular interactions with them and argue that NGOs contribute to their daily work by providing information and knowledge. There is no clear-cut definition of the term 'NGO' (Reinalda 2001; Betsill and Corell 2008; Bloodgood 2011; Vakil 1997). Definitions differ legally from country to country and also from discipline to discipline. For example, juridical studies require that NGOs display the features listed in the UN Resolution 1996/31, namely established headquarters, a constitution which is democratically adopted, someone who can speak on behalf of the members, an executive body and financial independence from governmental bodies. In contrast, sociological perspectives offer a variety of encompassing definitions, highlighting the autonomy of NGOs from the government, their not-for-profit and non-violent nature and the presence of an organisational structure (Martens 2002). In this book, NGOs are defined as not-for-profit NSAs, with a relatively clear organisational structure, which are concerned with the promotion of various goals, ranging from human rights (e.g., Human Rights Watch, the Euro-Mediterranean Human Rights Network) to development (e.g., Oxfam, APRODEV), to environmental issues (e.g., Friends of the Earth Middle East) or specific problems and issues related to the conflict such as settlements (e.g., Peace Now). This category is, therefore, broad and comprises a variety of actors that display different features in terms of their size, the location of their headquarters, their organisational structure and their capacity to perform lobbying and advocacy at various levels.

Unlike business groups, NGOs are constantly lobbying. The most frequent issues covered by these NSAs are human rights, developmental issues, environmental issues, specific aspects related to the conflict such as house demolition, settlements and prisoners, but also topics related to the relationship between the EU and Israel.[16] Although some issues are constantly on the NGOs' agenda (e.g., settlements, human rights), there are events that generate peaks in lobbying, such as the conflict in Gaza in December 2008–January 2009 or the recognition of Palestine as a member of the UN. On those occasions, the energy of most NGOs is concentrated on the specific issue raised by an event and lobbying becomes very punctual and focused. For example, the European Coalition for Israel (EC4I) mounted a strong lobbying action in the EU called 'Give Peace a Chance', explaining Israeli rights to the land in the Middle East to prevent the recognition of Palestinian statehood by EU member states (European Coalition for Israel 2013).

While information is always double-checked, EU and national officials consider NGOs as a precious resource in their job (Interviewees 13, 17, 27, 68). Given the overwhelming amount of emails or meetings that officials and policy-makers have to deal with on a daily basis, the message of NGOs is most useful when it goes straight to the point, and provides precise information (Interviewees 13, 27, 58). Professionalisation of NSA activities is crucial to be able to convey the message effectively (cf. Grossman and Saurugger 2004; Klüver and Saurugger 2013). According to some observers, the quality of the material provided by many NGOs has increased over time, with information being offered in a well-structured and tailored way that considers the needs of each institution (Interviewees 13, 27, 29). In this regard, some NGOs are developing 'training activities' and 'lobbying toolkits' that can be used by other groups when they approach officials and policy-makers. For example, both Crisis Action and the EMHRN have begun to develop a 'methodology of lobbying', thereby providing other NGOs with the instruments and strategies to carry out lobbying (Interviewee 60). The EMHRN is particularly active in organising workshops with national NGOs to help them to do effective lobbying, so that the work of Brussels-based NGOs is facilitated and the different levels of EU policy-making are better coordinated (Euro-Mediterranean Human Rights Network 2013).

While NGOs are often divided into pro-Israel and pro-Palestinian groups, this division into two camps is misleading and is also rejected by both officials and NSAs (e.g., Interviewees 11, 82). The dichotomy entails the idea that the other party does not have rights, a position rejected by the majority of NGOs and only adopted by radical groups. Moreover, it would not allow for considering Israeli or Jewish groups that, in the name of Israel's interests and security, want to address the situation in the Occupied Territories and ensure respect for international law. They recognise the rights of the Palestinians to live side-by-side with Israel and see Israeli policies in Palestine as a serious obstacle to peace. The landscape of NGOs is better described on the basis of the type of requests and claims they make to the EU (or the national government, if acting nationally).[17] On the one hand, a group calls on the EU to use its leverage on the parties to the conflict to ensure respect for human rights, international law and international humanitarian law. This often translates into a call to the EU for adopting a tougher stance towards Israel and for forcing it to comply with international law. On the other hand, the second group aims to disentangle the political dimension of the conflict from the bilateral relations between the EU and Israel. These NGOs are often portrayed as the pro-Israel lobby (cf. Mearsheimer and Walt 2007; Cronin 2011). In comparison to their American counterparts, however, these NSAs are less organised and resourced. For instance, the European Friends of Israel (EFI) is an NGO that works to support the cross-party group of national MPs and MEPs that openly sympathise with Israel. To a certain extent, it attempts to replicate the model of the American Israel Public Affairs Committee (AIPAC) (Interviewees 6, 62; Cronin 2011). However, given the different institutional structure of the EU, the EFI does not support electoral campaigns, but mainly organises dinners for parliamentarians or trips to the region, or provides policy briefs. Other NSAs are the Brussels-based branches of American groups. For example, the Transatlantic Institute is one of the European offices of the American Jewish Committee, which has offices in other European capitals. As the former director Emanuele Ottolenghi said, 'The whole point of our activities in Europe is of engaging thoughtfully in the battle of ideas. … It is about adding a voice to the debate. In America, the lobby is a lot more entrenched' (as quoted in Cronin 2011: 143).

According to some EU officials (Interviewees 13, 19), these pro-Israel NGOs can be fairly confrontational in their approach. For example, the Israeli NGO Monitor published a report in 2008 in which it accused the EU of financing NGOs whose activities are in conflict with EU policies and principles, and of granting money in a way that is not transparent and accountable (Steinberg 2008). The Commission was also summoned by NGO Monitor (Interviewee 29). During the Second Intifada, similar accusations were raised by some NGOs, claiming that the EU's money was used to finance Palestinian terrorism (Funding for Peace Coalition 2004). Another instance of this confrontational stance dates back to 2002, when the Centre for Monitoring the Impact on Peace accused the EU of financing Palestinian textbooks which contained anti-Israeli and anti-Jewish biases and incitements (Council of the European Union 2002; Palestinian Ministry of Education 2005).

In terms of targets, recent studies focusing on the EU show how the choice of targets varies on the basis of the institutional constraints, the stage in the policy-making process and the nature of the policy at stake (Gullberg 2008; Marshall 2010). In the case of EU foreign policy towards Israel and Palestine, evidence suggests that NGOs prefer to lobby their 'friends' in the European Parliament, instead of approaching those policy-makers who oppose their positions. According to EU officials (Interviewees 11, 35), NGOs lobby those MEPs who are already convinced and are thus more likely to take up their message, given that they share similar political views on the situation. For example, one MEP (Interviewee 36) maintained that he is rarely approached by NGOs that call for a stronger engagement with Israel, as they know that he is unlikely to give credit to their views and claims. Another MEP (Interviewee 66) has good personal relationships with the chief of the European Coalition for Israel, a Christian NGO with the goal of improving the relations between Israel and the EU, with whom he shares information and views on the subject. These strong links between NGOs and some politicians can even reach the point where some MEPs are seen as spokespeople of certain NSAs. Some MEPs are particularly sensitive to certain arguments, so that some ideas and issues have more resonance among MEPs than in other institutions (Interviewees 11, 35).

Solidarity movements

The category of 'solidarity movement' shares some characteristics with NGOs, but differs in terms of the core activity and of some of its constitutive elements. Solidarity movements tend to act via public protests – that is, by mobilising the public. They aim to exert influence through the indirect pressure of public opinion and, most of the time, have a less structured organisation than NGOs. They are mainly based on people volunteering for a cause they feel important and for showing solidarity towards the people in the region. They might have different organisational structures (e.g., be small and based at the national level or diffused across countries) and might campaign on different topics. For example, the Association Belgo-Palestinienne (ABP) is listed in the database as a solidarity movement, as it aims to raise awareness among Belgian citizens by carrying out a campaign per year, organising events and going to schools to talk about the topic. Despite having a full-time employee, the contribution of volunteers to spreading the values of ABP is a crucial element for the survival of the group.

Given the topics they work on (e.g., human rights, occupation of Palestine), solidarity movements, like NGOs, lobby officials and policy-makers constantly, with an intensification of lobbying activities if specific events occur. For example, the French group Plateforme des ONG françaises pour la Palestine promoted the campaign 'Un bateau français pour Gaza' to replicate the Freedom Flotilla attacked by Israel on 31 May 2010 (Plateforme des ONG françaises pour la Palestine 2012). Unlike NGOs, however, solidarity movements do not have the same level of professionalisation.[18] This is mainly due to the lack of trained and permanent staff, which prevents them from carrying out in-depth research, and of resources (e.g., time) to be spent on lobbying actions.

Moreover, solidarity movements are mainly active at the national level. This does not mean that supranational movements do not exist. The Boycott, Divestment and Sanctions movement (BDS), which was born in Palestine in 2005 when civil society organisations called for the boycott of, divestment from and sanctions against Israel, is now a worldwide movement with 'branches' in most EU countries. While each national BDS group carries out its activities taking into consideration the specificities of the country in which it operates, there is an attempt to coordinate these activities at the supranational level.[19]

Think tanks

Think tanks, the fourth category, carry out research that is meant to be policy-relevant. Their way of contributing to the policy-making process is by generating and shaping the debate among policy-makers through the provision of new ideas. They produce documents based on research (policy briefs, papers, reports, etc.) that focus on specific issues related to the situation on the ground or in relation to EU foreign policy towards the Israeli–Palestinian conflict. For example, the International Crisis Group (ICG) has teams of experts (generally composed of local people and one international person) on the ground in charge of writing reports and providing recommendations to international actors such as the EU. Given its strong network on the ground, the ICG's material represents a source of information for Western policy-makers. For example, the ICG is in touch with all sides of the conflict, including Hamas, so that EU officials can get information that would otherwise be difficult to receive (Interviewee 25). Another instance of work carried out by think tanks is offered by the Israeli–European Policy Network (IEPN). Established in 2003, the IEPN is a network of scholars, policy-makers and practitioners that provides a structured forum for meetings and discussions on relevant issues linked to EU–Israeli relations. By producing papers and briefs, as well as favouring dialogue among people, the IEPN contributes to shaping the debate in the long run (Interviewee 92). For instance, in November 2011 it organised a conference on the topic of Palestinian statehood and its recognition in the UN. Various policy-makers, practitioners and academics participated in this conference, which offered the opportunity to debate about this crucial issue and the implications that the recognition of Palestine as a state would have at the international level (Israeli–European Policy Network 2013).

The distinction between think tanks and NGOs is sometimes very difficult to draw, given that many NGOs also base their work on evidence and research.[20] However, analysis and research are the core activity of think tanks, which do not represent any constituencies. Although think tanks are often registered as NGOs, they are classified as a separate category in the database. German foundations[21] are also included in this category as they are very active in stimulating the debate and providing research-based documents to policy-makers. While foundations also carry out work on the ground like NGOs, the Israeli–Palestinian conflict is an aspect on which the research-based component is particularly evident, especially at the EU and German level, making them very similar to think tanks.

The media

The media are also part of the NSA landscape, as they participate in shaping the debate at the political and public opinion level. Newspapers and broadcasts are clearly the main channels through which these activities take place. However, the database does not focus on the mainstream newspapers or television programming, but on those actors that focus on Israeli–Palestinian issues (or devote a substantial part of their work to them). This category also includes those internet-based groups that focus on the provision of information in the form of articles, op-eds and so on, with the aim of providing specific interpretations of events. Some of them target journalists, check the content of newspaper articles or television programmes and aim to steer the debate. While some of these NSAs are active at the European level, the majority of them are based in member states. An example of this type of actor is the Britain Israel Communications and Research Centre (BICOM), a British NSA which aims at 'creating a more supportive environment for Israel in Britain' (BICOM 2013). Not only does BICOM provide news and analysis of events in Israel or in the region, it also tries to influence the media sector by 'building relationships with key journalists and editors, taking them on paid-for trips to Israel, and setting up high level meetings in Israel and the UK. They also provide journalists with daily briefings and suggest stories and angles to friendly contacts' (Oborne and Jones 2009: 33).

Other NSAs such as JNews or the European Jewish Press (EJP) provide information related to the conflict, Israel and EU foreign policy towards the region. JNews states on its website that it aims to encourage debates among the British public on matters related to Israel and Palestine thanks to articles and analyses (JNews 2013). In contrast, the EJP describes itself as the 'sole online Jewish news agency in Europe', which aims at offering 'balanced, up-to-date and reliable news reports about European Jewry and other issues of concern to the Jewish community', focusing on issues related to European Jews as well as EU–Israel relations (EJC 2013).

Individuals

Individuals form a very small category comprising those who have been mentioned in interviews or whose name has been found in reports, newspaper articles, etc. due to their activism regarding the Israeli–Palestinian conflict. For example, Simone Susskind is a Jewish Belgian woman who is very active on issues related to Jewish culture, identity and so on, as well as on the Israeli–Palestinian conflict. She has established contacts within the EU institutions, organises various events in Brussels that target the general public, maintains a blog (Susskind 2013) and used to circulate weekly emails with articles or analysis on Israel and Palestine. Another NSA categorised as 'individual' is the 'European Former Leaders Group', a group formed of 26 former European leaders from 12 EU member states and Norway. In December 2010 they sent a letter to the European Council President Herman van Rompuy, the High Representative Catherine Ashton and all EU heads of government and ministers of foreign affairs.

They asked EU member states and institutions to give concrete application to the Council Conclusions on the Middle East Peace Process of December 2009, as the only way to show credibility and ability to act (European Former Leaders Group 2010, 2013).

Trends in NSA lobbying

Some key trends can be found in the population of the dataset. If we look at the 'location' of NSAs – that is, where NSAs are based – five different categories have been identified in the database. The category 'EU/Europe-based' means that NSAs are based in the EU or in Europe (e.g., Switzerland). It refers to both NSAs that are located exclusively in one country (and might have an office in Brussels) or that are based in different EU or European states, but not present in other geographical areas. In contrast, the category 'cross-country' implies that their geographical scope is multinational and not limited to the EU/Europe. For example, the European Jewish Congress is an EU/Europe-based NSA, given that its headquarters is in France and all offices are in Europe. In contrast, Oxfam, Amnesty International and Human Rights Watch are cross-country NSAs because they are present around the world. The category 'Israel/Palestine' indicates that NSAs are based either in Israel or in the Occupied Territories; 'other' is used when NSAs do not fall under any of the previous categories (e.g., Lebanon) and 'n/a' when information about the location is not available. As shown in Table 3.2, the majority of NSAs are either EU/Europe-based (49 per cent) or cross-country (33 per cent), while only 16 per cent of the NSAs in the database are exclusively based in Israel or Palestine.

In this regard, it is also worth pointing out that NGOs rarely come from the new EU member states (Interviewee 68; see also Table 3.3). The cross-country NGOs such as Amnesty International usually have a branch in new member states, but civil society there is not particularly active on the Israeli–Palestinian dossier (Interviewee 2, 72).

Clearly, the location of NSAs can also have an impact on their activities and their outreach capacity. Not all NSAs are based in Brussels or have a representation there. As Table 3.4 shows, 73 per cent of them are not present in the EU capital. If we cross this feature with their 'location', it emerges that Europe/

Table 3.2 Frequency of NSAs by location

	Frequency	*%*
EU/Europe-based	159	49%
Cross-country	108	33%
Israel/Palestine	51	16%
N/A	5	2%
Other	2	1%
Total	**325**	**100%**

Table 3.3 Frequency of NSAs by location of headquarters

Location of headquarters	Frequency
UK	74
Israel	52
Belgium	39
France	27
Germany	26
USA	19
Palestinian Territories	16
Netherlands	14
N/A	10
Switzerland	9
Sweden	7
Ireland	6
Italy	5
Denmark	4
Spain	4
Austria	2
Germany/Israel	2
Cyprus	1
Finland	1
Israel/USA	1
Lebanon	1
Luxembourg	1
Norway	1
UK/Lebanon	1
Israel/Palestinian Territories/Jordan	1
Israel/Palestinian Territories	1
Total	**325**

EU-based or cross-country NSAs in the database are almost the only actors that have an office in Brussels. Only two of the Israel/Palestine-based NSAs are also present there, as shown in Table 3.4. While this does not prevent NSAs based in Israel or Palestine from going to Brussels when it is necessary, they are, in principle, in a less privileged position to interact with the EU, compared to those NSAs that are based in the EU capital. For Brussels-based actors it is easier 'to

Table 3.4 Frequency of NSAs by presence in Brussels and location

	Cross-country	EU/Europe-based	Israel/Palestine	N/A	Other	Total
Office in Brussels	35% (38)	27% (43)	4% (2)	20% (1)	0% (0)	26% (84)
No office in Brussels	65% (70)	72% (114)	96% (49)	60% (3)	100% (2)	73% (238)
N/A	0% (0)	1% (2)	0% (0)	20% (1)	0% (0)	1% (3)
Total	**100% (108)**	**100% (159)**	**100% (51)**	**100% (5)**	**100% (2)**	**100% (325)**

be involved in the policy-making process, to be informed about what is going on, to act on short notice, [and] to collect information' (Voltolini 2012: 28). While being present in Brussels is seen as an important factor, even EU/Europe-based and cross-country NSAs with an office there are relatively few, with percentages of 27 per cent and 35 per cent respectively. Needless to say, the costs involved in having an office in Brussels are not always affordable, especially in the case of small NGOs or solidarity movements, while it is slightly easier for cross-country NSAs thanks to the larger resources at their disposal.

The registration of NSAs in the Transparency Register seems to be related to their location. Of all NSAs listed in the database, only 65 (20 per cent) are registered (see Table 3.5). However, by crossing this information with the presence in Brussels, it emerges that 62 per cent of NSAs present in Brussels are in the Register, in comparison to only 5 per cent of those that do not have an office there. From the data available, presence in Brussels seems to increase the likelihood of being registered in the Transparency Register.

While presence in Brussels is important in lobbying activities targeting the EU, a different type of advantage benefits NSAs on the ground. Because they have their fingers on the pulse of the situation on the ground and often are better placed to understand changes and facts occurring in Israel and Palestine, they can provide EU officials with first-hand information. Moreover, Israeli and Palestinian NSAs are seen as the voices of local civil society whose information and expertise is indicative of the main issues and concerns on the ground (Interviewees 23, 47, 68). For example, the work carried out by Peace Now, an Israeli NGO that supports peace with the Palestinians, is appreciated by EU and national officials, as this NGO does an invaluable job in tracking the construction or expansion of Israeli settlements, in drawing detailed maps of the settlements and in offering constant updates from the region (Interviewee 101). Similarly, the online database *Who Profits?*, created by the NGO Coalition of Women for Peace, lists the names of the business groups that contribute to Israel's occupation of Palestine via commercial activities linked to the settlement industry (e.g., trade of settlement goods), economic exploitation (e.g., use of Palestinian resources) and the control of the population (e.g., provision of technology used at checkpoints) (Interviewee 27).

Even when NSAs are not in Brussels, they can access the EU in different ways. First, NSAs can use the internet (websites, emails, newsletters, etc.) to transmit

Table 3.5 Frequency of NSAs by registration in the Transparency Register and presence in Brussels

Transparency Register	Presence in Brussels			
	Office	*No office*	*N/A*	*Total*
Registered	62% (52)	5% (13)	0% (0)	20% (65)
Non-registered	38% (32)	95% (225)	100% (3)	80% (260)
Total	**100% (84)**	**100% (238)**	**100% (3)**	**100% (325)**

their information and requests. Second, NSAs based on the ground can exploit the channel offered by the EU Delegations in Israel and Palestine. Delegations have a key role in collecting relevant information from civil society and passing it to Brussels, where the officials and policy-makers decide if and how to use these inputs (Interviewee 23). Finally, they can go to Brussels either alone or via an umbrella or partner organisation there.[22] EU officials tend to be receptive to the requests of local NSAs and the information they bring. Meetings with officials and policy-makers, especially MEPs, can be particularly effective, as most people feel the duty to reply and take the issue into consideration (Interviewee 53). For example, the European Parliament (2010b) took action in favour of the Jordan River, by issuing the 'European Parliament resolution of 9 September 2010 on the Situation of the Jordan River with Special Regard to the Lower Jordan River Area', after contacts with the Israeli-Palestinian-Jordanian NGO called the Friends of the Earth (FoE) Middle East. The first meeting between FoE and some MEPs occurred in September 2009, when a Delegation was on a mission to the region. It was followed by a workshop in the European Parliament in June 2010, during which MEPs were informed about the situation of the Jordan River and felt compelled to support the initiative of FoE Middle East in their work to prevent the river from running dry (Interviewee 45; Voltolini 2012). Moreover, as long as the message given by Western and local NSAs is consistent, there is a multiplier and strengthening effect when these two types of NSAs work together, as Western-based NSAs benefit from the credibility of their local partners (Interviewee 68, 91).

In relation to their location and their lobbying activities, it is interesting to note that interviewees mentioned the names of certain NSAs more frequently than others, to the extent that it is possible to identify a 'core group'. This group is formed of NGOs based in Brussels and on the ground. It includes the big cross-country NGOs (e.g., Amnesty International, Human Rights Watch and Oxfam), some umbrella organisations (e.g., EMHRN, APRODEV, CIDSE and Crisis Action, FIDH) and some groups that want stronger EU–Israel relations (e.g., EFI, Transatlantic Institute, the European Coalition for Israel, B'nai B'rith and the European Jewish Congress). As for the NGOs on the ground, some of the frequently named NGOs are Adalah and the Mossawa Centre (both working on the Arab minority in Israel), Breaking the Silence (composed of former Israeli soldiers who denounce occupation) and B'Tselem and Al-Haq (focusing on human rights in the Occupied Territories). Members of this 'core group' tend to work in cooperation with each other or, at least, they coordinate their activities.[23] This is especially true in the case of Brussels-based NGOs, with around 15–20 NGOs[24] interacting on a regular basis. The people who work for these NGOs know each other, share information and work together (Interviewees 2, 4, 11). Moreover, this cooperation, both in formal and informal ways, allows for a better division of labour and more professionalised lobbying (cf. Grossmann and Saurugger 2004; Klüver and Saurugger 2013).

Networking and working in coalitions is important for NSAs, especially in Brussels. 'Ad hoc issue coalitions' are groups 'characterised by low levels of formalisation (compared to formal interest group organisations) and high levels of autonomy for the coalition's members. They are established in the short to medium term for the duration of a single legislative or regulatory debate' (Mahoney 2007: 367–8; on coalition, see also Klüver 2013). This way, NSAs send a common signal to policy-makers and pool resources together. In the case of lobbying on EU foreign policy towards the Israeli–Palestinian conflict, both NGOs and solidarity movements tend to form ad hoc coalitions. EU officials prefer to receive a shared message from NGOs and they also find it particularly useful if local NGOs on the ground are included (Interviewee 68).

Cooperation is at times limited by the different focus of activity, mandate and priorities of each NSA. NGOs work on a variety of different topics and from different perspectives (e.g., human rights, development). These differences lead to heterogeneous coalitions or coalitions with a variable geometry that changes on the basis of the issue on which lobbying is carried out. For example, Crisis Action is an NGO that coordinates the work of other NGOs by providing a platform for cooperation and interaction. An example of this is the advocacy work on the blockade of Gaza in 2009 and 2010 (Crisis Action 2010) or on the labelling of settlement products since 2012 (Rettman 2012a). Moreover, the size of coalitions varies enormously as there are instances in which many NGOs participate in the same lobbying action and others in which only few NGOs work together on an advocacy action and, for example, produce a report. For instance, the EMHRN and APRODEV (2012) co-produced the report *EU–Israel Relations: Promoting and Ensuring Respect for International Law*, which was released in February 2012.

Ad hoc issue coalitions also allow for an informal division of labour. Not only can NSAs maximise their resources (time, money and staff), but they can also work on those issues where they have a comparative advantage in terms of expertise or that are part of their mandate. By avoiding the overlapping of lobbying, they also manage to cover more issues thanks to this better allocation of lobbying actions. In addition, the coalitions that form around each topic represent a stronger and unified voice when it comes to lobbying the EU. For example, the EMHRN has been working extensively on the Goldstone Report and on the issue of impunity, while Crisis Action has focused on Gaza (Interviewee 2).

In other cases, NSAs opt to become members of umbrella organisations that represent their interests, which is a way to deal with the multi-level policy-making of the EU and to directly lobby the EU.[25] They lobby at the EU level on behalf of their members and collect information on EU policies to be passed to their member organisations. Both business groups and NGOs form umbrella organisations. For instance, BusinessEurope is an umbrella organisation representing 41 member federations across Europe. On the NGO side, there are NSAs such as EMHRN, APRODEV and CIDSE. While the scope of these umbrella organisations is quite broad, all three have a working group on Israel/Palestine consisting of one or two people. The EMHRN works on human rights issues and has member organisations from the region, while the other two are developmental organisations related to the Protestant and Catholic churches respectively, which put together organisations based in Europe. Some NSAs are composed of sub-sections (especially at the national level) or have many offices at the national and international level. Unlike umbrella organisations, the local or national or inter-national offices are only branches of the general headquarters: they stick to the same principles and pursue the same types of objectives. For example, Amnesty International, Oxfam and Human Rights Watch have offices around the world, including Brussels, which is used as the basis for lobbying the EU. Even if each branch has a degree of autonomy, they still need to coordinate and adhere to some criteria and common guidelines that come from the headquarters.[26]

'Embedded' lobbying

NSA lobbying activities do not occur in a vacuum, but within the boundaries and parameters of the policy field defined in Chapter 2. As suggested in Chapter 1, lobbying can be imagined as a stage: all actors are interconnected and their actions develop and are shaped as a result of these interactions. Many officials state that NSAs bring important pieces of information and new knowledge to them, as they offer new views and inputs for the work of EU or national institu-tions (Interviewees 11, 13, 17, 27, 29, 35, 79, 80, 87, 101, 107, 109). At the same time, information and knowledge also go the other way round: NSAs receive insider information about the next steps one institution is planning to take or about certain policy aspects that they would not be aware of; they get to know details about political debates, diplomatic information and other information that NSAs might not have access to (Interviewees 4, 88). Moreover, by drawing on EU tenets and principles, some NSAs also define their own constitutive traits. As will be shown in Chapter 5, the EMHRN refers to EU principles and discourses when defining its constitutive traits. Put differently, there are frequent social and cooperative interactions between NSAs and EU/national officials during which the two sides engage in discussions and redefine and adjust to each other's knowl-edge and behaviour.

If we zoom in on the EU institutions, the European Parliament is a clear exam-ple where these patterns of social interactions emerge. The in-house knowledge and expertise in the European Parliament are not sufficient to enable MEPs and officials to have a precise view and make judgements on every issue, given that the European Parliament's competences range over a broad number of policy areas (e.g., Bouwen 2004; Marshall 2012). Therefore, reliance on external infor-mation and on frames to interpret events and build a more complete overview of the situation becomes a necessity to perform their tasks (e.g., Interviewees 24, 45, 53). It follows that it is not infrequent that political advisors or officials prepare a draft resolution and ask NSAs for feedback and inputs on it (Interviewee 32). An example of this is provided by the European Parliament (2010a) 'European Parliament resolution of 17 June 2010 on the Israeli Military Operation against the Humanitarian Flotilla and the Gaza Blockade', when offi-cials and political advisors asked NGOs for inputs, figures and examples (Interviewee 35).

As said, the flow of information also occurs in the other direction – that is, MEPs and officials pass information on to NSAs. For example, some MEPs are particularly active on issues related to the Israeli–Palestinian conflict and share their information and knowledge with NSAs, by telling them, for example, about the results of a fact-finding mission (Interviewee 32). Moreover, some MEPs and officials establish strong personal relationships with some NSAs, so that a circular flow of information and knowledge becomes an integral component of these links. Therefore, frequent interactions between MEPs or officials and NSAs also shape the way in which NSAs perceive events and frame their lobbying activities. For instance, an MEP of the Alliance of Liberals and Democrats for Europe (ALDE) political group has personal and frequent contacts with the director of the European Coalition for Israel: discussions about Israel and the conflict are thus frequent (Interviewee 66).

Besides the European Parliament, the Commission and, since the Lisbon Treaty, the EEAS are also a favourable context in which NSAs and EU officials can develop strong social interactions. NGOs often prepare good documents and material that EU officials can use in their work, especially in terms of offering concrete examples or further evidence that the Commission can use to support its general message towards Israel or the Palestinian Authority (Interviewee 68). Moreover, EU officials also consult certain NSAs when they have to deal with specific topics or policies. For example, one official argued that he worked with NGOs providing information about administrative detention, as this gave him concrete and specific elements on which he could establish an effective discussion with Israeli officials during bilateral meetings in the sub-committee on political dialogue and the informal working group on human rights (Interviewee 17). Another official maintained that the involvement of civil society organisations before the review of the ENP or other ENP-related occasions is of crucial importance for the work of the Commission as it gives valuable inputs and information (Interviewee 27).

While strong ties between MEPs/officials and NSAs can be based on friendship and other personal reasons, in the majority of cases closer contacts are the result of the credibility, professionalism and trustworthiness of NSAs. Various officials indeed stressed that NSAs have become more and more professional in their lobbying over the years (Interviewees 11, 29, 36). In the case of NGOs, they are often able to produce very detailed and well-researched reports and provide timely information that contributes to framing EU positions. For example, in 2010 many Israeli NGOs approached the EEAS as regards the bill on the activities and funding of NGOs, which would curtail freedom of association. These NGOs discussed with the Commission the problems that the bill would cause and presented various convincing arguments (Interviewee 29). Following repeated contacts and meetings with different NGOs, the Commission developed its position on the issue and included a few paragraphs on it in the 2010 Progress Report on Israel. It also raised the issue with Israel in their bilateral meetings (Interviewee 29, 68). This increased professionalisation seems to be the result of the repeated interactions and contacts that NSAs have with EU officials and policy-makers.

By establishing mutual trust and becoming credible partners, NSAs shape their own behaviour and their defining traits. For example, the importance that the EMHRN gives to the development of a proper methodology to lobby the EU seems to be the result of interactions that have progressively changed the nature and main functions of this umbrella NGO.

Conclusions

This chapter presented the key features of the population of NSAs that is (potentially) interested in lobbying the EU on its foreign policy towards the Israeli–Palestinian conflict, revealing that NSAs are active and engaged in lobbying. The high density of NSAs thus refutes the 'null hypothesis' of no or limited lobbying activities in EU foreign policy. Not only does it provide relevant counter-evidence to the expectation that EU foreign policy is a domain which is predominantly in the hands of EU member states, it also shows that the EU is viewed as a relevant actor in the Israeli–Palestinian conflict by NSAs.

On the basis of their core activity and their organisational features, NSAs have been divided into six categories: business groups, NGOs, solidarity movements, think tanks, the media and individuals. An evident difference is between business groups and NGOs and solidarity groups as far as the topics and frequency of lobbying are concerned. Business groups concentrate their lobbying efforts on specific pieces of legislation or on the policy frameworks that impinge upon their interests in a specific sector. In contrast, NGOs and solidarity groups are engaged in lobbying on a regular and constant basis. The topics they work on are 'ongoing' issues, ranging from conflict-related aspects (e.g., house demolition, prisoners, etc.), to human rights, development and the like. Clearly, their activities become more focused when certain events take place on the ground or at the EU/international level. For example, some NGOs and solidarity groups were very active on the recognition of Palestinian statehood at the UN and on Operation Cast Lead. Moreover, their lobbying intensifies before the meetings of the Association Councils or the sub-groups between the EU and Israel or the Palestinian Authority or when new policy guidelines are drafted, as these are considered as key moments by both NGOs and solidarity movements.

Not only do business groups lobby the EU in a more punctual way than the other NSAs, they also have a relatively easier access to EU institutions than the other categories. This is determined by the multiplicity of forums and consultations that the Commission organises to hear the voices of stakeholders. Moreover, many interviewees believe that business groups do not need to lobby the EU on Israeli–Palestinian issues, as the circumstances are already favourable to their activities. Even when they have to face obstacles, they seem to prefer business-to-business relations to deal with problems or they rely on their national governments to protect their interests at the EU/international level.

As for NGOs, they are the category that is mentioned most frequently in interviews. Their work is appreciated by officials and policy-makers as it often helps them to get a better understanding of an issue they have to deal with. Interviewees have also maintained that NGOs are more professional nowadays and are able to provide the EU with punctual information, precise analyses and frames to interpret events on the ground. This is a crucial aspect that distinguishes NGOs from solidarity groups, which tend to be less professional and to base their lobbying on voluntary work done by sympathisers and members.

The other categories of the database, namely think tanks, the media and individuals, also display peculiar features. The media, which are more present and active at the national level, target public opinion or journalists with the aim of shaping the debate taking place around the Israeli–Palestinian conflict. In contrast, think tanks are very active at the EU level. They play a crucial role in shaping the contours of the debate at the policy level and in providing ideas and guidelines as far as EU policies towards the Israeli–Palestinian conflict are concerned. Finally, individuals are a residual category, given that lobbying is predominantly carried out by organisations or business actors. However, the individuals listed in the database represent examples of people who are active and engaged on EU foreign policy towards the Israeli–Palestinian conflict.

Another aspect that emerged from the chapter is the existence of a 'core group' of actors formed by NGOs. This group is partly composed of Brussels-based NGOs and partly of NGOs on the ground, which have regular contacts with officials (e.g., Adalah, Mossawa Centre, Breaking the Silence, B'Tselem, Mattin Group and Al-Haq). Brussels-based NGOs also tend to form a sort of smaller community which is particularly active on Israel/Palestine and consists of around 15–20 NGOs. This favours the development of strong relationships among NGOs, the sharing of information and the possibility of cooperating on various initiatives. Cooperation among NGOs is a key feature in Brussels, even if it is limited to specific issues or events. Ad hoc issue coalitions are also frequent among NSAs, with a view to maximising their impact and using the resources at their disposal in the most efficient way. The informal division of labour that takes place in Brussels is thus indicative of this trend.

While being in Brussels is clearly an advantage for carrying out lobbying activities, many NSAs are not present there, probably due to the costs involved. To overcome this problem, some NSAs have become part of umbrella organisations that are meant to represent the interests of their member organisations at the EU level.

To conclude, this chapter has provided an overview of the complexity of the NSA population interested in EU foreign policy towards the Israeli–Palestinian conflict. By highlighting the main features that NSAs display as well as the key trends that characterise their lobbying, the background components of the policy field and the actors involved in EU external policies towards Israel and Palestine have been identified. The following chapters will look at specific instances of lobbying, which took place within the broader framework described in Chapters 2 and 3.

Notes

1 For example, on the involvement of civil society organisations in EU policies, see Marchetti and Tocci (2011); Challand (2011); Jünemann (2003).

2 To a certain extent, selecting NSAs on the basis of their relevance in each case study can be considered as akin to the 'attributed influence method' (Dür 2008; Arts and Verschuren 1999). According to this method, the researcher measures influence on the basis of the self-perception of an actor, the perception of other actors and the researcher's own evaluation, which is normally based on secondary sources and process tracing.

3 EU scholars do not have a 'single, systematic source of data on lobbying activities in the form of lobbying registration', so that they are forced to use different sources, which however do not measure the same population of interest groups (Berkhout and Lowery 2008: 490). Wonka *et al.* (2010) built a dataset with the aim of establishing a complete list of EU interest groups in 2008, which could serve as a common platform for all EU scholars. Recently, the project INTEREURO built a new dataset which has also the purpose of serving as a basis for studies related to EU lobbying. See www. intereuro.eu and the Special Issue of *Interest Groups and Advocacy*, 3, (2), 2014, where further details are provided.

4 The website of CONECCS was no longer accessible when this research started.

5 The only incentive to register was related to the possibility of being informed about EU initiatives. For an assessment of the Commission's Register, see Alter EU (2009).

6 For an overview of the rules on lobbying in the European Parliament, see Kluger Rasmussen (2011) and the European Parliament's website.

7 E.g., in 2011 some MEPs accepted money to table certain amendments on EU legislation on banking regulation (see Bryant 2011). In 2012 the Maltese Commissioner John Dalli resigned due to allegations with regard to his involvement with the tobacco industry (Rettman 2012b).

8 I was able to get information as long as the languages in which information was provided were Italian, English, German, French, Spanish and, to a certain extent, Dutch.

9 See Appendix 1 for the database.

10 There is not a fixed typology provided in the literature. A key distinction is often made between business groups (or concentrated interests) and actors pursuing a collective good (or diffuse interest).

11 For some member states (e.g., the United Kingdom and the Netherlands) more information was available. Although a broad range of sources has been used to minimise the possible over-representation deriving from this, this cannot be excluded. However, this is not a problem given that no statistical analysis is conducted and the study has an exploratory nature, thus mapping this terrain for the first time.

12 See http://www.me-economy-oxford.org/ (accessed 10 February 2011; web address no longer live).

13 Public consultations are often held by the Commission when it launches new policies, negotiations, etc. In certain cases, consultations are open to all stakeholders, in others they are targeted to specific actors such as the industrial sector. Each DG has the consultations listed on its website.

14 See European Commission (2013). According to Interviewee 23, in the EIDB the Commission mainly works as a mediator among various entrepreneurs and businessmen. Interactions take place between business groups, more than as an institutionalised form of communication between the EU and companies.

15 See Lipkin (2006). According to Interviewee 23, the Chamber is not an important instrument for lobbying, as it is more a façade and a sign that EU–Israeli relations are good.

16 The list of topics covered by NGOs is vast, but the above-mentioned categories summarise the main types of arguments (based on interviews with officials and NSA representatives, see Appendix 2).

17 Business groups do not really fit into this dichotomy either. Their approach is mainly based on their economic activity, so that their requests to the EU rarely concern the political relationships between the EU and the parties to the conflict.

18 Some of them prepare brochures and informative documents for their members (either other organisations or individuals). For example, the French group Plateforme des ONG françaises pour la Palestine produces online material as well as publications on the Israeli–Palestinian conflict. See http://www.plateforme-palestine.org/ (accessed 19 March 2013).

19 For further information, see www.bdsmovement.net

20 On think tanks, see Stone (2000) and Rich (2004). Rich argues that think tanks are often perceived as more credible in the eyes of policy-makers, given that they do not speak on behalf of a specific constituency. This neutrality can, however, be questioned due to the fact that certain think tanks propose visions that serve the interests of certain sectors of the society.

21 This type of organisation is peculiar to the German system and no similar entities have been found in other countries. Foundations have a special status in Germany. They are generally associated with a political party (and they receive public money according to the electoral power of each political party), but they are independent from political power and work autonomously.

22 In this research, umbrella organisations are understood as those NSAs that are composed of more organisations, with each organisation maintaining its specificities and its autonomy.

23 Clearly, they work together as long as they share the same interests/goals (i.e., those that aim to promote EU–Israel relations do not work with those of the other side).

24 There are around 40 NGOs in Brussels that work on Israeli–Palestinian issues.

25 The member organisations of the umbrella organisations have been listed in the database only if there was evidence that they were also carrying out separate lobbying. This choice was explicitly made to avoid overinflating the number of NSAs.

26 The various branches have not been listed in the dataset.

References

Alter EU. 2009. *The Commission's Lobby Register One Year On: Success or Failure?* Brussels: Alter EU.

Arts, Bas and Piet Verschuren. 1999. 'Assessing Political Influence in Complex Decision-Making: An Instrument Based on Triangulation'. *International Political Science Review* 20 (4): 411–24.

Baroni, Laura, Brendan J. Carroll, Adam William Chalmers, Luz Maria Muñoz Marquez and Anne Rasmussen. 2014. 'Defining and Classifying Interest Groups'. *Interest Groups & Advocacy* 3 (2): 141–59.

Berkhout, Joost and David Lowery. 2008. 'Counting Organised Interests in the European Union: A Comparison of Data Source'. *Journal of Public Policy* 15 (4): 489–513.

———. 2010. 'The Changing Demography of the EU Interest System since 1990'. *European Union Politics* 11 (3): 447–61.

Betsill, Michele Merrill and Elisabeth Corell, eds. 2008. *NGO Diplomacy: The Influence of Nongovernmental Organizations in International Environmental Negotiations.* Cambridge, MA: MIT Press.

BICOM. 2013. 'BICOM – About'. http://www.bicom.org.uk/about/

Bloodgood, Elizabeth A. 2011. 'The Interest Group Analogy: International Non-Governmental Advocacy Organisations in International Politics'. *Review of International Studies* 37 (1): 93–120.

Bouwen, Pieter. 2004. 'The Logic of Access to the European Parliament: Business Lobbying in the Committee on Economic and Monetary Affairs'. *Journal of Common Market Studies* 42 (3): 473–95.

Bryant, Chris. 2011. 'MEP Resigns over Claims of Lobbyist Payments'. *Financial Times*, 20 March. http://www.ft.com/intl/cms/s/c34e40a4-5324-11e0-86e6-00144feab49a,Authorised= false.html?_i_location=http%3A%2F%2Fwww.ft.com%2Fcms%2Fs%2F0%2Fc34e40a4-5324-11e0-86e6-00144feab49a.html&_i_referer=#axzz2Loj757wN

Challand, Bénoit. 2011. 'Coming Too Late? The EU's Mixed Approaches to Transforming the Israeli-Palestinian Conflict'. In *The EU, Civil Society and Conflict*, edited by Nathalie Tocci. Abingdon/New York: Routledge. 96–125.

Chari, Raj, John Hogan and Gary Murphy. 2010. *Regulating Lobbying: A Global Comparison*. Manchester: Manchester University Press.

Coen, David and Jeremy Richardson, eds. 2009. *Lobbying the European Union: Institutions, Actors and Issues*. Oxford: Oxford University Press.

Council of the European Union. 2002. 'Palestinian Schoolbooks'. http://www.consilium. europa.eu/uedocs/cms_data/docs/pressdata/en/misc/70923.pdf

Crisis Action. 2010. *Crisis Action Annual Report 2009/2010*. Crisis Action. http://crisisaction. org/wp-content/uploads/2010/10/crisis-action-2009-10-annual-report-english.pdf

Cronin, David. 2011. *Europe's Alliance with Israel*. London: Pluto Press.

Dür, Andreas. 2008. 'Measuring Interest Group Influence in the EU: A Note on Methodology'. *European Union Politics* 9 (4): 559–76.

EJC, European Jewish Congress. 2013. 'About Us'. http://www.eurojewcong.org/about-us/

EU Delegation to the West Bank and Gaza Strip. 2013. 'EU Assistance to the Palestinians'. http://eeas.europa.eu/delegations/westbank/index_en.htm

Euractiv. 2008. 'EU Lobbyists Scramble over Their Exact Numbers'. *EurActiv.com*, 10 June. http://www.euractiv.com/pa/eu-lobbyists-scramble-exact-numb-news-219932

Euro-Mediterranean Human Rights Network (EMHRN). 2013. 'EMHRN Training Guide and Advocacy Toolkit'. 15 January. http://euromedrights.org/publication/emhrn-training-guide-and-toolkit-on-eu-advocacy/

Euro-Mediterranean Human Rights Network (EMHRN) and APRODEV. 2012. *EU–Israel Relations: Promoting and Ensuring Respect for International Law*. Brussels.

European Coalition for Israel. 2013. 'Give Peace A Chance'. http://www.ec4i.org/index. php?option=com_content&view=article&id=128:give-peace-a-chance&catid=74: press-releases&Itemid=53

European Commission. 2010. 'Local Market Access Teams Under the Market Access Partnership'. http://trade.ec.europa.eu/doclib/docs/2010/june/tradoc_146233.pdf

———. 2012. 'Trade – Israel'. 23 October. http://ec.europa.eu/trade/policy/countries-and-regions/countries/israel/

———. 2013. 'International Affairs: Round Tables and Business Dialogues'. 5 February. http://ec.europa.eu/enterprise/policies/international/listening-stakeholders/round-tables/ index_en.htm

European Former Leaders Group. 2010. 'Letter to the President of the European Council', 14 December. http://occupiedpalestine.wordpress.com/2010/12/14/full-letter-by-the-26-former-european-leaders/

European Parliament. 2010a. 'European Parliament resolution of 17 June 2010 on the Israeli Military Operation against the Humanitarian Flotilla and the Gaza Blockade' Strasbourg.

———. 2010b. 'European Parliament resolution of 9 September 2010 on the Situation of the Jordan River with Special Regard to the Lower Jordan River Area' Strasbourg.

Finke, Barbara. 2007. 'Civil Society Participation in EU Governance'. *Living Reviews in European Governance* 2 (2).

Funding for Peace Coalition. 2004. *EU Funding of the Palestinian Authority: The European Parliament Working Group Report Raises More Questions Than It Answers*.

FCP Report. Funding for Peace Coalition. http://www.eufunding.org.uk/accountability/EUWorkingGroupReport.html

Greenwood, Justin. 2003. *Interest Representation in the European Union*. Basingstoke: Palgrave Macmillan.

Greenwood, Justin and Joanna Dreger. 2013. 'The Transparency Register: A European Vanguard of Strong Lobby Regulation?' *Interest Groups & Advocacy* 2 (2): 139–62.

Grossman, Emiliano and Sabine Saurugger. 2004. 'Challenging French Interest Groups: The State, Europe and the International Political System'. *French Politics* 2 (2): 203–20.

Gullberg, Anne Therese. 2008. 'Lobbying Friends and Foes in Climate Policy: The Case of Business and Environmental Interest Groups in the European Union'. *Energy Policy* 36: 2964–72.

Hecker, Marc. 2005. 'Les groupes pro-Israéliens en France: une typologie'. *Politique Étrangère* 2 (Été): 401–10.

———. 2010. 'Les acteurs transnationaux face à l'état: l'exemple du militantisme, en France, Lié au conflit Israélo-Palestinien'. Doctorat de science politique, Paris: Université Paris 1 Panthéon-Sorbonne.

Israeli-European Policy Network. 2013. 'IEPN Events'. http://www.iepn.org/index.php?option=com_content&view=article&id=3&Itemid=3

JNews. 2013. 'About Us'. http://www.jnews.org.uk/about-us

Jünemann, Annette. 2003. 'The EuroMed Civil Forum: Critical "Watchdog" and Interncultural Mediator'. In *A New Euro-Mediterranean Cultural Identity*, edited by Stefania Panebianco. London/Portland: Frank Cass. 84–107.

Kluger Rasmussen, Maja. 2011. *Lobbying the European Parliament: A Necessary Evil*. CEPS Policy Brief 242. CEPS: Brussels.

Klüver, Heike. 2013. *Lobbying in the European Union Interest Groups, Lobbying Coalitions, and Policy Change*. Oxford: Oxford University Press.

Klüver, Heike and Sabine Saurugger. 2013. 'Opening the Black Box: The Professionalization of Interest Groups in the European Union'. *Interest Groups & Advocacy* 2 (2): 185–205.

Kohler-Koch, Beate and Barbara Finke. 2007. 'The Institutional Shaping of EU–Society Relations: A Contribution to Democracy via Participation?' *Journal of Civil Society* 3 (3): 205–21.

Lipkin, David. 2006. 'New Israeli–EU Chamber of Commerce Established'. *Ynetnews*, 13 July. http://www.ynetnews.com/articles/0,7340,L-3275204,00.html

Mahoney, Christine. 2007. 'Networking vs Allying: The Decision of Interest Groups to Join Coalitions in the US and the EU'. *Journal of European Public Policy* 14 (3): 441–66.

Marchetti, Raffaele, and Nathalie Tocci. 2011. *Civil Society, Conflicts and the Politicization of Human Rights*. Tokyo: United Nations University Press.

Marshall, David. 2010. 'Who to Lobby and When: Institutional Determinants of Interest Group Strategies in European Parliament Committees'. *European Union Politics* 11 (4): 553–75.

———. 2012. 'Do Rapporteur Receive Independent Policy Advice? Indirect Lobbying via the European Parliament's Committee Secretariat'. *Journal of European Public Policy* 19 (9): 1377–95.

Martens, Kerstin. 2002. 'Mission Impossible? Defining Nongovernmental Organizations'. *Voluntas: International Journal of Voluntary and Nonprofit Organisations* 13 (3): 271–85.

Mearsheimer, John J. and Stephen M. Walt. 2007. *The Israel Lobby and US Foreign Policy*. London: Allen Lane.

Oborne, Peter and James Jones. 2009. 'The Pro-Israel Lobby in Britain'. *Open Democracy*, 13 November. http://www.opendemocracy.net/ourkingdom/peter-oborne-james-jones/pro-israel-lobby-in-britain-full-text

Palestinian Ministry of Education. 2005. 'The Myth of Incitement in Palestinian Textbooks'. *The Electronic Intifada*. 13 June. http://electronicintifada.net/content/myth-incitement-palestinian-textbooks/5626

PIBF. 2013. *Palestine International Business Forum*. http://www.pibf.net/

Plateforme des ONG françaises pour la Palestine. 2012. 'Un bateau français pour Gaza'. http://www.plateforme-palestine.org/spip.php?rubrique127

Profundo. 2006a. *Dutch Economic Links in Support of the Israeli Occupation of Palestinian and/or Syrian Territories*. Profundo.

———. 2006b. *Riwal and the Israeli Separation Wall*. Profundo.

———. 2010. *Update of 'Dutch Economic Links in Support of the Israeli Occupation of Palestinian And/or Syrian Territories'*. Profundo.

Reinalda, Bob. 2001. 'Private in Form, Public in Purpose: NGOs in International Relations Theory'. In *Non-State Actors in International Relations*, edited by Bas Arts, Math Noortmann and Bob Reinalda. Non-State Actors in International Law, Politics, and Governance Series. Aldershot, Hants, England Burlington, VT: Ashgate. 11–40.

Rettman, Andrew. 2012a. 'EU Working on Consumer Labels for Israeli Settlement Products'. *EUobserver*, 14 September. http://euobserver.com/foreign/117547

———. 2012b. 'EU Commissioner Resigns in Tobacco-Lobby Dispute'. *EUobserver*, 16 October. http://euobserver.com/institutional/117887

Rich, Andrew. 2004. *Think Tanks, Public Policy, and the Politics of Expertise*. Cambridge/New York: Cambridge University Press.

Saurugger, Sabine. 2008. 'Interest Groups and Democracy in the European Union'. *West European Politics* 31 (6): 1274–91.

Steinberg, Gerald. 2008. *Europe's Hidden Hand: EU Funding for Political NGOs in the Arab Israeli Conflict: Analyzing Processes and Impact*. NGO Monitor Monograph Series 2. NGO Monitor. http://www.ngo-monitor.org/article/ngo_monitor_releases_groundbreaking_report_on_eu_funding_of_ngos

Stone, Diana. 2000. 'Think Tank Transnationalisation and the International Market for Non Profit Analysis, Advice and Advocacy'. *Global Society* 14 (2): 153–72.

Susskind, Simone. 2013. 'Simone Susskind'. *Simone Susskind*. http://www.simonesusskind.be/

The Coalition of Women for Peace. 2010a. *Financing the Israeli Occupation*. Tel Aviv: Who Profits from the Occupation.

———. 2010b. *Crossing the Line: The Tel-Aviv-Jerusalem Fast Train*. Who Profits. Tel Aviv: Who Profits from the Occupation.

———. 2011a. *SodaStream: A Case Study for Corporate Activity in Illegal Israeli Settlements*. Tel Aviv: Who Profits from the Occupation.

———. 2011b. *The Case of G4S: Private Security Companies and the Israeli Occupation*. Tel Aviv: Who Profits from the Occupation.

Tocci, Nathalie. 2005. *The Widening Gap between Rhetoric and Reality in EU Policy towards the Israeli–Palestinian Conflict*. 271. CEPS Working Paper Document. Brussels: CEPS.

Vakil, Anna C. 1997. 'Confronting the Classification Problem: Towards a Taxonomy of NGOs'. *World Development* 25 (12): 2057–70.

Van Gelder, J. W. and H. Kroes. 2009. *UK Economic Links with Israeli Settlements in Occupied Palestinian Territories*. Profundo.

Van Kuppevelt, Marloes. 2009. *Stakeholder Analysis: European Policy on the Middle East*. Brussels: IKV Pax Christi.

Voltolini, Benedetta. 2012. *The Role of Non-State Actors in EU Policies towards the Israeli–Palestinian Conflict*. Occasional Paper 99. Paris: EU ISS.

Woll, Cornelia. 2012. 'The Brash and the Soft-Spoken: Lobbying Styles in a Transatlantic Comparison'. *Interest Groups & Advocacy* 1 (2): 193–214.

Wonka, Arndt, Frank R. Baumgartner, Christine Mahoney and Joost Berkhout. 2010. 'Measuring the Size and Scope of the EU Interest Group Population'. *European Union Politics* 11 (3): 463–76.

4 Trade relations between the EU and Israel

Lobbying on the territorial scope of the EU–Israel Association Agreement

This chapter analyses EU–Israel trade relations with specific attention to the issue of goods produced in the settlements, which caused tensions between the EU and Israel. The point of contention discussed in this chapter concerns the treatment that these goods receive when imported to the EU. On the basis of the provisions contained in the Association Agreement and in the attached Fourth Protocol on the rules of origin, only goods that are produced or processed either in the EU or in Israel are entitled to receive preferential treatment – that is, enter the market paying reduced or zero customs duties. However, the EU and Israel give different interpretations to the 'territorial scope' of the Agreement (Article 83). While Israel defines the territorial scope of the agreement as encompassing the entirety of the territories that it has controlled since 1967, including settlements in the West Bank, East Jerusalem and Golan Heights, the EU does not recognise Israeli-occupied territory as part of the state of Israel. This implies that the goods produced in the Occupied Palestinian Territories (OPTs) cannot be exported to the EU under preferential treatment. Although the issue of trade with settlements is central here, it has to be noted that this aspect has much broader political implications in relation to the Peace Process. Settlements and territorial issues are indeed a very sensitive element of the conflict and of its resolution.

Given the centrality of the issue, it does not come as a surprise to find evidence of lobbying from NSAs. Many NGOs and solidarity movements have been calling for the boycott of Israeli goods or, at least, of settlement goods, arguing that settlements represent a violation of international humanitarian law. For example, the BDS movement has been calling for the boycott of Israeli goods and the complete ban of Israeli products from EU markets (together with a policy of divestment from settlements and the imposition of sanctions). Other NSAs have mixed the issue of preferential treatment with that of labelling of products, while still others prefer to deal with the broader implications of settlements for the Middle East Peace Process. In this chapter the focus will be on the specific issue of the rules of origin that apply to goods exported from Israel under the provisions of the EU–Israel Association Agreement. The choice of focusing on the issue of the rules of origin is due to the fact that the EU has exclusive competence on Common Commercial Policy and the Customs Union. Moreover, the problem emerging from this case extends to the general issue of the territorial scope of EU–Israel agreements, thus involving an aspect of crucial importance to the EU and its member states. While problems in trade relations between the EU and Israel date back to the Israeli policy of occupation following the 1967 Six-Day War and the subsequent establishment of Israeli settlements, lobbying actions on the rules of origin emerged in the second half of the 1990s. Due to the very technical and legal nature of the issue, few NSAs lobbied the EU. Two can be singled out for their activism: the MATTIN Group, a Palestinian NGO, and Brita GmbH, a German business group.[1]

This chapter shows that the MATTIN Group mainly played the role of dialogue-builder and employed technical frames (with a legal argument), thus managing to establish good relationships with EU officials. Through a dense set of social interactions, the MATTIN Group and the EU ended up framing the issue of goods coming from the settlements from a legal perspective that differs significantly from the mainstream understanding of the problem. In contrast, Brita GmbH, a German business actor trading with the Israeli company Soda Club, adopted the role of the opponent by challenging the EU in court. While it also used a technical (legal) frame, the confrontational attitude employed did not lead to cooperative interactions aimed at developing a mutual understanding of the issue at stake.

In order to demonstrate the different roles played and the frames used, this chapter is structured as follows. The first section provides an overview of the issue of the preferential treatment of goods and the rules of origin, delineating the key moments of EU–Israel relations. The following two sections deal with the types of role played and with the frames employed by the two NSAs. I then explain what happened at the national level and conclude with a discussion of the main findings of the chapter.

Preferential treatment and settlement goods

After the establishment of the European Community (EC), Israel was among the first countries to demand the establishment of diplomatic and economic relations with the newly formed Community. In 1958 Gideon Rafael, Israeli Ambassador to Belgium, became a non-member observer to the Commission, the same role played by the representatives of Britain and Ireland (Sachar 1999). Israel also established a full diplomatic mission with ambassadorial status in Brussels in light of the growing importance of the European market and the opportunities that the EC would provide. Ties between the EU and Israel started to get stronger very quickly. In 1964 the two parties signed a commercial agreement on the reduction on duties on certain agricultural products, followed by another agreement in 1970 that was meant to work as a transitory step before establishing a free trade area. The latter began to emerge with the 1975 agreement, signed within the 'Global Mediterranean Policy' framework: this agreement paved the way for the progressive elimination of trade barriers in both the industrial and agricultural sectors. A further boost to the bilateral relationship occurred in 1978, when the parties signed additional protocols on cooperation in industrial, technological, scientific, agricultural and financial sectors. While both parties were interested in strengthening their bilateral relationships for economic, cultural and political reasons, the EC also used these agreements and protocols to exert leverage on Israel with regard to the conflict (Bertrand-Sanz 2010; Greilsammer 1991; Sachar 1999). The increased cooperation was not, however, accompanied by evidence of specific problems related to the territorial scope of these agreements. Only in the 1980s did the first signs of tensions over trade relations begin to emerge.

A negative peak in EU–Israel bilateral relations was reached in 1986, when the Council of the European Communities (1986) issued Regulation 3363/86, granting preferential customs treatment to agricultural products from the West Bank and Gaza. Through this Regulation, the EU started treating Israel and the OPTs as two separate entities under EU law. Palestinian exporters were supposed to have direct relations with European importers and the Arab Chamber of Commerce was responsible for issuing certificates of origin, as the Palestinian Authority did not exist at the time. Yet, Israel denied the right of Palestinians to export their products directly, as Israeli law granted the monopoly of export of agricultural products to Agrecxo.[2] As a result, the European Parliament decided to block the approval of three of the protocols to the 1975 Agreement that were still pending, namely those on financial cooperation, transitional measures following the accession of Spain and Portugal and the harmonisation of duties on Israeli products and those coming from the acceding countries. The then Commissioner for the Mediterranean Countries, Claude Cheysson, tried to delink the ratification of the protocols from the implementation of the regulation. Eventually, the crisis was solved in the autumn of 1988, when Israel accepted that Palestinian agricultural exports could directly deal with EC importers (Greilsammer 1991; MEDEA Institute 1997). Although the issue was settled at the time, problems lingered on into the 1990s and 2000s. The peaceful settlement of the dispute at the end of the 1980s was followed by the strengthening of bilateral relations: Israel was granted a 'special status' in 1994 (European Council 1994).[3] The following year the two parties signed the Association Agreement as part of the Barcelona process/Euro-Mediterranean Partnership (EMP), which, however, entered into force in 2000 due to delays in ratification by the French and Belgian parliaments (Bertrand-Sanz 2010).

The Agreement has been the legal basis for all subsequent protocols and further agreements between the EU and Israel that followed. Importantly, it also defines the rules of the free trade area between the EU and Israel. In a free trade area goods can circulate freely without being subject to duties when they enter the market of another state – that is, they are entitled to preferential treatment. Only the goods produced or significantly processed in the territories of the signatories of a free trade agreement can benefit from this special access. Goods therefore have to comply with the so-called 'rules of origin', a set of criteria which indicate when traded goods exported to the other market are entitled to preferential treatment. In the case of the EU–Israel Association Agreement, the rules of origin are contained in the Fourth Protocol to the Agreement. According to Article 2 of the Protocol, products originate from the territory of the parties if they are 'wholly obtained or substantially transformed' either in the territories of the member states of the EU or in the territory of the state of Israel. The Association Agreement further provides, in Article 83, that the Agreement applies 'on the one hand, to the territories in which the Treaties establishing the European Community and the European and Steel Community are applied and under the conditions laid down in those Treaties and, on the other hand to the territory of the State of Israel'. However, no specific definition is provided as for what is meant by 'territory of the State of Israel'. As drafted, the Association Agreement thus gives Israel the right to interpret the term according to its domestic legislation.

In essence, these two articles define the 'territorial scope' of the Agreement – that is, the areas to which it applies – and clarify which goods are entitled to preferential treatment. Products that are obtained or substantially processed in the territory of one of the two parties can enjoy preferential treatment when being exported to the partner's market. In the case of Israeli goods, Israel's customs authorities are in charge of issuing the certificates of origin EUR.1, as required by the procedure for preferentially exporting goods to the EU under the Association Agreement.[4] The customs authorities of EU member states rely on the certificates issued by their Israeli counterparts, and make some random ex-post facto verifications. If they are not sure about the origin of products, they can ask for clarification or confirmation from the authorities of the exporting country. Similarly, EU exporters rely on the same procedure and on EU customs authorities to receive a certificate proving that their goods are eligible under the conditions specified in the Protocol. Thus, the system is based on mutual trust between the parties (Paasivirta 1999).

Although these provisions seem straightforward, signs of an incorrect implementation of the Association Agreement by Israel emerged in the second half of the 1990s. At that time, the Commission suspected that Israel-labelled orange juice was in reality a mixing of Israeli juice and Brazilian juice concentrates. By stating that it originated in Israel, Israeli exporters and EU importers were benefitting from preference treatment under the Agreement, thus violating the provisions of the Fourth Protocol. The Commission published a Notice to Importers 'warning [them] of non-originating products coming from Israel', as customs debt might be recovered from them if certificates proved to be false (ibid.: 322). Moreover, the Commission questioned the validity not only of the certificates related to the export of orange juice, but also of all EUR.1 certificates issued by Israeli authorities. It stated that 'various elements have come to light which confirm a lack of effective administrative cooperation ... and in particular certain substantial errors in the application of [the] agreements, to the extent that the validity of all preferential certificates issued by Israel, for all products, are put in doubt' (European Commission 1997).

In 1998 the Commission published a Communication in which it stated that Israeli settlements were not part of the state of Israel, as defined in international law (European Commission 1998). Were exports under the Association Agreement from these territories to be confirmed, Israel was supposed to end them soon.

Through two fact-finding missions in September 1998 and October 1999, the Commission confirmed Israel's breach of the Agreement. Israel's reply to the Commission's position was that East Jerusalem and the Golan Heights were part of Israel according to Israeli law. Israel further claimed that the settlements in the West Bank and Gaza, although they were not annexed to Israel, were, in practice, under its sovereign jurisdiction. Finally, the OPTs were part of its territory in customary terms, as there had been no complaint by the EU over the issue, and as the result of the 1994 Paris Protocol on Economic Relations between Israel and the PLO, which created a single customs envelope (Bertrand-Sanz 2010; Pardo and Peters 2010).

The contention of the late 1990s revolved around the different interpretation that Israel and the EU give to Article 83, due to its lack of specificity regarding the borders of the state of Israel. Following the position adopted by the international community, the EU recognises the state of Israel as the territory within the Green Line – that is, the pre-1967 borders. Consequently the Occupied Territories could not be considered to be part of Israel under the terms of the EU–Israel Association Agreement, as Israel's exercise of sovereignty over these territories is considered illegal by the EU. This means that goods produced in East Jerusalem, the Golan Heights or the West Bank cannot be granted preferential treatment under the Agreement, as they do not comply with the rules of origin of the Fourth Protocol. In contrast, Israel conceives the OPTs as part of its jurisdiction, as it has *de facto* extended its jurisdiction to the settlements and has made them part and parcel of the economic life of the country (although it has never annexed the West Bank *de jure*). Moreover, Israel justifies its practical incorporation of the West Bank under its treaty-making competences on the basis of WTO provisions and international trade rules that apply to administered territories. It also claims that these areas can be incorporated within the territorial scope of its trade agreements on the basis of the Paris Protocol between Israel and the PLO (Bertrand-Sanz 2010; Zemer and Pardo 2003). In practice, Israel implements its trade agreements without distinguishing between the territory of Israel, as internationally recognised, and the Occupied Territories (Interviewee 1).

In 2000 the issue reached the European Parliament as well. Members of the European Parliament (MEPs) started addressing questions concerning the issue of settlement goods and preferential treatment to the Commission and the Council.[5] In the same year, the first round of verifications on the goods exported from Israel began. In combination with pressure exerted from national customs authorities, especially Belgium and the United Kingdom, which were in need of guidance on how to deal with the settlement goods, the findings of the verification procedures confirmed the Commission's suspicions about Israeli violations. Following an unsuccessful meeting of the EU–Israel Customs Cooperation Committee in July 2001, during which the parties did not manage to find an agreement on how to solve the issue of settlement goods due to the different position on the OPTs (Hauswaldt 2003), the Commission decided to issue a second Notice to Importers in November 2001. It stated that goods from the settlements were not entitled to any preferential treatment and importers were subjected to tariff liability also retroactively.[6]

In 2003 the issue of settlement goods appeared again on the agenda of the EU, as the pan-European system of cumulation of origin for the Mediterranean area was under discussion. The EU invited Israel to find a solution to the problem of settlement goods; otherwise the cumulation of origin could not be implemented. A temporary solution, which is still in place today, was reached with the so-called 'Olmert Arrangement' or 'Technical Arrangement', according to which Israeli exporters would indicate the name of the place where the goods were produced or processed. Upon the Arrangement's entry into force in February 2005, the Commission and the Council stated that it was only a temporary device which would not solve the problem.[7] Basically, customs authorities of member states could recover duties on the products originating from the settlements, if the name on the EUR.1 was part of the list of settlements. At the same time, Israel was allowed to continue to issue the certificates of origin to the goods produced in the settlements, without being asked to implement the Association Agreement correctly.

While the issue remained in a sort of stand-by following this Arrangement, an important event in the story took place in 2009, when the Tribunal of First Instance issued its opinion on a case about the denial of preferential treatment to some Israeli goods imported by Brita GmbH in 2002. The final ruling by the European Court of Justice (ECJ) was issued in February 2010 and confirmed that goods produced in settlements cannot benefit from preferential treatment under the EU–Israel Association Agreement. Although the judicial ruling has not solved the problem of the different interpretation of the territorial scope of the Association Agreement and of its incorrect application by Israel (which was treated as a political matter), it provided clear legal references as far as the EU's position and its policies are concerned. In August 2012 the Commission issued a further Notice to Importers (European Commission 2012), putting the onus of checking the origin of goods claimed as Israeli on European importers. The list of ineligible places of origin was made public and importers need to consult it before lodging a claim for preferential treatment. If the postal code of the goods they are importing is on this list, they should refrain from sending a request to the customs authorities.[8]

Against this backdrop, two NSAs became very active and tried, with different means, to influence EU policies. The next section analyses the roles played by the MATTIN Group, a small NGO based in Ramallah (West Bank), which began its involvement in the origin rules issue by promoting the adoption of the 1986 Council Regulation and participating in its implementation, and Brita GmbH, a German water filtration company with 14 subsidiaries and one joint venture located in different parts of Europe and the world, which started its lobbying only in the early 2000s.

'Dialogue-builder' vs 'opponent': who wins?

In their lobbying actions on the issue of preferential treatment, the MATTIN Group and Brita GmbH played two different roles: the former that of the dialogue-builder and the latter that of the opponent. This section shows that NSAs adopting a more consensual role (dialogue-builder) develop cooperative forms of social interactions with EU officials and politicians. This allows for frames to be conveyed and for meaning to be shared. In contrast, an adversarial role (opponent) limits the possibility for NSAs to engage with EU policy-makers, given that the parties delegitimise each other. In this case, it becomes impossible for the parties to develop shared understandings and for frames to be developed and travel.

The MATTIN Group, which aims to influence EU foreign policy-making with a view to upholding international law and changing the situation on the ground for the Palestinians, has been lobbying the EU for the past 20 years and was known to many of the interviewees (e.g., Interviewees 13, 17, 20, 28, 29, 68). The NGO combines a 'passive enforcement'[9] approach, which it developed around the idea of holding a state or, in the case of the EU, an international organisation accountable to its existing legal obligations under international law, international humanitarian law and human rights law, with an access approach based on the provision of documents, analyses and face-to-face meetings. Instead of looking for public attention and exerting indirect pressure through public opinion and the media, the MATTIN Group focuses on the venues where the administrative processes and the political bargaining take place and on direct contacts with policy-makers (Beyers 2004; Bouwen and McCown 2007). Building on the advocacy initiated through Al-Haq and the Centre for International Human Rights Enforcement (CIHRE), which was based on the concept of third state responsibility in relation to the Israeli's occupation of the West Bank and Gaza Strip, the MATTIN Group relies on argumentation and deliberation as modes of interaction. It investigates the consistency of EU and third state dealings and practice with the responsibilities each has accepted and aims at establishing dialogue and cooperation with their officials that lead to a common understanding of an issue on the basis of the facts and the validity of the arguments presented.

The case of the rules of origin and preferential treatment to settlement goods was a sort of 'laboratory' for the MATTIN Group, and the first focus of its systematic lobbying of the EU. Its lobbying actions were developed and modified through constant interactions with both national and EU officials and politicians (Interviewee 1). While this lobbying began in the late 1980s, in connection with the 1986 Council Regulation establishing an EU preferential import regime for the West Bank and Gaza Strip and Israel's obstruction of its implementation, it was only with the issue of the rules of origin and settlement goods that the MATTIN Group started to develop a more coherent and organised approach to the EU, with a clearer frame in place. The consensual role that the NGO has developed is the result of continuous interactions that progressively altered the MATTIN Group's approach and role in engaging the EU (Interviewee 1).

The MATTIN Group's activities took place at two levels: the EU and the national. The use of the national level, which will be analysed in the fourth section, was complemented by a direct engagement with the Commission and the European Parliament. On the one hand, this NGO established contacts and had several interactions with the staff of the Commission, especially with the people working in the Directorates General (DGs) of TAXUD (Taxation and Customs Union) and the former RELEX (External Relations). Interestingly, the MATTIN Group also cooperated with MEPs to table oral and written questions to the Commission and the Council, as a way to raise the issue of settlement goods and hold these institutions accountable. As various EU officials confirmed (Interviewees 13, 17, 20, 29, 68), putting pressure on the Commission via the European Parliament forces the Commission to, at least, reply and recognise an issue. It is, therefore, a way to force the EU to take action (Interviewee 28). Other EU officials who sooner or later met with representatives of the MATTIN Group stated that they began to receive many questions from MEPs on the issue of settlement goods and preferential treatment; they knew these questions were written by the MATTIN Group, as the type of points raised reflected the argument that they had already listened to in meetings with MATTIN Group representatives (Interviewee 17, 20, 68). For example, in June 1998, MEP Mary Banotti asked the Commission how the EU was going to ensure that settlement goods did not benefit from preferential treatment under the EU–Israel Association Agreement.[10] The wording of the question was akin to the language and form used by the MATTIN Group, and it seems to confirm what was stated in interviews, namely that the NGO was providing MEPs with questions to be addressed to the Commission or the Council. Similarly, in January 2000 MEP Luisa Morgantini asked questions to both the Council and the Commission concerning the practical steps that EU institutions were taking to prevent the incorrect application of the Agreement and the illegal preferential importation of settlement products under the Agreement.[11] At the same time, the Delegation for relations with the Palestinian Legislative Council invited the MATTIN Group to give a presentation on the issue of settlement products. Moreover, the NGO met with people in the Customs Code Committee responsible for dealing with the rules of origin.[12]

While the issue of settlement goods was not new to the Commission, which was already seeking Israel's agreement to establish some mechanisms of control, the role of the MATTIN Group was important in keeping the issue alive and pushing the Commission, also via parliamentary questions, to take action (Interviewee 28). Interestingly, as will be explained in the third section of this chapter, there was a progressive shift from dealing with EU–Israel agreements in only political terms to a more legal understanding of the problem of the territorial scope of the Agreement and repercussions that it would have on the EU's legal system. For instance, in March 2000, a group of MEPs filed a question to the Commission on the 'Irregular Application of the EC–Israel Agreement' during the plenary debate.[13] By referring to obligations under international law and the applicability of the EU–Israel Association Agreement to the internationally recognised territory of Israel, MEPs questioned the Commission about the policies implemented in order to deal with the alleged violations of the provisions in the Agreement by Israel.

As a result of strong pressures from both the European Parliament and the customs authorities of member states, the Commission became more active.

The MATTIN Group entered into frequent exchanges with OLAF (the Commission's anti-fraud office) and DG TAXUD and presented empirical evidence that various products coming from Israel were actually originating from the OPTs. Faced with this evidence, the Commission was forced to consider the issue of settlement goods in a different light. More frequent contacts with the MATTIN Group were established, as the NGO was increasingly seen as an inter-locutor by the EU thanks to the information provided and the use of a legal frame to make sense of EU–Israel trade relations more in general.[14]

While questions to the Commission and the Council also continued in the following months, the European Parliament issued a resolution in May 2001 in which MEPs raised the improper implementation of the Association Agreement by Israel. In the resolution, the Commission and member states were urged to take action to end this wrongful situation (European Parliament 2001). Further pressure on the Commission was also exerted by national customs authorities, which asked for guidance on the issue of settlements products, after the launch of verification procedures between 2000 and 2001.[15] Eventually, the Commission confirmed its suspicions about Israeli violations and decided to issue a second Notice to Importers in November 2001, stating that goods from the settlements were not entitled to any preferential treatment and importers were subjected to tariff liability also retroactively (European Commission 2001).

Given that the Notice did not tackle the core of the problem – that is, Israel's different interpretation of the territorial scope – the MATTIN Group continued to discuss with member states, MEPs and the Commission the EU's need to imple-ment its legislation correctly in order to enable them to come up with an adequate solution. Between 2001 and 2003 the MATTIN Group helped MEPs and MPs to formulate parliamentary questions to clarify Commission and member states' positions,[16] and national customs authorities continued to carry out verification procedures on products imported from Israel (Interviewees 1, 17, 20).

EU officials confirm that they met the MATTIN Group several times and they all recall the 'territorial scope' clause as the NGO's main argument (Interviewees 13, 17, 20, 29). Interestingly, these interviews point out how the MATTIN Group evolved during the years as a result of constant interactions with EU policy-makers. While those officials that met representatives of the MATTIN Group in recent years argue that this NGO knows what to do, when and where to intervene (Interviewee 29), some officials who had meetings in the early stages argue that the initial behaviour of the MATTIN Group was accusatory, often lacking a clear understanding of how the EU worked and doing unnecessary overwork in lobby-ing (Interviewee 13). Interviewees 13 and 20 also shared a sense of 'pushiness' in the MATTIN Group's approach. Nevertheless, through frequent interactions with EU policy-makers and officials and a deepening of the mutual knowledge of each other, the MATTIN Group enhanced its credibility as a partner with whom EU policy-makers could have a dialogue and cooperate. These relations between the MATTIN Group and EU policy-makers also allowed for the definition of a common understanding concerning the problem of the rules of origin, as will be shown later.

Unlike the MATTIN Group, Brita GmbH played the role of the opponent. While it also used a legal argument, as will be shown in the following section, it turned to a German court with a view to achieving policy change through judicial ruling. As explained in Chapter 1, the use of litigation is a confrontational mode of interaction in which the two sides do not negotiate or establish a dialogue on the issue of contention. Via litigation NSAs challenge the EU through a judicial procedure that does not lead to mutual understanding or cooperation, but to a mutual delegitimation. In other words, NSAs relying on litigation aim to change EU policies through the ruling of a court, which either restores the status quo or paves the way for policies that had been previously opposed in the policy-making process.

It is important to point out here that Brita GmbH had obviously economic interests when it brought the case to the court, as it wanted to import goods from Soda Club, an Israeli company with factories in the settlements, without paying customs duties. There was probably an interest to recover and protect its interests and get the money of the duties back. However, the political dimension of the case cannot be ignored, given the rather small amount of money to be paid. It revolves first and foremost around the application of the EU–Israel Association Agreement and the status of settlement products. Indeed, Brita GmbH was selling the distribution rights for Soda Club and it was in its interest to defy the duties applied on settlement products. The aim was thus to change EU legislation in this regard, by claiming that the law of treaties supported Israel's application of the Association Agreement. In an interview (Interviewee 28), it was even suggested that Soda Club and the Israeli government might have been behind the case, as they were both interested in reversing the situation of the preferential treatment for settlement goods. Given the dissatisfaction of Israel as far as the status of settlement goods was concerned, the Israeli government might have looked for a legal procedure to change the situation implemented at the political level.[17]

What is also known as the 'Brita case' revolves around the denial of preferential treatment to Brita GmbH's imports of Soda Club's goods. In 2002, Brita GmbH imported water-carbonating machines and drink-makers for sparkling water and syrups produced by Soda Club in the company's factory in Mishor Adumin, an Israeli settlement in the West Bank. Between February and June 2002, Brita GmbH filed 62 declarations, stating that the goods it imported had originated in Israel, as proved by the EUR.1 certificates issued by Israeli customs authorities. Following the provisions of the EU–Israel Association Agreement, the goods were, in Brita GmbH's view, eligible for preferential treatment. The Hauptzollamt (customs office) Hamburg-Hafen provisionally accepted Brita GmbH's application and granted the exemption from customs duties. At the same time, however, it started a verification procedure, requesting Israeli customs authorities to indicate the exact origin of the goods, on the basis of Article 32 of the Fourth Protocol of the EU–Israel Association Agreement.[18] In their reply, Israeli customs authorities stated that the goods were manufactured in an area under Israeli customs responsibility. The Hauptzollamt considered this indication insufficient and decided to ask for supplementary information about the exact location of production, especially to verify whether the goods had been produced in the Occupied Territories of the West Bank, the Gaza Strip, East Jerusalem or the Golan Heights. Because Israeli customs authorities failed to reply, the Hauptzollamt Hamburg-Hafen refused to grant entitlement to preferential treatment to the goods imported by Brita GmbH in a notice of 25 September 2003. The reason was that it was not possible to establish with certainty if the imported goods were produced in an area where the EU–Israel Association Agreement applied. As provided for by the Notice to Importers of 2001, the Hauptzollamt sought post-clearance recovery of customs duties for an amount of €19,155.46.

Although Brita GmbH appealed against this decision, its appeal was dismissed by decision as being unfounded in June 2006. Therefore, the company brought an action for annulment before the Finanzgericht (financial court) Hamburg. The latter, unsure about the interpretation of the relevant trade agreements, referred the case to the ECJ for a preliminary ruling in 2008. More specifically, it asked for advice about the interpretation of the EU–Israel and EU–PLO Association Agreement as far as entitlement to preferential treatment is concerned, and how national customs authorities should behave when dealing with EUR.1 certificates issued by their Israeli counterparts (European Union 2008).

In October 2009 the Advocate General Bot gave a legal opinion on the case, maintaining that settlement goods are not entitled to preferential treatment under the EU–Israel Agreement. The final ruling by the ECJ was issued in February 2010: it stated that the goods coming from the Occupied Territories do not fall within the territorial scope of that EU–Israel Agreement and therefore do not qualify for duty exemption under that agreement, even if the Israeli customs authority issues a certificate of origin stating that the products originate in Israel. Therefore, Brita GmbH would have to pay the duties for the goods it imported (Hamburger Justiz 2010).

In referring to the court, Brita GmbH was not only trying to recover its money, but also challenging the legitimacy of EU policies towards Israel and Palestine. Despite its economic aspects related to the duties imposed on the company's imports, the 'Brita case' had strong political relevance as it aimed at changing EU legislation. Had the ECJ ruled in Brita's favour, it would have reversed one of the key pillars of EU policy, namely respect for international law, humanitarian law and international human rights law. Not only was Brita GmbH in disagreement with the policies of the EU, it was also challenging them without identifying possible alternatives to the current situation.[19] In other words, a legal ruling is a black-or-white position that either supports an implemented policy or delegitimises it. Unfortunately, it is not possible to elaborate on the reasons that pushed Brita GmbH in this direction, given that Brita's representatives refused to be interviewed and the EU and national officials interviewed could not elaborate on this issue.

The cases of the MATTIN Group and Brita GmbH have thus offered the possibility of investigating two different roles, the dialogue-builder and the opponent respectively. The MATTIN Group interacted directly with officials and politicians with a view to establishing cooperation and dialogue. This, in turn, progressively led to a new and shared understanding of the issue of settlement goods, as will be shown below. The progressive shift from a more accusatory approach to a cooperative mode of interaction shows that playing a consensual role when lobbying allows for cooperative social interactions on the basis of which frames can travel and get developed. In contrast, the case of Brita GmbH demonstrates that an adversarial role, which challenges EU policies, prevented the possibility of a positive cooperation and the establishment of mutual trust. Given this confrontational stance, the EU and Brita GmbH could not reach a common understanding on the issue, as any room for dialogue was precluded.

Technical frames to open the door of EU policy-making?

NSAs relying on technical frames are more likely to play a significant role, to be involved in EU foreign policy-making and to develop deep interactions with EU officials and politicians. This is due to the nature of the EU's policy-making process, which is characterised by a limited level of politicisation and a consensus-driven policy mode. Interestingly, both the MATTIN Group and Brita GmbH used technical and, more specifically, legal frames, but they had opposite results. On the one hand, the MATTIN Group managed to develop strong ties with EU policy-makers and to reach a new and shared understanding of the issue of the rules of origin in EU–Israel agreements. On the other hand, Brita GmbH was not able to convey its frame and interact with the EU on this basis.

In the case of the MATTIN Group, it is possible to identify a very articulated and complex technical frame, which revolves around the idea of the 'territorial scope' of the EU–Israel Association Agreement. More specifically, the EU cannot recognise as lawful or give legal effect within its legal system to an Israeli action that it considers unlawful under international law (Voltolini 2015). The incorrect application of the Agreement by Israel in the case of settlement goods – due to the different interpretation of Article 83 – leads to the violation by the EU of its own law and its obligations under international law, international humanitarian law and human rights. The frame is rooted in solid legal bases and has a high degree of technicality, with numerous references to international treaties such as the Vienna Convention, the Geneva Conventions and articles in the Association Agreement.[20]

The legal and technical dimension is still linked to key principles and interests of the EU, namely respecting its own legal system and its commitments under international law. According to the frame proposed by the MATTIN Group, the EU cannot accept that settlement products are imported under the preferential treatment, as this would lead to the violation of its own law and would endanger the Commission's role as 'guardian of the treaties'. In particular, the Commission would not be in the position to ensure the correct application of EU law and the proper collection of duties by national customs authorities (ibid.). The Association Agreement provides for the possibility of addressing the problem of different interpretations of the wording of the agreements through an arbitration mechanism, which would ensure that the EU does not accommodate to Israel's position regarding the status of the Occupied Territories (Interviewee 1; Euro-Mediterranean Human Rights Network 2006). These references to the *raison d'être* of the EU thus ensure that the resonance of the frame is strong, as suggested in Chapter 1. Besides its resonance, the frame by the MATTIN Group was supported with empirical evidence of Israeli violations of the Agreement: Israel exported settlement products (such as Ahava cosmetics, wine from the Golan Heights and cut flowers) under preferences in violation of EU law. By providing concrete examples in support of its argument, the MATTIN Group strengthened the empirical credibility of its frames, thus ensuring that it resonated more with EU officials and policy-makers (Snow and Benford 1992).

While the evidence collected on settlement goods was functional to the MATTIN Group's argument that the EU was violating its own law and its obligations under international law and humanitarian law, lobbying was generally based on the provision of policy briefs and legal documents offering details about international law, Israeli law and the rules of origin for the EU.[21] In essence, due to the different interpretations of the territorial scope of the EU–Israel Agreement, the EU risked creating a situation that would have compromised its position under international law, had measures to prevent this not been taken. By allowing Israeli actions that the EU considers illegal under international law to determine how EU law is implemented, the EU would give legal effect to these acts, losing the possibility of contesting them later on (in legal terms, this is called acquiescence). In some interviews, it was pointed out that the explanation was very detailed and important to raise the issue of preferential treatment to settlement goods and in exerting pressure on the Commission (Interviewees 13, 17, 20). However, some also lamented that the argument was sometimes too technical and legal, thus being difficult to understand (Interviewees 17, 20).

Despite the difficulties of the frame due to its highly technical and legal nature, the MATTIN Group's argument was well-structured and its content referred to pressing issues that the EU could not ignore or avoid tackling. Importantly, the EU and the MATTIN Group managed to collectively reach a new understanding of the situation. Through interactions based on mutual recognition as legitimate and trustworthy partners, argumentation and persuasion shaped the framing process (Tocci 2011; Beyers 2010; Nye 2004; Finnemore and Sikkink 1998; Hindess 1996). Interpretation and the construction of a new frame for EU–Israel relations was the result of a socially embedded process, where argumentation prevailed. Moreover, the frame proposed by the MATTIN Group differed substantially from the majority of the frames used by NSAs. These did not deal with the problem of the rules of origin and preferential treatment, and legal frames were not used due to the difficulties and technicalities involved (see Interviewee 2). The focus of many NSAs, including solidarity movements like the BDS movement, mainly revolves around the banning of Israeli products, new forms of labelling of goods and, in certain cases, the suspension of the Agreement. In contrast, the MATTIN Group proposed that the Agreement and the subsequent protocols be redrafted, and that Israel be forced to apply the Agreement with the EU according to EU law, so that the EU does not breach its obligations under

EU law, which also implies respect for international law, international humanitarian law and human rights law.[22]

Interestingly, the 'Brita case' also revolved around the territorial scope of the EU–Israel Association Agreement and whether settlement goods should be granted preferential treatment under the Agreement. Although the legal frame was in practice produced by the German Finanzgericht to which Brita GmbH appealed, it was an obvious consequence of the appeal to the court. As mentioned above, the Finanzgericht Hamburg referred the case to the ECJ, given that it had doubts about the interpretation of the EU–Israel Association Agreement. More specifically, it raised four issues:

1   The German Court asked whether preferential treatment should be granted anyway for goods coming from the West Bank, since this treatment is provided under both the EU–Israel and the EU–PLO Association Agreements, even if the certificates were issued by the Israeli customs authority.
2   It also enquired if the certificates of origin issued by the Israeli customs authority were binding for the national customs authorities of the EU.
3   It further questioned whether national customs authorities were authorised to refuse to grant entitlement to preferential treatment, if the Israeli authority fails to reply once asked for clarifications as far as the exact origin of the goods is concerned.
4   The Finanzgericht also wondered whether preferential treatment could be denied outright if it was sure that the goods imported were produced in the West Bank. (European Union 2008)

In his opinion, in October 2009, Advocate General Bot regrouped the questions under two main issues. On the one hand, the issue was whether the customs authorities of the importing state are bound by the results of the verification procedure carried out by the exporting state and whether any dispute has to be submitted to the Customs Cooperation Committee before taking measures unilaterally. In Bot's opinion, this was a problem of rules of origin and, more precisely, 'ascertaining whether that origin falls within the scope of the EC–Israel Agreement (point 86)' (Bot 2009). Therefore, the dispute is not over a question of fact, but relates to the territorial scope of the Agreement and its interpretation. The Association Council is the competent authority to deal with this issue.

On the other hand, the question relates to 'whether goods certified as being of Israeli origin but which prove to originate in the Occupied Territories, more specifically the West Bank, were entitled without distinction either to the preferential treatment under the EC–Israel Agreement or to that under the EC–PLO Agreement (point 105)'. According to Bot, the EU–Israel and EU–PLO Agreements have their territorial scope, namely the state of Israel and the territories of the West Bank and Gaza Strip respectively. The EU–PLO Association Agreement has been precisely signed in order to differentiate between Israel and the West Bank/Gaza Strip and to stimulate trade between these territories and the EU. Therefore, goods coming from these areas are not entitled to any preference under the EU–Israel Association Agreement. They are not allowed to be granted preferential treatment under the EU–PLO Agreement either, if the certificates of origin are issued by the Israeli customs authorities. The only valid certificates of origin that customs authorities in EU member states can accept for goods originating in the West Bank are those issued by Palestinian customs authorities, as provided by in the EU–PLO Association Agreement. In conclusion, the Advocate General maintained that those goods that are certified as being of Israeli origin by Israeli customs authorities, but which prove to originate from the Occupied Territories, are not entitled to preferential treatment either under the EU–Israel or the EU–PLO Association Agreement.

The ECJ's judgment on 25 February 2010 reached similar conclusions, but the ruling was based on different legal grounds, namely the existence of two different agreements, the EU–Israel and EU–PLO Association Agreements, which have mutually exclusive territorial scopes and pursue the same objective of developing free trade between the parties (point 48) (European Court of Justice 2010a). Therefore, 'products originating in the West Bank do not fall within the territorial scope of the EC–Israel Agreement and do not therefore qualify for preferential treatment under that agreement' (European Court of Justice 2010b).[23]

While the frame was structured by the national and EU courts, it seems reasonable to argue that Brita GmbH was looking for a legal way to change the situation of the rules of origin. In a different way from the frame proposed by the MATTIN Group, this ruling also offered a strong legal basis and made references to the founding principles of the EU, namely its legal framework. The case was likely to have been driven by intentions different from the simple recovering the duties on imports, but more as an attempt to change EU policies. Recalling again the interview with an EU official (Interviewee 28), the Israeli government was supposedly behind the case, as having a legal ruling favourable to duty-free exports from the OPTs would have been a possibility to solve the issue of settlement goods.

Interestingly, both NSAs used technical (legal) frames in representing their interests with regard to trade relations with Israel, but with opposite results. The MATTIN Group's frame of the territorial scope of agreements, which was shared with EU officials and politicians through cooperative forms of social interactions, led to the reframing of the EU's stance. As shown in the Statement of the European Union after the Tenth Meeting of the EU–Israel Association Council, the EU maintained that '[t]he elaboration of an operational cooperation agreement between Israel and Europol has also advanced. The first comprehensive draft was submitted to Israel for consideration in December 2010. The necessary provisions are made for the *correct territorial application* of this and other instruments' (European Union 2011, emphasis added). In December 2012, the Council Conclusions further stated that

> The European Union expresses its commitment to ensure that – in line with international law – all agreements between the State of Israel and the European Union must unequivocally and explicitly indicate their

inapplicability to the territories occupied by Israel in 1967, namely the Golan Heights, the West Bank including East Jerusalem, and the Gaza Strip. Recalling its Foreign Affairs Council Conclusions adopted in May 2012, the European Union and its member states reiterate their commitment to ensure continued, full and effective implementation of existing European Union legislation and bilateral arrangements applicable to settlement products. (Council of the European Union 2012)

Moreover, the publication in July 2013 of the 'Guidelines on the eligibility of Israeli Entities and their activities in the territories occupied by Israel since 1967 for grants, prizes and financial instruments funded by the EU from 2014 onwards'[24] seems to be the codification of this idea on a broader and more general level. In contrast, the frame used by Brita GmbH did not lead to a new understanding or reframing of the EU's position, nor did it bring about a shared understanding of the issue at stake. The German company lost the case and the ECJ clearly stated that goods imported from Israeli settlements cannot benefit from the preferential treatment granted by the EU–Israel Association Agreement. Approaching the issue in a very confrontational way did not allow for new frames to be conveyed and get codified.

The use of the national channel

In the EU's multi-level foreign policy system, member states also represent one of the possible contexts where NSAs conduct their lobbying on EU policies. In the case of the rules of origin, the MATTIN Group and Brita GmbH represent two different instances of the use of the national channel. On the one hand, the MATTIN Group, whose main activities were concentrated on Brussels, also relied on the national channel as a complementary lobbying strategy. On the other hand, the fact that Brita GmbH's headquarters are in Germany made the national venue congenial to its lobbying activities. Moreover, most of the time reliance on a litigation approach requires NSAs to go through the national channel, by referring to the ECJ via national courts (see Chapter 1). By recalling the patterns identified in Chapter 1, we could consider it as a form of internalisation – that is, the inclusion of the EU dimension/policy into interest representation at the national level.

Together with other European and Palestinian NGOs,[25] the MATTIN Group addressed the governments of France, Belgium, the United Kingdom and the Netherlands to make them aware of the problems concerning the ratification of the Association Agreement, especially in terms of Israel's violations of human rights (Bertrand-Sanz 2010).[26] The MATTIN Group also began to target the customs authorities of some member states and to provide evidence of their incorrect implementation of the Agreement, as well as by Israel, with regard to settlement products. In particular, the MATTIN Group worked with the Dutch, British, French and Belgian customs authorities and confronted them with the fact that they were granting preferential treatment to settlement goods in violation of EU legislation, even if the goods were being exported by Israel with a EUR.1

certificate issued by Israeli customs authorities that declared the goods were of Israeli origin (Interviewee 1).[27] More specifically, the customs authorities of Belgium, France, the United Kingdom and the Netherlands were confronted with clear evidence that some goods that were preferentially imported into European markets as merchandise originating in Israel were actually coming from the Golan Heights and the West Bank. By carrying out *a posteriori* verification on these files, customs authorities had to admit that some of these products entered the market without paying the customs duties.[28] By not collecting duties on the imports in question, there was a violation or deficient implementation of EU law. In this way, the MATTIN Group put them in a situation where they had to take action or call for action from the Commission to perform their responsibilities correctly and bring such violations to an end.[29] By providing a frame of interpretation for these pieces of information, the MATTIN Group was able to open a channel to make this issue of the territorial scope of agreements become part of the discourse at the EU level.

The reliance on the national level was partly forced by the nature of the issue. Trade agreements with third parties, and their relative rules of origin, are implemented at the national level by the customs authorities of the country to which Israeli goods are exported. Therefore, customs authorities represented an easy gateway to the Commission: once it was proved that settlement goods were entering EU markets without paying customs duties, national authorities were forced to refer to the Commission and ask for guidance in terms of what actions were to be taken in these cases. National delegations in the Customs Code Committee reported the results of their investigations and confirmed that they were in touch with the MATTIN Group, which had provided them with the relevant evidence.[30]

At the same time, lobbying efforts with national customs authorities were also complemented with actions with members of national parliaments (MPs). These had a similar role to that of the MEPs: they put questions to their governments in order to raise member states' awareness of the EU–Israel Association Agreement and the problems related to it. For example, questions were asked in the United Kingdom[31] and Germany.[32] In an interview, it was argued that the meetings with and documents sent by the MATTIN Group were important, as they provided useful information for parliamentarians by raising the specific legal issues involved in the case (Interviewee 87). However, the problem with the frame proposed by the MATTIN Group was, for many parliamentarians, the absence of a political dimension they considered meaningful, which is a necessary component in any debate in a national parliament (Interviewee 87). Therefore, the national channel proved to be a way to exert indirect pressure on the EU via member states. Like the European Parliament, national parliaments function as a form of control over their governments: they force ministers and their staff to answer questions about certain policies or positions, thus justifying the choices of the government. Similarly, MEPs target the Commission and the Council to exert indirect pressure on them, by forcing them to justify and explain the reasons behind certain policies. Basically, the MATTIN Group's approach when acting at the national level did not change if compared to its lobbying at the EU level.

A tentative explanation for this would be that the MATTIN Group has predominantly interacted with the Commission (with the national level being secondary and complementary), so that it has been socialised to the EU context and logics.

In the case of Brita GmbH, the litigation strategy required the involvement of the national level, as private disputes tend to reach the ECJ through the preliminary reference mechanism (Bouwen and McCown 2007). Brita GmbH thus exploited the national court to raise an issue in front of the ECJ: it was almost inevitable that the case would be referred to the ECJ, as it involved the interpretation of EU law on an issue that was extremely unclear from a legal point of view. The national level was undoubtedly a channel through which the company aimed to target the EU. In this sense, it can also be considered a case of internalisation – that is, the inclusion of EU policies in the representation of interests at the national level. Given the centrality of the EU in this policy domain (commercial policy is an EU-level competence), Brita GmbH mobilised over an EU issue at the national level. As it was not possible to discuss the issue with representatives from the company and in the absence of any additional evidence, it is difficult to assess whether Brita conducted other lobbying activities at either the national or the EU level.

This case shows that the national level is important to NSAs' lobbying. Both the MATTIN Group and Brita GmbH used the national channel to conduct their lobbying actions. In the case of the MATTIN Group, the national level has complemented the NGO's activities at the EU level. As for Brita GmbH, it has not been possible to ascertain whether litigation via a national court was the only form of lobbying used. Nevertheless, these examples show that NSAs based or active in Brussels, like the MATTIN Group, use the national level to complement their primary engagement with the EU level. In the case of NSAs based in member states, such as Brita GmbH, there is evidence of internalisation, whereby the EU dimension enters their lobbying at the national level and lobbying is conducted with the aim of indirectly lobbying the EU.

Conclusions

This chapter shows that NSAs lobbied the EU on the issue of the rules of origin. In particular, the role of the MATTIN Group was significant in instilling the issue of the territorial scope into EU policies, bringing the legal dimension of the issue to the forefront. This had clear implications in terms of the actions undertaken and the frame on which the EU's policy was based was significantly shaken and questioned. This led to some changes, whose effects can be seen in more recent decisions (e.g., the Guidelines) in which the broader issue of the territorial scope of agreements become prominent. Had the MATTIN Group not lobbied on this issue and not been involved in the policy-making process, it would have been very unlikely for the EU to take these steps. Keeping good relations with the Israeli government would have taken precedence over other concerns (e.g., legal aspects), so that the latter might have not reached the agenda at all. Therefore, the MATTIN Group proved crucial in raising the issue, contributing to a reformulation of the frame underpinning EU policies and in keeping the topic 'alive'.

While this chapter has shown that NSAs play a role in EU foreign policy towards the Israeli–Palestinian conflict, the type of role played is also important. Being a dialogue-builder is more suitable for lobbying the EU, as it offers the possibility of developing cooperative social interactions with it and influence its policies. Consensual and cooperative interactions based on argumentation allow for frames to travel and get developed. In contrast, playing the role of the opponent does not favour the engagement of NSAs with EU officials and politicians: the two sides delegitimise each other and there are no conditions for cooperative interactions to take place. Therefore, it is more difficult for frames to travel and for a shared understanding to be developed.

The MATTIN Group managed to establish trust-based relationships with EU officials and politicians and to develop dialogical and cooperative forms of interactions based on frequent meetings and email exchanges. This consensual form of interaction led to the progressive cooperation between the EU and the MATTIN Group. The two sides engaged in argumentation and reached a common understanding on the issues of the rules of origin. By being a dialogue-builder, the legal frame proposed by the MATTIN Group favoured a reframing of the EU's stance towards the issue of settlement products. This frame revolves around the territorial scope of EU–Israel agreements and how the different interpretation of this aspect has repercussions for the EU's legal system. By accepting that goods originating in the settlements (which Israel considers as part of its territory) benefit from preferential treatment, the EU would violate its own law and its obligations under international law and humanitarian law. Interestingly, not only has this frame been at the basis of a redefinition of the EU's position on the issue of settlement goods and EU–Israel agreements more generally, the MATTIN Group has also changed during its interactions and frequent contacts with the EU. From an approach that, while still consensual, was perceived as accusatory and not entirely fitting into the mode of EU policy-making, the MATTIN Group has become increasingly cooperative and has acquired a position as a partner.

In contrast, Brita GmbH played the role of the opponent by adopting a litigation approach. Therefore, it did not engage in cooperative forms of interaction with the EU, but challenged the legitimacy of its policies and did not aim to establish a dialogue whereby the two sides could try to reach a shared understanding of the situation at stake. The German company relied on a legal frame that challenged EU policies. Although the frame was formulated by the European and national courts, the decision by Brita GmbH of bringing its case to the German Finanzgericht was aimed at changing EU positions on the issue. Given the legal uncertainty surrounding the territorial scope of the EU–Israel Association Agreement, it was inevitable that the court would refer the case to the ECJ for an interpretation of the provisions of the Agreement. Although it was not possible to verify this with Brita GmbH's representatives, the litigation approach adopted did not seem to have only economic implications, namely the willingness to recover the duties on the imported goods. It is plausible to argue that, by creating a legal case, the aim was to change the EU's policy towards the settlements in a way that was favourable to Brita GmbH. Despite the use of a legal frame, lobbying by Brita GmbH had different outcomes compared to the MATTIN Group. This can be explained by the adoption of an adversarial approach: by preventing any possibility of cooperation and dialogue, it was not possible to convey the legal frame and work towards a redefinition of the EU's stance together with EU officials and politicians.

Lobbying also took place at the national level, but in different ways. On the one hand, the MATTIN Group complemented its Brussels-based activities with actions in member states. In the case of Brita GmbH, the choice of a litigation approach partially forced the business group to choose the national level to file its legal claim. The lobbying done by Brita GmbH is also an example of internalisation: a case of Europeanisation whereby NSAs incorporate the EU dimension/policy into their lobbying activities. EU issues have been brought into the lobbying efforts at the national level and the national channel has been the way for the business groups to pursue its interests and convey its demands and views.

Notes

1 No evidence of lobbying by business groups beyond Brita GmbH has been found. While a few other NGOs have done some lobbying on this issue, they have been mainly driven by the MATTIN Group, which took the lead and provided the expertise that was necessary to work on the issue. APRODEV, an umbrella NGO based in Brussels, has also been active on this issue. Yet, its lobbying on the rules of origin has been conducted in coordination with the MATTIN Group, which has provided the inputs and expertise necessary to carry out such activities (Interviewee 4). The Euro-Mediterranean Human Rights Network also tried to do some work on this topic and to adopt the MATTIN Group's approach in its lobbying actions, but it then decided to focus on other issues; this was partly due to the different requests from its member organisations (human rights) (Interviewee 2). For these reasons, the MATTIN Group is the only NGO considered here, as the other NGOs have relied on its work.
2 While it did not stop the export of industrial products, Israel obstructed trade via paperwork.
3 The wording of the Declaration does not exactly define what 'special status' means. It only says that 'Israel, on account of its high level of economic development, should enjoy special status in its relations with the European Union on the basis of reciprocity and common interests.'
4 In the media and public opinion, this technical and legal aspect is often confused with the 'labelling' of products, i.e., with the indication of the place where goods are produced, so that consumers are aware of what they buy. The fact that the rules of origin and the labelling are often confused derives from the fact that both problems refer to the goods coming from the settlements. See Interviewee 20.
5 E.g., Questions by MEP Luisa Morgantini to the Council (H-0017/00) and the Commission (H-0018/00) on Products imported from Israel: possible violations of the rules of origin in January 2000; Question by MEP Luisa Morgantini to the Council (H-0069/00) in July 2000; Written Question by MEP Alain Lipietz to the Commission (P-2786/00) in September 2000.
6 Notice to Importers, Importations from Israel into the Community, *Official Journal, OJ 2001 C 328*. On this point, see also Bertrand-Sanz (2010).
7 Written Question by Caroline Lucas to the European Commission, 6 July 2005, P-2496/05 and Oral Question by Said El Khadraoui to the Council, 22 June 2005, H-0544/05.
8 The list was updated in 2013, following a change in the postal code system in Israel. See http://ec.europa.eu/taxation_customs/customs/customs_duties/rules_origin/preferential/israel_ta_en.htm, accessed 10 January 2014.

9 The term was first introduced by the MATTIN Group, but it is also used in the literature now (e.g., Tocci 2007).
10 Question by MEP Mary Banotti to the Commission (H-0522/98), as listed in a confidential document seen by the author.
11 Questions by MEP Luisa Morgantini to the Council (H-0017/00) and the Commission (H-0018/00) on Products imported from Israel: possible violations of the rules of origin.
12 Confidential document seen by the author.
13 Oral question by several MEPs (O-0018/00) on Irregular Application of the EC–Israel Trade Agreement.
14 Unfortunately, the documents of Committee meetings, correspondence between the MATTIN Group and the EU Commission were not available for public consultation. The evidence presented here is therefore based on interviews and confidential documents that the author saw during interviews by courtesy of the interviewees.
15 Austria, Belgium, Italy, Sweden, Spain, France, Germany, UK and the Netherlands. See Bertrand-Sanz (2010) and a working document supplied to the author by the MATTIN Group.
16 E.g., during the European Parliament session of 13 May 2003, seven Question Time questions were asked to the Commission on the irregular application of EC–Israel trade-related agreements. The MEPs who submitted the questions were: H-0266/03 by Alain Lipietz, H-0268/03 by Mary Banotti; H0270/03 by John Cushmatian; H-0272/03 by Luisa Morgantini, H-0278/03 by Bartho Pronk, H-0283/03 by Jan Daehne, H-0287/03 by Ulla Sandaek. On the national level, as one example, Danish MP Jeppe Kofod wrote a letter to the Danish Minister of Taxes, 12 March 2003.
17 It was not possible to further investigate the issue with representatives of Brita GmbH or the Israeli government, as they refused to be interviewed for the purpose of this book and comment on the events.
18 According to this article, the authorities of the importing state are authorised to request verification of the EUR.1 certificates, had they doubts on the origin of the products.
19 It has to be noticed that Brita GmbH did not have many other possibilities than acting in this way, as the EU had already started a process of revision of its policies towards Israel (see previous discussion on the MATTIN Group's role).
20 Various documents produced by the MATTIN Group and seen by the author by courtesy of the NGO. These documents are confidential and they cannot be reproduced here.
21 Confidential documents seen by the author by courtesy of the MATTIN Group.
22 While interviewees were generally sharing the view that the MATTIN Group makes a valid and interesting point, Interviewee 20 found the argument too convoluted, with actually limited inputs on how to translate it in practical terms.
23 For different interpretations of the case, see, for example, Cardwell (2011).
24 Official Journal of the European Union, 2013/C 205/05. 19 July 2013. Available at: http://eur-lex.europa.eu/LexUriServ/LexUriServ.do?uri=OJ:C:2013:205:0009:0011: EN:PDF (accessed on 30 September 2013).
25 Human Rights Watch, ICCO, Save the Children, Pax Christi Belgium, CIHRE.
26 The Agreement was signed in 1995, but it entered into force only in 2000, given the delay in the ratification procedure in some member states.
27 Working document supplied to the author by the MATTIN Group.
28 Working document supplied to the author by the MATTIN Group.
29 The Commission, in its function of guardian of the treaties, has to guarantee that EU law is applied correctly. Therefore, deficient implementation of EU law due to the accommodation of wrong practices by third countries in their relationship with the EU could not be accepted.
30 Working document supplied to the author by the MATTIN Group.

31 E.g., Questions by MP Phyllis Starkey to the Secretary of State and Commonwealth Affairs, 12 January 1998, available at: http://www.publications.parliament.uk/pa/ cm199798/cmordbk1/80112w01.htm (accessed 30 March 2011).

32 E.g., Written questions by Dr Jürgen Gehb (CDU/CSU), *Anerkennung rechtmäßig vorgenommener Ursprungsbeurteilungen der Behörden des Ausfuhrlandes durch die Zollverwaltung des Einfuhrlandes gemäß geltendem Gemeinschaftsrecht, insbesondere für israelische Siedlungsprodukte*; Ralf Göbel (CDU/CSU), *Verstoß israelischer Ursprungszeugnisse für Exportwaren gegen das Assoziierungsabkommen der EU mit Israel*; Joachim Hörster (CDU/CSU), *Beurteilung der Ursprungszeugnisse für aus Israel in die EU exportierte Waren.* 8 August 2003. Available at: http://dipbt.bundestag.de/dip21/btd/15/014/1501474.pdf (accessed 20 March 2013).

References

Bertrand-Sanz, Agnes. 2010. 'The Role of the European Union in the Resolution of the Israeli–Palestinian Issue: Towards an Engagement Based on Respect for International Law and Human Rights'. PhD, London: School of Oriental and African Studies.

Beyers, Jan. 2004. 'Voice and Access: Political Practices of European Interest Associations'. *European Union Politics* 5 (2): 211–40.

———. 2010. 'Policy Issues, Organisational Format and the Political Strategies of Interest Organisations'. In *Interest Group Politics in Europe*, edited by Jan Beyers, Rainer Eising and William Maloney. West European Politics Series. London/New York: Routledge. 86–109.

Bot, Advocate General. 2009. Opinion – Brita GmbH v. Hauptzollamt Hamburg-Hafen. European Court of Justice.

Bouwen, Pieter and Margaret McCown. 2007. 'Lobbying versus Litigation: Political and Legal Strategies of Interest Representation in the European Union'. *Journal of European Public Policy* 14 (3): 422–43.

Cardwell, Paul James. 2011. 'Adjudicating on the Origin of Products from Israel and the West Bank: Brita GmbH v. Hauptzollamt Hamburg-Hafen (C-398/06)'. *European Public Law* 17 (1): 37–50.

Council of the European Communities. 1986. 'COUNCIL REGULATION (EEC) No 3363/86 of 27 October 1986 on the Tariff Arrangements Applicable to Imports into the Community of Products Originating in the Occupied Territories'. Brussels.

Council of the European Union. 2012. 'Council Conclusions on the Middle East Peace Process – 3209th FOREIGN AFFAIRS Council Meeting'. http://www.consilium.europa.eu/ uedocs/cms_data/docs/pressdata/EN/foraff/134140.pdf

Euro-Mediterranean Human Rights Network. 2006. *A Human Rights Review on the EU and Israel: Mainstreaming or Selectively Extinguishing Human Rights? 2004–2005.* Copenhagen: EMHRN.

European Commission. 1997. 'Notice to Importers. Importations from Israel into the Community'. Brussels.

———. 1998. 'Communication on the Implementation of the Interim Agreement on Trade and Trade-Related Matters between the European Community and Israel SEC(98) 695'. Brussels.

———. 2001. 'Notice to Importers. Importations from Israel into the Community'. Brussels.

———. 2012. 'Notice to Importers. Imports from Israel into the EU'. Brussels.

European Council. 1994. 'Presidency Conclusions, Essen, 9–10 December 1994'. Essen: European Union.

European Court of Justice. 2010a. Judgment of the Court (Fourth Chamber) in Case C-386/08, Reference for a preliminary ruling under Article 234 EC, from the Finanzgericht Hamburg (Germany), made by decision of 30 July 2008, received at the Court on 1 September 2008, in the proceedings Brita GmbH v. Hauptzollamt Hamburg-Hafen. European Court of Justice.

———. 2010b. 'Press Release No. 14/10'. Luxembourg, 25 February 2010.

European Parliament. 2001. 'European Parliament resolution of 17 May 2001 on the Situation in the Middle East'. Strasbourg.

European Union. 2008. 'Reference for Preliminary Ruling from the Finanzgericht Hamburg (Germany) Lodged on 1 September 2008 – Brita GmbH v. Hauptzollamt Hamburg-Hafen, OJ of the EU'. Brussels.

———. 2011. 'Tenth Meeting of the EU–Israel Association Council Statement of the European Union'. http://eeas.europa.eu/delegations/israel/press_corner/all_news/news/2011/20110222_01_en.htm

Finnemore, Martha and Kathryn Sikkink. 1998. 'International Norm Dynamics and Political Change'. *International Organization* 52 (4): 887–917.

Greilsammer, Ilan. 1991. 'The Non-Ratification of the EEC–Israel Protocols by the European Parliament (1988)'. *Middle Eastern Studies* 27 (2): 303–21.

Hamburger Justiz. 2010. 'EuGH Zum Zoll-Präferenzabkommen Der EG Mit Israel'. *Hamburger Justiz.* 8 March. http://justiz.hamburg.de/finanzgericht/4374022/eugh-zum-zollpraeferenzabkommen-eg-israel/

Hauswaldt, Christian. 2003. 'Problems under the EC–Israel Association Agreement: The Export of Goods Produced in the West Bank and the Gaza Strip under the EC–Israel Association Agreement'. *European Journal of International Law* 14 (3): 591–611.

Hindess, Barry. 1996. *Discourses of Power: From Hobbes to Foucault.* Oxford: Blackwell.

MEDEA Institute. 1997. 'EU–Palestinian Exports, Preferential Arrangement Granted Unilaterally by the EC'. http://www.medea.be/en/themes/euro-mediterranean-cooperation/eu-palestinian-exports-preferential-arrangement-granted-unilaterally-by-the-ec/

Nye, Joseph S. 2004. *Soft Power: The Means to Success in World Politics.* 1st edn. New York: Public Affairs.

Paasivirta, Esa. 1999. 'EU Trading with Israel and Palestine: Parallel Legal Frameworks and Triangular Issues'. *European Foreign Affairs Review* 4 (3): 305–26.

Pardo, Sharon and Joel Peters. 2010. *Uneasy Neighbors: Israel and the European Union.* Lanham, MD: Lexington Books.

Sachar, Howard Morley. 1999. *Israel and Europe: An Appraisal in History.* 1st edn. New York: Alfred Knopf.

Snow, David A. and Robert D. Benford. 1992. 'Master Frames and Cycles of Protest'. In *Frontiers in Social Movements Theory*, edited by Carol McClurg Mueller and Aldon D. Morris. New Haven: Yale University Press. 133–55.

Tocci, Nathalie. 2007. *The EU and Conflict Resolution: Promoting Peace in the Backyard.* Abingdon/New York: Routledge.

———. 2011. *Turkey's European Future: Behind the Scenes of America's Influence on EU–Turkey Relations.* New York/London: New York University Press.

Voltolini, Benedetta. 2015. 'Territorial Borders and Functional Regimes in EU–Israeli Agreements'. In *Fragmented Borders, Interdependence and External Relations. The Israel-Palestine-European Union Triangle*, edited by Raffaella A. Del Sarto. Basingstoke: Palgrave Macmillan. 67–85.

Zemer, Lior and Sharon Pardo. 2003. 'The Qualified Zones in Transition: Navigating the Dynamics of the Euro-Israeli Customs Dispute'. *European Foreign Affairs Review* 8 (1): 51–75.

5 The Goldstone Report

To endorse or not to endorse it?

While the previous chapter focused on trade relations between Israel and the EU, this chapter analyses lobbying activities concerning a more politicised issue that regards the EU's stance on human rights and humanitarian law. It focuses on the EU's position towards the Goldstone Report, the fact-finding mission (FFM) report that the United Nations (UN) commissioned to Judge Richard Goldstone, following Operation Cast Lead. After the Israeli attack on the Gaza Strip in response to the launch of rockets by Hamas in December 2008–January 2009, the United Nations Human Rights Council (UNHRC) decided to establish an FFM, chaired by Judge Goldstone, in April 2009. The team had the task of investigating alleged violations of human rights, international law and international humanitarian law that were committed during the conflict. The work of the FFM and the publication of the report generated much attention and several NSAs worked very intensively on it. Many NGOs and solidarity groups tried to influence the position adopted by the main international actors, including the EU and its member states. Business groups were not involved in lobbying due to the political nature of the report, which focuses on human rights and international law. The UN was also one of the main battlefields of NSA lobbying, but this chapter will only deal with this arena to the extent that this is linked to NSAs' lobbying aimed at shaping the EU's position within this context.

Lobbying on the Goldstone Report was exceptionally polarised. While some NSAs lobbied the EU and its member states to ensure their support for the Report and its recommendations, others argued that the Report was biased against Israel and its findings lacked credibility. To the former camp belongs the Euro-Mediterranean Human Rights Network (EMHRN), a human rights umbrella organisation based in Brussels which works on human rights in the Mediterranean region. Although the EMHRN has a broad focus on the entire Mediterranean region, it has a thematic working group composed of European, Israeli and Palestinian NGOs that focuses specifically on Israeli–Palestinian issues. The Goldstone Report was one of the priorities of the EMHRN, which took the lead on lobbying actions in Brussels. In this regard, it is important to note that NGOs in Brussels tended to divide and coordinate their work to avoid duplications or over-lapping in their lobbying activities (see Chapter 3).[1] In the camp against the report, the European Jewish Congress (EJC) and the European Friends of Israel (EFI) were the main actors engaged in lobbying. The EJC is an umbrella organisation that represents the Jewish communities in Europe,[2] while the EFI is an NGO that has been established by MEPs and MPs to support parliamentary initiatives that favour EU–Israel bilateral relations. The Goldstone Report was one of the topics on which the efforts of these NGOs were particularly evident and intense.

The chapter shows that, according to what was suggested in Chapter 1, the more consensual their role is and the more technical their frames are, the more likely it is for NSAs to be involved in the policy-making process. All three NGOs shifted between the dialogue-builder and voice-articulator roles, as they adopted both the approaches of access and information politics. However, the EMHRN used mixed frames, while the EFI and EJC mainly framed their arguments in political terms. Finally, the EMHRN also relied on the national level to carry out its activities as a way to complement its lobbying in Brussels. Lobbying in member states occurred when the goal was to influence national positions at the UN, while the EU level was privileged when the EMHRN aimed at swaying the European Parliament's position.

This chapter is structured as follows. The first section provides background information on Operation Cast Lead and the Goldstone Report. The second section contextualises these issues within the broader context of EU foreign policy. The third section focuses on the roles played by the three NSAs analysed in this chapter, and the fourth is devoted to analysis of the frames they employed. Before concluding with the summary of the main findings of the chapter, the fifth section analyses the use of the national level by the three NGOs.

Operation Cast Lead and the Goldstone Report

Since the coup d'état by Hamas in the Gaza Strip in June 2007 and the closure of the Strip from the rest of the world imposed by Israel, tensions between the Hamas-led government and Israel had mounted. They erupted on 27 December 2008, when Israel launched an attack on the Gaza Strip. Officially, the Israeli government justified the military operation as a response to, and a form of prevention against, the launch of rockets and mortars towards its towns in south Israel. Codenamed Operation Cast Lead, the attack lasted until 18 January 2009, when Israel and Hamas declared a unilateral ceasefire.[3] Numerous appeals from the international community called on the parties for the immediate termination of violence, the establishment of a ceasefire and the withdrawal of Israel from the Gaza Strip (UNSC 2009). In addition, many states intervened diplomatically with a view to finding a solution to the conflict (European Union 2008).

As shown in Chapter 2, Operation Cast Lead was the moment when the penny dropped and the EU (and the majority of its member states) slowly began to change their attitude towards the Israeli government and to be less willing to unconditionally support Israel (Interviewees 4, 91). In June 2009 the EU decided to freeze the upgrading of the Association Agreement/ENP, which was agreed upon in June 2008, but it continued to exploit the potential for cooperation under the existing framework. When Operation Cast Lead took place, the EU's reaction was extremely confused and, in the beginning, there was not a common stance in response to the events (Euro-Mediterranean Human Rights Network 2009a). The French presidency, which was in its very last days in this position, issued a declaration on 30 December 2008, calling for an immediate ceasefire and for the reopening of all borders (European Union 2008). Other member states issued separate, and sometimes contradicting, declarations. Diplomatic efforts were scattered and, despite the shared vision on the key pillars that shape the EU's position towards the conflict (see Chapter 2), the stance adopted with regard to the responsibilities of the attack on Gaza varied significantly. As Table 5.1 illustrates, there was a three-fold split within the EU. According to the EMHRN's report (2009a), member states' positions ranged from condemnation of Operation Cast Lead (Ireland and Belgium), to supporting Israel's military intervention as a necessary response to Hamas's attacks on Israeli cities close to the border with Gaza (Italy and Germany), to the adoption of a middle position condemning both sides (United Kingdom and France).

Following the end of hostilities, the President of the UNHRC established the UN FFM on the Gaza conflict on 3 April 2009, on the basis of UNHRC Resolution S-9/1 adopted on 12 January 2009. The FFM, led by Justice Richard Goldstone and composed of three other experts (Professor Christine Chinkin, Ms Hina Jilani and Colonel Desmond Travers), was tasked with 'investigat[ing] all violations of international human rights law and international humanitarian law that might have been committed at any time in the context of the military operations that were conducted in Gaza during the period between 27 December 2008 and 18 January 2009, whether before, during or after'.[4] To perform its mandate, the FFM had several meetings with various stakeholders (UN member states, NSAs, UN agencies), used the information concerning events since June 2008 coming from all interested persons and organisations, organised three fieldwork missions (two in Gaza and one in Jordan) and relied on public hearings, videos and photos to conduct its investigation of the violations of human rights committed by the parties involved in the Gaza war.[5]

The findings of the FFM were published in a report, known as the Goldstone Report, in which evidence of violations of human rights, international law and humanitarian international law by Israel, the Palestinian Authority and Hamas was provided. The Report also recommended that the parties carry out domestic

Table 5.1 Member states' positions on Operation Cast Lead

Condemnation of Operation Cast Lead	Support for Israel's action	Mixed/balanced stance
IE, BE, SE, LU, CY, FI, MT	DE, IT, CZ, NL, DK, RO	GB, FR, ES

Source: Information retrieved and adapted from Euro-Mediterranean Human Rights Network (2009). This source does not list the positions of all member states due to the lack of media sources and the impossibility of carrying out interviews in all member states. The same applies to my efforts to identify the positions of the missing member states.

investigation into, and eventually prosecution of, the ascertained violations. In the FFM's view, it was important to 'prevent ... the development of a climate of impunity' and to conduct investigations that were impartial, independent, prompt and effective (UN Human Rights Council 2009a).[6] The United Nations General Assembly (UNGA) endorsed the report on 5 November 2009, when the plenary passed Resolution A/RES/64/10, calling on the parties to implement its recommendations and asking the Secretary General to transmit the document to the Security Council. On 26 February 2010, the UNGA voted on a second and follow-up Resolution (A/RES/64/254), reiterating its support for calling on the parties to implement its recommendations. Further resolutions related to the report followed in March 2010, September 2010 and March 2011 (UN Human Rights Council 2010a, 2010b, 2011).[7]

The EU, the UN and the Goldstone Report

Against this backdrop, the EU became one of the targets of NSA lobbying. Its position on the Goldstone Report did indeed matter, and for two reasons. First, the EU is one of the main players on the Middle East chessboard, so that its declarations and policies towards the Israeli–Palestinian conflict are taken into consideration by the actors on the ground. In the case of the Goldstone Report, the key issue was the international support and legitimacy of the findings of the FFM. The EU's position in favour of or against the Report was crucial from a diplomatic and symbolic perspective. Second, the EU has the status of observer in the UN, with delegations both in Geneva and New York.[8] The main players, however, remain EU member states, which have a seat and voting power in the UN. All EU members sit in the UNGA, only the United Kingdom and France are permanent members in the UNSC, and representation in the UNHRC is based on regional quotas, so that EU member states rotate. When discussing the role of the EU within the UN, the coherence and coordination of the policies of its member states are therefore the main concerns, given these different forms of representation.

Member states make an attempt to coordinate their positions and reach a common EU stance on the issues under discussion in the UNHRC and the UNGA. Most coordination efforts among member states take place in Geneva and New York, although some preparatory work is also carried out in Brussels, in the Council Working Group on Human Rights (COHOM) or the Political and Security Committee (PSC) (Smith 2006; Basu 2012). According to interviewees (Interviewees 2, 60), however, the Goldstone Report was not discussed in Brussels: decisions on the position to be adopted on the Report were taken in each member state's capital and attempts to reach a common EU position were made in Geneva and New York. Although some studies (Luif 2003; Birnberg 2009) identify a coherent position with regard to the Middle East, the Goldstone Report proved to be quite divisive, confirming Smith's (2006, 2010) view on the UNHRC. A common EU position was indeed never reached in the UNHRC and the UNGA, with voting patterns showing splits all but once (when member states abstained), as shown in Table 5.2.

Table 5.2 Votes of member states in the UNHRC and UNGA on the Goldstone Report

Resolution	In favour	Against	Abstention	No vote
UNHRC 12th Special Session, The human rights situation in the Occupied Palestinian Territory, including East Jerusalem, 16/10/2009, A/HRC/ S-12/L.1		IT, HU, NL, SK	BE, SI	FR, GB
UNGA on the Follow-up to the report of the United Nations Fact Finding Mission on the Gaza Conflict, 05/11/2010, A/RES/64/10	CY, IE, MT, SI, PT	CZ, DE, HU, IT, NL, PL, SK	LV, LT, RO, BG, AT, BE, DK, EE, FI, FR, GR, LU, ES, SE, GB	
UNGA on the Second follow-up to the report of the United Nations Fact-Finding Mission on the Gaza Conflict, 26/02/2010, A/RES/64/254	AT, BE, CY, DK, EE, FI, FR, GR, IE, LU, ES, SE, GB, MT, SI, PT		CZ, DE, HU, IT, LV, LT, NL, PL, RO, SK, BG	
UNHRC on the Follow-up to the report of the Committee of experts, 29/09/2010, A/HRC/RES/15/6			BE, ES, FR, GB, HU, PL, SK	
UNHRC on the Follow-up to the report on the United Nations Fact-Finding Mission on the Gaza Conflict, 13/04/2011, A/HRC/RES16/32		SK, UK	BE, FR, HU, PL, ES	

Sources: UNGA and UNHRC minutes of sessions. Available at: www2.ohchr.org/english/bodies/ hrcouncil/; www.un.org/en/ga (accessed 12 January 2012).

Although the EU had stated that it considered investigations of utmost importance, not all the EU member states that were members of the UNHRC on 16 October 2009 endorsed the Goldstone Report. There was a three-fold split, with four states voting against, two abstaining and two not voting at all. A similar pattern also occurred in the UNGA vote of 5 November 2009. Again, member states split in three, despite the attempts by the Swedish presidency to reach a common position. On 26 February 2010, the UNGA voted on a follow-up resolution on the Goldstone Report. Interestingly, this time member states' votes were only divided into two, with no vote against the resolution. Compared to the previous vote, 11 member states changed their previous vote either from 'against' to 'abstention' or from 'abstention' to 'in favour'.[9]

The issue of the Goldstone Report was also taken up by the European Parliament. While member states discussed it in Geneva and New York, MEPs issued two resolutions in 2010, inviting the EU to show a common stance at the

UN level. The resolution of 25 February 2010 pointed out what the European
Parliament considered as the priorities for the EU in the upcoming session of the
UNHRC (European Parliament 2010b). On 10 March 2010, the European
Parliament issued a second resolution on the Goldstone Report, stressing the
importance of implementing the recommendations of the Report (European
Parliament 2010c). As will be highlighted in this chapter, this resolution became
a battlefield among NSAs and was very divisive among MEPs. Although the
European Parliament's resolutions are less relevant from a diplomatic perspective than statements issued by the Council or the High Representative, they still
have an impact in terms of legitimising a third country's actions. In this case, the
symbolic importance of the resolutions is also due to the fact that this was the
main forum in Brussels where the Goldstone Report was discussed. According
to some NGO representatives (Interviewees 2, 60), it was a deliberate choice of
member states to avoid dealing with the Goldstone Report in the Foreign Affairs
Council or in the Council's working groups, and to leave the matter for discussions and coordination in Geneva, New York and in member states' capitals.
In contrast, the European Parliament took a position on the issue, showing an
attention that had not been paid before to the Report, and aimed to exert further
pressure on other EU institutions and member states.

Therefore, the politics of the Goldstone Report was played on multiple levels.
The key forum was the UN, given that the FFM was established by the UN and
the Report was endorsed by the UNGA. In this context, the EU position was
shaped by the decisions of its member states and NSAs were therefore forced to
lobby either in Geneva/New York or in member states' capitals. At the same
time, the European Parliament played an important diplomatic role in the EU
context, as it issued two resolutions dealing with the Report. The activism of the
European Parliament was accompanied by lobbying actions by the NGOs
mentioned before. Against this backdrop, the following sections analyse the roles
and frames used by NSAs in lobbying on the Goldstone Report, while the final
section focuses on the use of the national level in lobbying efforts.

Swinging between dialogue-builder and voice-articulator

In the case of lobbying on the Goldstone Report, the EMHRN, the EJC and the
EFI swung between the roles of dialogue-builder and voice-articulator in their
interactions with the EU, as their lobbying activities were characterised by both
access and information politics approaches. Starting with the EMHRN, this NGO
is headquartered in Copenhagen, but has a representation office in Brussels. The
latter is tasked with the collection of information concerning EU policies and all
activities targeting the EU. The two-person staff that composes the working group
focusing on Israel/Palestine coordinates the activities and interests of the EMHRN
member organisations, which are NGOs based in Israel, Palestine and Europe.
Being a human rights NGO, its advocacy focuses on violations of human rights,
international humanitarian law and international law in the region, calling on the
EU to comply with its declarations on the Israeli–Palestinian conflict. Most EU

officials (Interviewees 11, 27, 29, 32, 35, 40, 45, 53, 68) maintained that they met frequently with the EMHRN and received regular emails with information, reports and calls for action from this NGO. For example, an EU official (Interviewee 35) stated that she was often in touch with the EMHRN to have inputs on issues that were of particular importance in the case of Israel–Palestine and with which the European Parliament should deal. The Goldstone Report was one such issue, confirming the existence of cooperation between MEPs or officials in the European Parliament and NSAs. Given the thematic scope of the EMHRN activities, this NGO lobbied the EU and its member states to ensure the EU's support for the implementation of the recommendations contained in the Goldstone Report, providing what an EU official (Interviewee 53) defined as crucial information and knowledge to the officials in the European Parliament. The core of the EMHRN's lobbying revolved around the issues of impunity and accountability: those responsible for violations of human rights and humanitarian law had to be punished.

Combining the use of an access approach (based on the provision of information and knowledge behind the scenes) with information politics (based on the production of reports or notes that were published on its website or presented in workshops and seminars) (Beyers 2004), the EMHRN swung between the dialogue-builder and the voice-articulator roles when targeting both the European Parliament and the member states. During the conflict, the EMHRN mainly provided EU institutions with information on the development of the events on the ground, stressing the violations of human rights and humanitarian law that were committed during Operation Cast Lead. Its provision of information also continued after the ceasefire: by relying on its member organisations on the ground, the EMHRN was able to send timely, detailed and precise information about the human rights situation in Israel and the Occupied Territories, an aspect of utmost importance given that the international community (including the EU) needed information and knowledge to build its response (Interviewee 2, 53).[10] Frequent interactions between EU decision-makers and the EMHRN were based on emails including detailed reports, or on meetings where the issue was discussed in person. Working behind the scenes with the aim of establishing a cooperative relationship with policy-makers is thus indicative of a dialogue-builder role, whereby the parties trust each other and work cooperatively towards the solution of the issue at stake. The EU and the EMHRN established a cooperative dialogue which left space for argumentation and for the development of a shared understanding of the situation.

Simultaneously, the EMHRN relied on an information politics approach: interactions took place in the public arena, although they were not necessarily directed at the public at large. Its public statements and reports targeted a very restricted audience, namely EU and national officials and practitioners working on the issue of the Goldstone Report. For example, in May 2009, the EMHRN published a report entitled *Active But Acquiescent: The EU's Response to the Israeli Military Offensive in the Gaza Strip* (2009a) in which the NGO stressed the window of opportunity that had opened for the EU to assert human rights and humanitarian law in the case of the Israeli–Palestinian conflict, thus reducing the rhetoric–practice gap between its statements and the actions on the ground. The report was well informed and documented thanks to the information and data collected through interviews carried out with the parties directly involved in the events and experiencing the situation on the ground on a daily basis (Euro-Mediterranean Human Rights Network 2009a). Just before the EU–Israel Association Council of 15 June 2009, the EMHRN released a statement, together with the International Federation of Human Rights (FIDH), asking the EU to use this bilateral meeting to put pressure on Israel to 'allow access of the UN Human Rights Council fact-finding commission to Israel and to Israeli political and military officials to conduct its investigation into all violations committed during Operation Cast Lead in Gaza' (Euro-Mediterranean Human Rights Network and FIDH 2009). A further public statement was issued on 3 September 2009, when the EMHRN published a 'Note on the Human Rights Situation in Israel and the OPT' in view of the forthcoming EU–Israel Informal Working Group on Human Rights (Euro-Mediterranean Human Rights Network 2009b). A section of this document was devoted to Operation Cast Lead and its findings. In essence, by raising the issue and keeping it alive through constant information flows as well as specific lobbying actions, the EMHRN aimed to ensure that the issue of the Goldstone Report was kept on the EU's agenda (Interviewee 2).

After the publication of the Report, the EMHRN continued to play both roles, targeting the European Parliament in particular. Not only did the EMHRN provide information and knowledge through emails or meetings with MEPs, officials or political advisors, it also organised a hearing in the Human Rights Sub-Committee of the European Parliament on 3 February 2010. On that occasion, Al-Haq, B'Tselem and Adalah briefed the MEPs on the assessment made by civil society organisations of the local investigations carried out by Israel, the Palestinian Authority and Hamas.[11] Following this meeting, the European Parliament (2010a) held a debate on the Goldstone Report on 24 February 2010, which resulted in the resolution of 25 February 2010 that was mentioned above.

Frequent interactions were established between the EMHRN and the EU. An EU official working in the Parliament (Interviewee 53) maintained that she worked in close cooperation with the EMHRN, contacting it to gain information, analyses and indications on how the issue could be further supported within the European Parliament. In particular, the two sides actively cooperated in order to ensure that MEPs would support the Goldstone Report through a resolution. The EMHRN was recognised as a partner and there was trust between it and European Parliament officials, aspects that led to cooperation and the attainment of mutual and shared understanding of the main aspects concerning the Goldstone Report. Interestingly, straddling between the dialogue-builder and voice-articulator roles still granted the EMHRN access to the European Parliament. Arguably, what mattered more was its dialogue-builder role based on acting behind the scenes and establishing personal relationships with officials working in the European Parliament and MEPs. In interviews (Interviewees 40, 53) details referring to this role were recalled, while public statements did not seem to have shaped the interactions between the EU and the EMHRN.

On the other side of the spectrum, the EJC and the EFI acted as counter-lobbying to the EMHRN. While lobbying on the same side, these two NGOs are very different as far as their nature and organisational features are concerned. The EJC represents the Jewish communities in Europe and, '[a]s the sole representative body of democratically elected European Jewish communities throughout Europe, the EJC works with national governments, European Union institutions and the Council of Europe' (EJC 2013). The EJC's headquarters are in Paris, but it has offices in other European cities, namely Brussels, Berlin, Budapest and Strasbourg. It is a federation that coordinates the elected leaders of the Jewish communities in Europe, representing around 2.5 million Jews. The Brussels office was inaugurated in October 2009, because of the increasing importance of the EU for the activities of the EJC and the necessity to be closer to officials and policy-makers at the European level. Its primary concerns are the well-being and interests of Jews living in EU member states, focusing on issues like anti-Semitism, the Shoah and inter-religious dialogue. Parallel to these topics, the EJC is also active on matters concerning the legitimacy of Israel and its policies. More specifically, since 2008 the EJC has increasingly mixed the legacies of the Holocaust with Israel's current policies, thus departing from the initial stance of being a bridge between Europe, Israel and the Arab world (Interviewee 52). In contrast, the EFI is an NGO supporting the inter-parliamentary initiatives of MEPs who sympathise with Israel. Due to its nature, the EFI is tightly linked to the European Parliament, but also lobbies the other EU institutions. Its main task is to provide MEPs with information about issues related to EU–Israeli relations and to organise events and workshops where politicians, practitioners and various officials are invited (Interviewees 6, 62).

Unlike the EMHRN, the EJC and the EFI aimed to ensure that the relationship between the EU and Israel continued unabated and strengthened. In their view, the Goldstone Report was a tool to blame and delegitimise Israel in front of the international community. Therefore, they attempted to convince the EU and its member states to dismiss the Report, pushing member states not to support the Report in the UN, and MEPs not to pass any resolution or declaration in favour of the Report.[12] They adopted the roles of both dialogue-builder and voice-articulator, combining public statements and press releases with private meetings, especially with MEPs and officials working in the European Parliament.

On the basis of the evidence found, the EJC mainly concentrated its efforts on the European Parliament, especially when the resolution on the implementation of the Goldstone Report was discussed.[13] There is no evidence that the EJC had interactions with the Commission or the Council, while some lobbying at the national level aimed at influencing the voting patterns of member states in the UN (see final section of this chapter).[14] It combined an access approach based on emails and face-to-face meetings with a more public stance based on public statements in newspapers or through its website. Interestingly, and similarly to what the EFI did, at times the EJC adopted a stance that favoured interactions based on cooperation and agreement on a shared meaning of the issue at stake, while its approach was less cooperative when it issued public statements. Prior its intense lobbying activity in March 2010, the EJC had issued a statement in November 2009, just before the vote in the UNGA. On that occasion, the EJC president Moshe Kantor called on EU member states to vote against the Goldstone Report (EJC 2009). The majority of public statements and direct lobbying (via meetings and emails) of decision-makers were concentrated in March 2010, just before the vote in the European Parliament on the resolution on the Goldstone Report. For example, Moshe Kantor issued a declaration on 2 March 2010 in the online news-paper *European Jewish Press*, arguing that the European Parliament should not endorse a report that is damaging for EU–Israel bilateral relations (EJP 2010a).

Similarly, the EFI was also active on the Goldstone Report with initiatives mainly directed at MEPs. To a lesser extent, the EFI also targeted top-level offi-cials in the Commission and the Council (Interviewees 6, 62). Moreover, it worked as a bridge between the EU and the Israeli Representation Mission in Brussels, thus favouring an exchange of information between MEPs and the Israeli government (Interviewee 62). In the EFI's view, the Report was a biased document, with many parts copy-pasted from NGO reports (Interviewee 62; *Haaretz* 2010a). Again, on the basis of their general mode of action, it is supposed that they mainly lobbied through an access approach, given that public statements on the issue were scarce, especially in the initial phases of the policy-making process.[15]

Both the EJC and the EFI became more active shortly before the European Parliament issued a resolution in March 2010. When it became clear that the European Parliament would table a motion for resolution on the Goldstone Report during the upcoming plenary session, the EJC started to lobby. It aimed to block the adoption of a text that would endorse the findings of the FFM, because this would have amounted to the 'most meaningful international endorsement' (*Haaretz* 2010b). Therefore, the EJC decided to target key MEPs, especially the presidents of the political groups, in order to steer the content of the resolution. In particular, it heavily lobbied the European People's Party (EPP) and the Socialists and Democrats (S&D), which were the biggest parties in the Parliament (EJP 2010b). For example, Arie Zuckerman, Secretary General of the European Jewish Fund, an organisation which belongs to the EJC, declared that they had 'a very promising meeting' with the leader of the Christian Democratic Party (*Haaretz* 2010a; EJP 2010b). Not only did the EJC organise meetings with MEPs to provide information concerning the Report and to explain its reasons why the European Parliament should not support the Goldstone Report, it also bombarded MEPs with emails indicating how to vote. The pressure was so strong that on 9 March 2010, the day before the vote, MEP Proinsias de Rossa, Chair of the Delegation to the Palestinian Legislative Council (PLC), circulated an email among his colleagues in which he appealed to them to resist such strong lobbying and to support the resolution as 'a test of the credibility of [the] parliament's commitment to human rights irrespective of political considerations' (Phillips 2010).

To summarise, the three NGOs analysed played roles that swung between the dialogue-builder and the voice-articulator. On the one hand, they arranged meet-ings with EU officials and policy-makers and they interacted through email. Their actions were taking place behind the scenes without the involvement of the public sphere. Especially in the case of the EMHR, the role of dialogue-builder led to the establishment of cooperative and dialogical interactions with officials and MEPs. It is also likely that this consensual approach played by the EJC and the EFI gave them the opportunity to work closely and establish a dialogue with certain MEPs and officials. In contrast, the voice-articulator role did not seem to favour any significant involvement of the three NGOs. Public statements and press releases did not lead to any form of communication and interaction between the EU and the NGOs. Neither the MEPs nor the officials interviewed recalled these forms of information politics as leading to social interactions, argumentation and deliberation or shaping their views in any way.

A battle of words: fighting impunity or delegitimising Israel?

The provision of information to policy-makers is an important aspect of lobbying. However, the framing process that shapes the ways information is conveyed also matters. In particular, technical frames are more likely to favour the development of cooperative social interactions and the reframing of EU positions and policies. At the same time, the European Parliament also finds mixed frames useful, as MEPs are politicians with an electorate mandate and need to be responsive to their constituencies. From their perspective, ideational centrality and political claims can be useful. In the case of the Goldstone Report, the three NGOs relied on different types of frames, which led to different forms of interactions with officials and MEPs. The EMHRN relied on mixed frames, the EFI and EJC on political ones.

Since the beginning of the hostilities between Israel and Hamas, the EMHRN had been providing information to EU institutions. To start with, it detailed the violations of human rights and international humanitarian law; then, it explained the difficulties for the FFM to carry out an appropriate investigation due to Israel's limited cooperation with the team led by Goldstone and the lack of independent and credible domestic investigations by Israel, Fatah and Hamas. On the basis of sources among NGOs and international organisations on the ground, the EMHRN got information that it then used in its interactions with EU officials and policy-makers, providing precise figures and information that gave strong credibility to its message (Euro-Mediterranean Human Rights Network 2009b). More specifically, the frame proposed combined legal and political arguments, revolving around the concepts of impunity and accountability. The main idea was that those breaking human rights law and international law needed to be punished and held accountable for their action. It was the EU's duty to comply with its rhetorical commitments and its obligations under international law. For instance, in a statement in December 2009, the EMHRN wrote:

> Given its close relation with Israel and its position as main donor to the Palestinians, the EU and its 27 Member States have a particular responsibility to ensure that international human rights and humanitarian law are

respected in Gaza. They not only have obligations as High Contracting Parties of the Geneva Conventions to ensure respect for these conventions, but they must also adhere to EU treaty obligations. In particular, they must respect Article 11 of the Treaty on the European Union, which establishes the consolidation of the rule of law and the respect for human rights as one of EU's foreign policy objectives. (Euro-Mediterranean Human Rights Network 2009d)

In order to push Israel to follow the recommendations of the Report, the EMHRN (2009c) 'urge[d] the EU and its Member States to publicly support the recommendations of the Fact Finding Mission and to follow up on and implement them'.

Although legal arguments referring to international law were present, the predominant frame was based on the language of human rights and the rhetoric–practice gap of EU policies, restating well-known discourses about EU foreign policy. In particular, there were references to the idea of good/bad, right/wrong, but no alternative on how to deal with the issue at stake was proposed (see also Euro-Mediterranean Human Rights Network and FIDH 2009, 2010). The EMHRN's frame was therefore a mixed frame, referring to the narrative that the EU should put into practice its rhetorical commitment and not indulge Israel for more pragmatic interests.[16] It provided the EU with detailed and precise information about the situation on the ground and made relevant links and references to legal issues, thus establishing the empirical credibility to its frame. At the same time, it embedded information into a political narrative that recalled the standard NGO advocacy when it comes to Israel–Palestine, namely the need for the EU to exert pressure on Israel to make it stop committing crimes against human rights and violating international law.

Interestingly, the wording that is found in the EMHRN's frame is very similar to that used by the EU. This congruence is important as it shows the extent to which NSAs draw on the EU's main tenets in terms of identity, discourses and policies to define their own constitutive traits. For example, in the statement issued by the EU Presidency at the UNHRC on 29 September 2009, the Swedish Ambassador, on behalf of the EU, stressed that 'one of the European Union's overarching human rights priorities is combating *impunity*. On this basis, we call upon both parties to fully *adhere to international humanitarian and human rights law*. ... The principle of *accountability* demands that all allegations of serious human rights violations and violations of international humanitarian law must be thoroughly investigated' (European Union 2009, emphasis added). It would be difficult to argue for unidirectional influence, such as the act of copy-pasting the words of the EMHRN in EU declarations or, vice versa, the EMHRN's simple use of the language of EU institutions. In contrast, this congruence in expressions and wording seems to point to the social embeddedness of actors and the fact that they influence each other in the way in which issues are framed and discussed. In support of this point, an EU official (Interviewee 53) maintained that she worked in close cooperation with the

EMHRN. She asked for information and analyses concerning the Goldstone Report, offering also an insider perspective to the EMHRN. The role of wording is particularly crucial in the case of the European Parliament, given the struggle over the meaning and the use of words when motions for resolutions are drafted. The selection of words and expressions becomes a battlefield in which various positions confront each other. In the case of the Goldstone Report, the EMHRN aimed at influencing the wording of the resolution that the European Parliament voted on in March 2010, by introducing references to accountability and the fight against impunity (Interviewee 53). In the Resolution, the European Parliament stated that it 'considers that accountability can contribute to a peaceful solution of the Middle East conflict [and] calls on the EU not to tolerate the lack of accountability on behalf of Israel for crimes committed against the Palestinian civil population'. It further '[u]nderlines that the policy of the EU and other international actions to grant Israel impunity for violations of international and international humanitarian law has failed', thus inviting member states to support the Report at the UNGA (European Parliament 2010c).

In contrast to the EMHRN's mixed frame centred on the concepts of impunity and accountability, the EJC and the EFI lobbied the EU on the basis of a political frame.[17] Both NGOs were strongly against the endorsement of the Goldstone Report by the EU and its member states in either UN forums or any other form of declaration or statement. In the words of the EJC's president Moshe Kantor, by endorsing the Report the EU would negatively affect EU–Israeli relations as well as the Middle East Peace Process (Phillips 2010; EJP 2010a). He also argued that the Goldstone Report was part of the 'systematic and orchestrated attempt to delegitimize Israel'. In accordance with the Israeli government, the EJC had therefore decided to offer its assistance and cooperation to fight against the 'campaign initiated by Muslim and pro-Palestinian organizations and indirectly nations, who seek to use public opinion and political tools' (EJP 2010a). A similar argument had previously been made in November 2009, when the EJC called on EU member states to vote against the Goldstone Report in the UNGA. On that occasion, it argued that the UN Assembly was dominated by a 'tyrannical majority' and hoped that Europe could 'enlist like-minded nations to ensure that no democratic nation votes for a resolution on the Goldstone Report' (EJC 2009).

The key argument proposed by the EJC revolved around the principles concerning the democratic nature of EU member states and the authoritarian features of many states voting in the UN, which had managed to hijack the UN and its agendas. This frame had very limited empirical credibility, as it did not provide any specific figure with regard to Operation Cast Lead or any legal reference on the reasons why EU member states should not support the Report. The bulk of the argument was based on the idea that the UN had a biased attitude towards Israel, with a view to delegitimising it and further destabilising the Middle East. Basically, the EJC made leverage on ideational centrality: it evoked myths and beliefs that were already present in the minds of EU politicians and officials (Snow and Benford 1992). The view that Israel was treated unjustly, that it faced an existential danger and that it was the only democratic state in the Middle East are commonly used images by those NSAs lobbying in favour of Israel. The EJC's frame placed the issue of the Goldstone Report in the broader framework of anti-Semitism and anti-Israeli feelings, with implicit references to the past of European states, an issue that has often conditioned the policies of many member states, Germany *in primis*.

In a similar way, the EFI framed its opposition to the Goldstone Report on the basis that the fact-finding mission was biased against Israel and its findings were not credible because they relied on NGOs' reports, data and figures. In essence, the EFI attacked the credibility of the Report by highlighting its discriminatory nature and its unfair account of the events. In order to inform MEPs about the alleged mistakes and incompleteness of the Report, it also referred to information provided by the Israeli government, which gave a different interpretation of the issue (Interview 62). Moreover, both the EJC and the EFI aimed at shaping the language of the resolution (EJP 2010a). More specifically, they referred to the biased nature of the Report, to its lack of credibility and to the damage that would result for the EU–Israel relationship. Supporting the Goldstone Report would amount to a 'blow' to the peace process by pushing the Palestinians away from the negotiation table (EJP 2010c).

The two types of frames used by the EJC and the EFI, on the one hand, and by the EMHRN, on the other hand, can be identified in the parliamentary debate on 24 February 2010 (European Parliament 2010a). Some MEPs were against the Goldstone Report, questioning the credibility of Judge Goldstone and maintaining that the situation of human rights in Israel could not be compared to that of other countries in the UNHRC such as Pakistan or China. Moreover, they viewed Hamas as a terrorist organisation, thus justifying counter-attacks by Israel. For example, MEP Louis Bontes (NI) argued that:

> it was clear from the very start that Israel was going to be labelled as perpetrator and aggressor in the Gaza conflict. Goldstone and his working methods are endorsed by countries such as Egypt and Pakistan and we know the state of human rights in those countries. It is beneath any acceptable standard. (Ibid.)

Similarly, MEP Michał Tomasz Kamiński, on behalf of the ECR Group, stated that:

> the Goldstone report is exceptionally unbalanced and unfair. It comes from the United Nations Human Rights Council, whose members include countries such as Iran, Nicaragua, Somalia and Libya. What right do those countries have, where respect for human rights has been reduced to zero, to evaluate Israel, the only democracy in the Middle East? (Ibid.)

In contrast, other MEPs supported the Goldstone Report and argued that it documented serious violations of human rights and humanitarian law on both the

Israeli and Palestinian sides. The EU could not close its eyes in face of these violations. For instance, MEP Frieda Brepoels (Verts/ALE) maintained that

> the Goldstone report has clearly shown that both Israel and Hamas have committed human rights violations during the war in Gaza. ... I also ask myself why the European Union is not standing up for international law. Why does it allow impunity to reign in this region? Any credibility in our respect for international law will be lost if the EU leaves these war crimes unchallenged. This report is not about Israel's security. This report is about major human rights violations. There is therefore no conceivable argument why the recommendations of this report should not be implemented. (Ibid.)

Before the vote in the plenary, each political party tabled its own motion for resolution on the implementation of the Goldstone Report. Following negotiations among political groups, the Alliance of Liberals and Democrats of Europe (ALDE), S&D, Verts/ALE (Greens/European Free Alliance) and European United Left/Nordic Green Left (GUE/NGL) tabled a joint motion for resolution.[18] Although the text had to be voted on in the plenary session on 10 March, the EPP blocked it the evening before, leading to its removal from the agenda (*Haaretz* 2010b; Phillips 2010). According to media reports, the EJC was instrumental in this sense, as EJC president Kantor warned MEPs of the harm to EU–Israel ties were the resolution to be approved by the Parliament. In the Israeli newspaper *Haaretz*, Kantor is quoted as having told the MEPs that '[i]t appears inconceivable that while the United Nations itself hasn't yet officially adopted this report, the European Parliament, in this motion for a resolution, calls for and demands its implementation' (*Haaretz* 2010b). As a result of the EPP's move, the plenary was supposed to vote on various different motions, with the EPP's text having the highest chances of success given the majority of MEPs in the Parliament (*Haaretz* 2010b; Phillips 2010). Against all forecasts, the EPP's motion for resolution, which was voted on first, was rejected by 243 votes to 364 (with 60 abstentions), while the joint motion for resolution, which was eventually retabled, was adopted by 335 votes to 287 (43 abstentions).[19]

Interestingly, the text approved contained various references to the aspects raised by the EMHRN. The resolution underlined the need for 'respect for international humanitarian law and international human rights law by all parties under all circumstances' and called on the High Representative and member states 'to work towards a strong EU common position on follow-up to the report of the fact-finding mission – led by Judge Goldstone – on the conflict in Gaza and southern Israel, publicly demanding the implementation of its recommendations and accountability for all violations of international law, including alleged war crimes'. Moreover, they were asked to 'monitor actively the implementation of the recommendations set out in the Goldstone report by consulting the EU's external missions and NGOs working in the field' and to include the 'recommendations and related observations ... in EU dialogues with both sides, and in multilateral fora'. Finally, it reiterated the centrality of respect for international law and the rule of law, and supported the UN efforts to 'ensure accountability for all violations of international humanitarian law and international human rights law during the Gaza conflict' (European Parliament 2010c).

Following this result, the EJC expressed its disappointment with the result of the vote. Kantor argued that the EJC 'made it abundantly clear to those MEPs which we contacted that this resolution was against the overall objectives of Europe's role in the Middle East'. He further pointed out that 'the fact that over 45% of MEP's voted against the resolution is cause for some satisfaction. We can see our lobbying efforts bore fruit due to the fact that the resolution passed by only a narrow margin, and not the consensus that was expected' (Phillips 2010; EJP 2010c). Furthermore, the EFI and the EJC also considered as their success the fact that the roll-call vote on the recital in the motion which referred to Hamas as a terrorist organisation approved it by a landslide, with 580 MEPs voting in favour (Interviewee 6; VoteWatchEU 2010b).[20]

This case shows that the EMHRN's mixed frame provided MEPs and officials with an argument that was suitable for them to use in the resolution. In contrast, the political frame proposed by the other two NGOs did not lead to any significant reframing of the EU's position. Moreover, the evident congruence between the wording of the EU and the EMHRN's declarations, statements and documents can be seen as indicative of the strong embeddedness that characterises lobbying in the EU.

Using member states but aiming at EU foreign policy

The national channel can be used by NSAs to complement their lobbying on EU issues with a view to changing EU policies. The EMHRN, the EJC and the EFI relied on the national level in their lobbying, which was probably a consequence of the fact that the issue of the Goldstone Report was also played in the UN arena, where member states have voting power.

Given the relevance of the UN 'battleground', the EMHRN aimed to push for a single position among EU member states inside the UNHRC and the UNGA. Over time, however, the EMHRN modified its position: the new goal became to convince more and more member states to support the Report, instead of reaching a common stance at all costs. While abstention was seen as a likely outcome, the EMHRN attempted to increase the number of member states supporting the report at the UN (Interviewee 2).[21] Interestingly, an EU official made the same argument, thus supporting the idea of strong social interactions between the EU and the EMHRN as basis for frames to travel and for the achievement of a new and shared understanding (Interviewee 53). In the official's view, it was acceptable to have different perspectives among member states: what really mattered was that they were all pointing in the same direction – that is, progressively recognising the need to keep the parties to the conflict accountable for violations of human rights. In this sense, the change of position from 'voting against' to 'abstaining' within UN forums (see the change in voting patterns between November 2009 and February 2010) could be considered a step in this direction.

In order to influence member states' positions on the Goldstone Report, the EMHRN organised missions to national capitals. For example, at the beginning of February 2010 it organised a mission to Paris during which a delegation of Israeli and Palestinian NGOs had the chance to speak to French officials and policy-makers and to present the results of their investigations related to the situation in Gaza. Given France's role as one of the permanent members of the UNSC, French support for the Goldstone Report was important (Interviewee 2). Similarly, the EMHRN organised a mission to Geneva in September 2010 with the aim of building consensus for the resolution under discussion in the UNHRC session and of achieving a true commitment by member states to following the investigations and ensuring accountability (Interviewee 2, 60).[22] In parallel to carrying out lobbying in capitals, member states were also lobbied via their Permanent Representations in Brussels (Interviewee 2).

More importantly, the EMHRN coordinated lobbying activities by national NSAs, given its limited capacity to conduct direct lobbying in all EU member states. Therefore, it organised training seminars for NSAs based in member states, pointing out how they could contribute to lobbying efforts on the dossier, and it prepared strategies and lobbying documents that national NSAs could use in their advocacy work (Interviewee 2). Moreover, the fact that the Goldstone Report was barely discussed in Brussels, but mostly in national capitals and in Geneva/New York, made lobbying via the national channel of utmost importance (Interviewee 60).

As for the EJC and the EFI, there is limited evidence on their use of the national level. On the basis of their organisational structure and the general type of lobbying activities they carry out, it is extremely likely that they lobbied at the national level. In the case of the EJC, its federated nature and its extensive presence in various parts of Europe makes it very likely that it also relied on its local branches and the various Jewish communities to attempt to influence member states' positions on the Goldstone Report. For example, the Board of Deputies of British Jews, a member of the EJC, organised a lobby mission to Brussels to meet with British MEPs and convince them to vote against the resolution in the European Parliament (*Haaretz* 2010a; EJP 2010b). Unfortunately, the data available and the interviews conducted do not allow us to elucidate this point on the use of the national level.

To summarise, this section shows that the national level was used in lobbying on the Goldstone Report, also due to the fact that the Report was discussed in the UN, where member states have voting power. This made it vital to lobby EU member states' positions to ensure that the EU would adopt a common stance on the Goldstone Report. While the EMHRN initially aimed at reaching a single EU position, it progressively changed its goal and aimed to increase the number of member states supporting the Report, instead of reaching a common stance that would be one of abstention. In contrast, the EJC and the EFI wanted to prevent any European support to the Goldstone Report, as they perceived this endorsement as damaging for Israel and its international legitimacy.

Conclusions

In contrast to the previous case on EU–Israeli trade relations, the issue of the Goldstone Report was a much politicised topic dealing with respect for human rights and humanitarian law by the parties to the conflict. It was indeed linked to the conflict between Israel and Hamas between December 2008 and January 2009 and, therefore, to the broader issue of the Israeli–Palestinian conflict. This chapter has demonstrated that NSAs, in particular NGOs, played a role in the policy-making process concerning the issue of the Goldstone Report. More precisely, the EMHRN, the EJC and the EFI played a role that swung between the dialogue-builder and the voice-articulator. They relied on an access approach, whereby they lobbied behind the scenes, met officials in the European Parliament and MEPs face-to-face, interacted via emails and developed forms of interactions that created the possibility of establishing dialogue, mutual trust and cooperation. In turn, this had the potential to lead to the construction of a shared view and understanding of the situation at stake. At the same time, however, these NGOs made use of information politics by issuing public statements and relying on the media (e.g., newspapers) and the public sphere. In this case, possibilities for interaction were mainly precluded and the parties could not negotiate a shared meaning of the events and their interpretation.

Although all three NGOs combined these two roles in their lobbying, the EMHRN managed to influence the European Parliament's position thanks to its mixed frame, which favoured a redefinition of the EU's position. The frame proposed had significant resonance among MEPs and officials, and a similar language was used in both EU and EMHRN documents. At the same time, the development of cooperative and dialogical interactions also influenced the consti-tutive traits and the preferences of the EMHRN. First, this NGO relied on the EU's tenets to define itself and its requests. Second, its changed position in terms of member states' voting patterns also seemed to be the result of interactions with officials of the European Parliament. In contrast, the political frame used by the EJC and the EFI did not lead to any reframing. A purely ideological argument based on political claims without empirical evidence does not work at the EU level, not even in the European Parliament.

Finally, the three NGOs also relied on the national level to carry out their lobbying, as EU member states were crucial, especially in relation to the EU's position within the UN. The EMHRN conducted direct lobbying at the national level as well as training NSAs based in member states to carry out lobbying on EU foreign policy and the Goldstone Report. Unfortunately, it is difficult to draw precise conclusions as far as the EJC and the EFI were concerned as the data available and the interviews did not lead to definitive conclusions in this regard.

In conclusion, this chapter has demonstrated that NSAs playing a role of dialogue-builder based on an access approach have more possibilities of develop-ing shared frames and of mutually defining each other, as in the case of the EMHRN. However, this role alone is not sufficient and it needs to be combined with a technical or, at least, mixed frame. While the Parliament would have probably issued the resolution anyway, NSAs were crucial in determining and shaping its content. The issue of impunity would not probably have had such an important place in the text had the EMHRN not been active in interacting with MEPs and officials. These interactions indeed led to a new way of framing the conflict in Gaza: impunity should not be granted to those that violated human rights and committed crimes during the conflict. Despite being perfectly in line with the main stance of the EP, interviewees also confirmed that this new frame was also the result of their interactions with NSAs, who contributed to form a new frame to understand the issue at stake.

Notes

1 Amnesty International (AI) was also active on the issues of Operation Cast Lead and the Goldstone Report to guarantee that the parties to the conflict were held accountable for violations of human rights and humanitarian law and make sure that the issue of the Goldstone Report was not forgotten (Interviewee 8, 60).
2 Its establishment in Brussels only dates back to 2009, but the EJC has been present in Europe for a long time, with headquarters located in Paris.
3 More precisely, Israel declared a unilateral ceasefire on 17 January 2009. Hamas followed with its unilateral ceasefire the day after. For a short overview of the issue, see Defence for Children International (2009).
4 http://www.ohchr.org/EN/HRBodies/HRC/SpecialSessions/Session9/Pages/FactFindingMission.aspx (accessed 10 October 2012).
5 Ibid.
6 The report was endorsed by the UNHRC on 16 October 2009 by a majority of 25 out of 42 votes (UN Human Rights Council 2009b).
7 The resolutions dealt with the following: the establishment of a Committee of Independent Experts to monitor domestic investigations by Israel, the Palestinian Authority and Hamas; the discussion/conclusions on the report of this Committee; a follow-up resolution on the second report of the Committee.
8 The role of observer in the UN was originally granted to the European Community. Since the entry into force of the Lisbon Treaty, this position has been taken over by the EU, which has acquired legal personality. The Delegations of the Commission and the Council, which were previously distinct, have been merged into one single EU delegation.
9 Interestingly, the resolution contained references to potential actions by the UNSC. Despite this element, both France and the UK voted in favour.
10 Among its member organisations, B'Tselem (2009) and Al-Haq (2009) produced detailed reports on violations of human rights and international law during Operation Cast Lead.
11 No record of this hearing was found on the website of the European Parliament. The meeting was confirmed in interviews (Interviewees 2, 60, 69) and in an email exchange that the author had with one representative of the EMHRN on 12 January 2011. It was also mentioned in various confidential documents seen by the author by courtesy of the EMHRN.
12 Information and documents concerning the activities of these two NGOs are scarce. During interviews, few details about these events were given.
13 Limited information was available due to the fact that interviewees did not want to disclose certain details. This also made it necessary to derive certain patterns from general trends of the EJC. Unfortunately, interviewees remained extremely vague and it was not always possible to fill in the gaps with data available through other sources.

14 However, much of the lobbying at the UN level was left to the World Jewish Organisation, which is based in New York (Interviewee 77).

15 Like the EJC, it was very difficult to get detailed information from EFI representatives. The MEPs that are members of EFI refused to be interviewed.

16 This argument, which is often summarised in the expression 'business as usual' (Interviewee 4), is also recurrent in the academic literature. The basic idea is that EU policies towards the Israeli–Palestinian conflict are a clear example of a rhetoric–practice gap due to numerous factors, including the predominance of possession goals over milieu goals (Wolfers 1962). For instance, see Tocci (2005); Musu (2010).

17 While most of the attention will be given to the EJC's frame here due to the fact that more evidence was found in this case, the arguments presented by the EFI were very similar, at least on the basis of the information retrieved.

18 S&D, Verts/ALE and GUE/NGL are generally strong supporters of human rights and tend to be vocal against Israel's violations of human rights and international law. The ALDE is a divided group which has no common position on the issue: MEPs vote according to their preferences. Finally, the EPP and the other right-wing parties generally support Israel.

19 According to NGO sources, which cannot be quoted here for reasons of anonymity, the Verts/ALE and GUE/NGL voted in favour, in the S&D and ALDE only a tiny minority abstained or voted against, while around ten to 20 MEPs from the EPP also voted in favour of the joint motion. This was possible because there was no roll-call vote on the motion, so that MEPs were in the position to break lines with the party line. See also VoteWatchEU (2010a, 2010b).

20 It is important to remember that this vote is not particularly significant, as the EU had placed Hamas on the terrorist list already in 2003.

21 Working documents seen by the author by courtesy of the EMHRN. For reasons of confidentiality, these documents cannot be reproduced or quoted here.

22 Confidential documents seen by the author by courtesy of the EMHRN. Due to the confidentiality of the material, no quotations or specific references can be made to them.

References

Al-Haq. 2009. *Operation Cast Lead and the Distortion of International Law*. Position Paper. Israel: Al-Haq. http://www.alhaq.org/publications/publications-index/item/operation-cast-lead-and-the-distortion-of-international-law

Basu, Sudeshna. 2012. 'The European Union and the Human Rights Council'. In *The European Union and Multilateral Governance*, edited by Jan Wouters, Hans Bruyninck, Sudeshna Basu and Simon Schunz. Basingtoke: Palgrave Macmillan. 86–102.

Beyers, Jan. 2004. 'Voice and Access: Political Practices of European Interest Associations'. *European Union Politics* 5 (2): 211–40.

Birnberg, Gabriele. 2009. 'The Voting Behaviour of the European Union Member States in the United Nations General Assembly'. Thesis, London: London School of Economics and Political Science.

B'Tselem. 2009. *Fatalities during Operation Cast Lead*. Israel: B'Tselem.

Defence for Children International, Palestine Section. 2009. 'Operation Cast Lead: Legal and Political Background'. 16 April. http://www.dci-pal.org/english/display.cfm?DocId=962&CategoryId=1 (web address no longer live).

EJC (European Jewish Congress). 2009. 'European Jewish Congress Calls on European Nations to Challenge the "Automatic Tyrannical Majority" in the UN General Assembly as It Debates Goldstone Report', 3 November.

———. 2013. 'About Us'. http://www.eurojewcong.org/about-us/

EJP (European Jewish Press). 2010a. 'Goldstone Report at EU Parliament: "One Sided" Resolution Could Affect Israel–EU Relations, Jewish Leader Says,' 2 March.

———. 2010b. 'Intense Lobbying around the Goldstone Report Resolution in the European Parliament', 9 March.

———. 2010c. 'European Jewish Congress Concludes That the Middle East Peace Process Has Been Dealt a Blow after the Endorsement of the Goldstone Report in the European Parliament', 10 March.

Euro-Mediterranean Human Rights Network. 2009a. *Active But Acquiescent: The EU's Response to the Israeli Military Offensive in the Gaza Strip*. Brussels: EMHRN.

———. 2009b. 'Note on the Human Rights Situation in Israel and the OPT in View of the Fourth Meeting of the EU–Israel Informal Human Rights Working Group'.

———. 2009c. 'Press Release – The EMHRN Calls on the EU and Its Member States to Support the UN Fact Finding Mission Report on Gaza and Its Recommendations'.

———. 2009d. 'Statement – The Gaza Offensive One Year On'. Brussels: EMHRN.

Euro-Mediterranean Human Rights Network and FIDH. 2009. 'Open Letter on the Occasion of the EU–Israel Association Council 15 June 2009', 11 June. Brussels: EMHRN.

———. 2010. 'Open Letter in View of the EU–Israel Sub-Committee on Political Dialogue and Cooperation', 15 December. Brussels: EMHRN.

European Parliament. 2010a. 'Debate: Implementation of Goldstone Recommendations on Israel/Palestine'.   http://www.europarl.europa.eu/sides/getDoc.do?pubRef=-%2f%2fEP%2f%2fTEXT%2bCRE%2b20100224%2bITEM-017%2bDOC%2bXML%2bV0%2f%2fEN&language=EN

———. 2010b. 'European Parliament resolution of 25 February 2010 on the Parliament's priorities for the UN Human Rights Council'. Brussels.

———. 2010c. 'European Parliament resolution of 10 March 2010 on Implementation of the Goldstone Recommendations on Israel/Palestine'. Strasbourg.

European Union. 2008. 'Statement by the European Union on the Situation in the Middle East'. http://unispal.un.org/UNISPAL.NSF/0/43CE41745E64C27C85257530005109CD

———. 2009. 'Statement on Behalf of the European Union in the General Assembly on the Report of the Human Rights Council'. http://www.swedenabroad.com/Page____99162.aspx

Haaretz. 2010a. 'Jewish Leaders Work Furiously to Preempt European Adoption of Goldstone Report'. *Haaretz.com*, 5 March.

———. 2010b. 'Jewish Lobbying Sways EU against Support of Goldstone Gaza Report'. *Haaretz.com*, 10 March.

Luif, Paul. 2003. *EU Cohesion in the UN General Assembly*. Occasional Paper 49. Paris: EU ISS.

Musu, Costanza. 2010. *European Union Policy towards the Arab–Israeli Peace Process: The Quicksands of Politics*. Basingstoke: Palgrave Macmillan.

Phillips, Leigh. 2010. 'Despite Heavy Lobbying, EU Parliament Endorses Goldstone Report'. *EUobserver*, 10 March. http://euobserver.com/foreign/29650

Smith, Karen E. 2006. 'Speaking with One Voice? European Union Co-Ordination on Human Rights Issues at the United Nations'. *Journal of Common Market Studies* 44 (1): 113–37.

———. 2010. 'The European Union at the Human Rights Council: Speaking with One Voice But Having Little Influence'. *Journal of European Public Policy* 17 (2): 224–41.

Snow, David A. and Robert D. Benford. 1992. 'Master Frames and Cycles of Protest'. In *Frontiers in Social Movements Theory*, edited by Carol McClurg Mueller and Aldon D. Morris. New Haven: Yale University Press. 133–55.

Tocci, Nathalie. 2005. *The Widening Gap between Rhetoric and Reality in EU Policy towards the Israeli-Palestinian Conflict*. 271. CEPS Working Paper Document. Brussels: CEPS.

UN Human Rights Council. 2009a. 'Human Rights in Palestine and Other Occupied Territories. Report of the United Nations Fact Finding Mission on the Gaza Conflict A/HRC/12/48'.

———. 2009b. 'Resolution on the Human Rights Situation in the Occupied Palestinian Territories, Incuding East Jerusalem A/HRC/RES/S-12/L.1'.

———. 2010a. 'Follow-up to the Report of the United Nations Independent International Fact-Finding Mission on the Gaza Conflict, A/HRC/RES/13/9'.

———. 2010b. 'Follow-up to the Report of the Committee of Independent Experts in International Humanitarian and Human Rights Law Established pursuant to Council Resolution 13/9, A/HRC/RES/15/6'.

———. 2011. 'Follow-up to the Report of the United Nations Independent International Fact-Finding Mission on the Gaza Conflict, A/HRC/RES/16/32'.

UNSC. 2009. 'Resolution 1860 – Security Council Calls for Immediate, Durable, Fully Respected Ceasefire in Gaza Leading to Full Withdrawal of Israeli Forces'. New York: United Nations Security Council. http://www.un.org/News/Press/docs/2009/sc9567.doc.htm

VoteWatchEU. 2010a. 'VoteWatch Europe: European Parliament, Council of the EU'. http://www.votewatch.eu/en/implementation-of-goldstone-recommendations-on-israel-palestine-motion-by-ppe-group-motion-for-a-res.html (authorisation required to access website).

———. 2010b. 'VoteWatch Europe: European Parliament, Council of the EU'. http://www.votewatch.eu/en/implementation-of-goldstone-recommendations-on-israel-palestine-joint-motion-by-alde-s-d-greens-efa-.html (authorisation required to access website).

Wolfers, Arnold. 1962. *Discord and Collaboration: Essays on International Politics*. Baltimore: Johns Hopkins Press.

6 Framing the EU–Israel agreement on pharmaceutical products

Cheaper medicines, territorial scope or policy coherence?

More than three years after it was initialled, the Agreement on Conformity and Acceptance of Industrial Products (ACAA) between the EU and Israel was finally approved by the European Parliament in October 2012. Although NSAs did not pay much attention to this Agreement in the beginning, the situation changed once the ACAA reached the European Parliament in May 2010. From that moment, NSAs' activism increased exponentially, with various lobby groups competing to influence the European Parliament's decision. Unlike Chapter 5, where the role of the Parliament was symbolically relevant, in the case of the ACAA the European Parliament played a key role. The Lisbon Treaty has indeed attributed new powers and competences to the European Parliament in certain areas and the ACAA fell within the remit of these new powers. More specifically, the European Parliament was required to give its consent to the Agreement before it could enter into force. This chapter investigates how lobbying took place in this case. In particular, it focuses on the European Parliament, where most of the lobbying was concentrated, while very few lobbying actions were observed in the policy stages involving the Commission and the Council. By analysing the events that have occurred since 2009, when the preparatory stages for the ACAA started, this chapter shows that NSAs played a crucial role in framing the debate within the EP, while a less systematic involvement is found in the preparatory and negotiation stages of the Agreement.

The analysis shows that all types of roles (dialogue-builder, voice-articulator, opponent) were played in this case. Moreover, NSAs relied on all the categories of frames (technical, mixed and political) identified in Chapter 1. However, the extent to which NSAs were involved in the policy-making process and managed to influence EU policies varied on the basis of both the roles and the frames employed. As will be shown, those NSAs who played a more consensual role and used technical frames had more influence on policy-making. Nevertheless, NSAs proposing mixed frames were also partially involved due to the political nature of the European Parliament.

Two broad lobbying camps can be identified in this case: one side was in favour of the approval of the ACAA by the European Parliament while the other side was against it. In the latter case, as will be shown in the chapter, some NSAs rejected the ACAA entirely while others adopted a more nuanced stance aimed at modifying the text of the Agreement before approving it. Various actors were involved, but two NSAs, which were named more frequently in interviews, conducted systematic and organised lobbying on the issue of the ACAA: Teva and the MATTIN Group. The former is an Israeli pharmaceutical company, while the latter is the same NGO involved in the case in Chapter 4. In contrast, other actors such as the EMHRN or the European Jewish Congress (EJC) were less active on the issue and their lobbying activities more sporadic.

This chapter is structured as follows. The first part provides an overview of what an ACAA is, with specific reference to the agreement between the EU and Israel. The second section describes the policy-making process leading to the entrance into force of the ACAA. The third and fourth sections investigate which roles NSAs played and which frames they used in their lobbying activities. The fifth section refers to the national level, focusing on how Brussels-based NSAs relied on the national venue to complement their activities at the EU level. Finally, the conclusions summarise the main findings of this chapter.

The EU–Israel ACAA

An Agreement on Conformity Assessment and Acceptance (ACAA) of Industrial Products aims at facilitating trade between partners by removing technical barriers, thus making access to their respective markets easier. By signing an ACAA with the EU a third country agrees to align its legislative system, infrastructure, standardisation and assessment procedures for traded goods with the EU's legislation (European Commission 2013). In this way, markets are more accessible and costs are reduced thanks to the elimination of double-checks on batches of traded goods. The EU signs ACAAs in those industrial sectors where member states' legislations are harmonised, such as machinery, electrical products, construction products, pressure equipment, toys, medical appliances, gas appliances and pharmaceuticals (European Commission 2013; Hania 2010).

Negotiating an ACAA is a complicated procedure, which requires some preparatory stages aimed at the horizontal and sectorial alignment of the third country's legislation to the EU's as well as the establishment of appropriate infrastructure able to comply with procedures of standardisation, accreditation and metrology. Functioning and efficient market surveillance should also be ensured. Due to this cumbersome process and the numerous requirements that a third country has to comply with, the scope of ACAAs is normally limited to one industrial sector or even an aspect of it.

Preparation and negotiation of ACAAs have been underway for most Mediterranean partners. Given its advanced economy and its strong relations with the EU and on the basis of the provisions of the 2005 EU–Israel Action Plan, in which the EU proposes to 'accelerate progress towards bilateral negotiations leading to an ACAA, taking into account the specific nature of the Israeli economy and building upon the Palermo Action Plan' (Art. 2.3.1.4) (European Commission 2005: 10), the Commission started and initialled an ACAA with

Israel on good manufacturing practice (GMP) for pharmaceutical products in 2009. The ACAA was a Protocol to the Association Agreement with the aim of extending to Israel benefits granted by the internal market in sectors that were already aligned (European Commission 2009: 2). On the basis of the Protocol, pharmaceutical industrial products covered by the Protocol and attested as compliant with EU procedures can be placed on both Israeli and EU markets without any need for approval procedures. This means that products just need to be certified by one of the two parties (EU or Israel) in order to ensure their conformity to the legislation in place, instead of being double-checked and certified twice. The reduction in controls thanks to the application of the same standards and procedures in the two countries facilitates trade flows of pharmaceutical goods. In order to eliminate trade barriers, there are two mechanisms: 1) the recognition of equivalence in technical regulation, standardisation and conformity assessment for industrial products subject to equivalent regulation in both parties; 2) the mutual acceptance of industrial products not commonly regulated, but which are lawfully placed on the market in one of the parties, can be lawfully be traded in the other (European Commission 2009). The EU–Israeli ACAA includes an annex that makes the former mechanism operational, while the latter is not taken into consideration.

Israel was therefore asked to take appropriate measures to align its legislation and procedures to those of the EU. First, Israel had to modify its legislation in accordance to EU directive 2003/94/EC regulating the principles and guidelines for GMP in the case of medical products, and directive 2001/83/EC on the Community Code Concerning Medical Products for Human Use (European Commission 2003; European Parliament and Council of the European Union 2001). Second, the EU assessed the legislative changes introduced by Israel and checked if the modified legislative framework complies with the EU's requirements. Third, negotiations started with the involvement of the relevant DGs in the Commission (in this case, DG Trade, DG Enterprise and Industry and DG SANCO) and the Israeli Ministry of Industry, Trade and Labour and the Ministry of Health. Finally, once the text of the ACAA was ready, it had to be adopted and implemented.

The Commission's evaluation on the implementation of the ACAA identified advantages for both sides. EU and Israeli exporters would be allowed 'to test and certify their industrial products to the same (aligned) requirements prior to export, and then access that market without any further conformity assessment requirements' (European Commission 2009: 5). By carrying out the certification procedures only once, exports would be stimulated and time would be saved. The Commission admitted that there were difficulties in quantifying the benefits which would derive from the reduced time for accessing markets, from better predictability, less protectionism and the harmonisation of systems. According to the figures supplied by the European Federation of Pharmaceutical Industries and Associations (EFPIA), in 2007 the total trade in pharmaceutical products between the EU and Israel amounted to around 1 billion. The figures provided by EUROSTAT for the 2007–11 period show there was an increase in the bilateral trade, with the trade balance tilted in favour of Israel, as shown in Table 6.1. It is plausible to assume that the ACAA has a more beneficial impact for Israel, as its producers get easier access to the EU-27 market with its population of around 500 million people. In contrast, Israel is a small market for the EU, with its main potential being its advanced economic development. Through this agreement, Israeli generic pharmaceutical products enter the EU's market easily (Interviewee 30).[1]

The decision-making process of the ACAA

Before the entry into force of the Lisbon Treaty, the legal basis for an ACAA was Article 133 and Article 300 of the Treaty establishing the European Community (TEC). Accordingly, the Commission was tasked with the negotiation of the Agreement and was assisted by a committee appointed by the Council (133 Trade Committee) during the entire procedure. The Council was then in charge of deciding upon the signing and the conclusion of the Agreement on the basis of a proposal from the Commission. Under this legal basis, the European Parliament was only consulted, but had no formal power in the procedure (consultation procedure). Although Commissioner Verheugen wanted to conclude the ACAA during his mandate and before the entry into force of the Lisbon Treaty, this did not happen (Interviewee 63; Al Jazeera 2009). While the ACAA was initialled in 2009, the Council approved it only on 22 March 2010, after the Lisbon Treaty had entered into force (Council of the European Union 2010).

Thus, on the basis of Articles 207 and 218 of the Treaty on the Functioning of the European Union (TFEU), the European Parliament had a voice in the decision-making process on the ACAA. The Commission remained in charge of the negotiation stage on the basis of a Council's decision, but the conclusion and the entry into force of the Agreement also needed the consent of the European Parliament, in addition to the Council's approval. Accordingly, the dossier moved to the relevant Committee in the European Parliament, which in this case was the Committee on International Trade (INTA). Two other committees were appointed as Committees for Opinion, namely the Committee on Foreign Affairs (AFET) and the Committee on Industry, Research and Energy (ITRE), which could issue a non-binding opinion.

Table 6.1 Trade in pharmaceutical products between the EU and Israel (2007–11)

	Import	*Export*	*Trade balance*
2007	501,871,162	458,249,939	−43,621,223
2008	588,527,348	488,478,939	−100,048,409
2009	633,672,437	566,137,218	−67,535,219
2010	1,198,621,320	726,879,813	−471,741,507
2011	1,957,039,466	761,621,982	−1,195,417,484

Note: Values are expressed in euros. Import indicates imports from Israel to the EU-27. Export indicates exports from the EU-27 to Israel.

Source: EUROSTAT (2012).

Following the parliamentary legislative procedure, the INTA Committee had to draft a report on the ACAA to be presented in front of the plenary: the report would give indications to the MEPs on whether the European Parliament should give or withhold its consent to the ACAA. Withholding consent is perceived as a strong political act of opposition against the Council and the Commission, so it is rarely used (Interviewee 45). The European Parliament can, however, rely on two other options to express its disagreement. First, according to Article 81(3) of the European Parliament Rules of Procedure, the responsible committee 'may decide, in the interests of achieving a positive outcome of the procedure, to present an interim report on the proposal to Parliament including a motion for a resolution containing recommendations for modification or implementation of the proposed act' (European Parliament 2012). In essence, this procedure is a way for the European Parliament to show its disagreement with the Commission and Council's proposal and invite them to change it before the European Parliament gives its consent. Given that the consent procedure does not allow the European Parliament to modify the text of the agreement, the interim report offers MEPs a way to deal indirectly with this issue. Second, the opinion coming from the Committee can be accompanied by a political statement in which MEPs express their political views on the issue at stake, even if consent to the legislation or agreement is provided.[2]

The INTA Committee appointed the rapporteur, MEP Laim Liucija Andrikiene, on 19 April 2010, but the file was soon blocked due to political reasons (Interviewees 4, 45, 57).[3] Following Israel's attack on the flotilla intended to bring humanitarian aid to Gaza in May 2010, the INTA Committee decided to freeze the protocol due to concerns for human rights and postpone the discussion on the draft opinion until further notice.[4] MEPs in INTA felt that Israel's behaviour was not acceptable and that the EU could not continue to do 'business as usual' in the face of these violations of human rights and international law. In July 2010 there were attempts to retable the ACAA in INTA, but the Coordinators' meeting opposed this move. As a result, the European People's Party (EPP) gave back the report and Andrikiene stepped down.[5]

The stalemate was overcome in spring 2011, when the Coordinators' meeting decided to unfreeze the dossier on the ACAA and to discuss it in the INTA Committee. This change was determined by the new position adopted by the Alliance of Liberals and Democrats for Europe (ALDE). According to MEP Sarah Ludford, blocking the ACAA was inappropriate as the agreement did not represent an upgrade in EU-Israel bilateral relations, but only the implementation of the Action Plan (Ludford 2011).[6] ALDE was in the position to tip the scales in favour of the unfreezing of the calendar inside the Committee. Following these events, the Chair of the Committee, MEP Vital Moreira, was appointed rapporteur by default (ex officio rapporteur) on 24 May 2011.[7]

After a first exchange of views in the INTA Committee in July 2011, there was a second round on 11 October 2011. As will be explained later, MEPs sitting on the INTA Committee were extremely divided on the issue of whether or not the European Parliament should give its consent to the ACAA. While the debate did not lead to a clear majority in favour of either position, two things were decided. First, the MEPs agreed to invite the HR/VP Catherine Ashton, Commissioner Stefan Füle (Enlargement and Neighbourhood) and Commissioner Karel De Gucht (Trade) to address the broader issue of coherence among different EU external policies in relation to the ACAA. Second, the INTA Committee asked the AFET Committee to draft an opinion on the ACAA, given the political implications of the agreement.

The appointed rapporteur for the opinion in the AFET Committee was MEP Veronique De Keyser. As a first step, she wrote a working document that she presented to the Committee on 6 February 2012 (De Keyser 2012a). In this document she analysed the implications of the ACAA for the EU and suggested that the Committee request a legal opinion from the European Parliament's legal service. The AFET Committee agreed on this point, but also asked MEP De Keyser to draft her opinion by 17 February 2012. This draft opinion was then discussed on 27 March 2012, together with the legal opinion of the European Parliament's legal service issued in mid-March.[8] The vote on the draft opinion and tabled amendments scheduled for 24 April 2012 was cancelled, as the Chair of the AFET Committee, MEP Elmar Brok, explained that Commissioner Füle had promised that the Commission would soon issue a position paper on the ACAA in response to the European Parliament's legal opinion. Therefore, the Coordinators decided to wait for the Commission's position in order to have guarantees on the legal aspects of the agreement.

The INTA Committee worked in parallel to the AFET Committee. On 29 February 2012, Commissioner De Gucht attended the meeting and expressed the Commission's position concerning the agreement. The ACAA was part of the Action Plan package, so it was not an upgrade of EU–Israel relations, and would favour trade, thus being beneficial for the EU as well.[9] On 27 March 2012, the ACAA was again on the agenda in INTA, with Moreira presenting his draft recommendation. However, the Coordinators decided to postpone the vote in INTA to wait for the vote on the opinion in the AFET Committee. The latter eventually issued its opinion on 7 June 2012, recommending that the INTA Committee give its consent, if the requests concerning legal and political aspects made by the Chair of the AFET Committee to the Commission were met. On 18 September 2012, the INTA Committee's report was also in favour of giving the European Parliament's consent, even if by a tiny majority (15 voted in favour, 13 against and two abstained), so that the dossier passed to the plenary. The ACAA was finally approved by the European Parliament on 23 October 2012, thus closing the long decision-making process that characterised the story of the ACAA.[10] The ACAA passed by a majority of 379 votes (230 voted against, 41 abstained) (VoteWatchEU 2012). There was an attempt to table an amendment, asking the Council to issue an interpretative declaration in relation to the ACAA, but the EPP withdrew its support for it.[11] There was a debate in the plenary and lobbying continued until the vote, but there was no substantial change from previous positions. Table 6.2 provides an overview of the key moments described so far.

Table 6.2 Key dates of the ACAA policy-making procedure

October 2009	Commission's proposal on the ACAA with Israel
March 2010	Council decision
April 2010	INTA – MEP Andrikiene is nominated rapporteur
May/June 2010	Freezing of the ACAA
July 2010	Failed attempt to re-table the ACAA. MEP Andrikiene steps down as rapporteur
May 2011	Re-tabling of the ACAA on the agenda of the INTA Committee. MEP Moreira is nominated rapporteur
July 2011	First exchange of views in INTA
October 2011	Second exchange of views in INTA
February 2012	Working document in AFET
Mid-March 2012	Legal opinion by the European Parliament legal service
June 2012	Draft opinion in AFET
September 2012	Draft report approved in INTA
October 2012	Approval of the ACAA in the plenary session

Source: Author's own compilation.

Which role works best? The contention around the ACAA

Lobbying on the ACAA was not particularly strong when the agreement was negotiated by the Commission and approved by the Council, probably due to its technical nature and the fact that it was not a very visible issue. In contrast, there is evidence of extensive lobbying when the issue reached the European Parliament. Moreover, two main aspects characterised lobbying activities in the case of the ACAA. First, Teva, an Israeli business group, and the MATTIN Group, a Palestinian NGO, conducted very systematic and organised lobbying. In contrast, other NSAs did intermittent and more sporadic lobbying. Second, the ACAA gave rise to a polarised lobbying context, with one side in favour of the ACAA and the other against its approval (at least, as it was drafted).

Both Teva and the MATTIN Group played the role of dialogue-builder based on an access approach: they targeted EU officials and MEPs directly and in informal settings. This consensual role favoured the development of cooperative social interactions between the EU and NSAs based on trust and mutual legitimacy. In turn, this led to a shared framing of the EU–Israel ACAA. Other NSAs played less consensual roles, ranging from the voice-articulator to the opponent. This clearly did not allow for the establishment of positive interactions that would allow frames to travel and get codified.

Besides Teva, other European and Israeli business actors (e.g., EFPIA and the European Association of Euro-Pharmaceutical Companies [EAEPC]) were not lobbying the EU on the ACAA (Interviewees 1, 55, 56, 63).[12] The EFPIA was consulted by the Commission in the preparatory stages and was asked to provide data which were used in the Commission's proposal on the ACAA (European Commission 2009) as part of the normal consultation procedure with stakeholders to ensure that agreements are implemented smoothly once in force (Interviewee 55). In contrast, Teva, the biggest pharmaceutical company in Israel and one of the biggest worldwide, showed strong interest in the ACAA.[13] It is headquartered in Israel, has a European headquarters in the Netherlands and is also present in Brussels with a one-person staffed office. This person is responsible for the contacts with EU institutions and for promoting Teva's interests within and in relation to the EU. It comes as no surprise that Teva had a strong interest in the ACAA, as this would benefit its trade with the EU. By facilitating the entrance of Israeli pharmaceutical products into EU markets, opportunities for Teva's generic medicines would be opened. Although Teva has European branches, there would be no competition between the goods produced in Israel (and thus benefiting from the agreement) and in the EU as the lines of production are complementary (Interviewee 63).

Unlike Brita GmbH (see Chapter 4), Teva played the role of dialogue-builder, providing information and knowledge to MEPs and EU officials through direct contacts and often in informal ways. Teva's lobbying, especially when the ACAA reached the European Parliament, was also conducted through a professional lobbying consultancy, D&D Consulting Services, which supported Teva's representative in designing an effective lobbying strategy and in organising meetings with MEPs and EU officials working in the Commission and the European Parliament.[14] Teva's case was dealt with by the General Manager of D&D Consulting Services, Mr Dimitri Dombret, whose past experiences provided him with particular added-value for Teva's purposes. He specialised in Middle East studies at the Tel Aviv University and worked for the Belgian Ministry of Foreign Affairs at the Embassy in Israel, experiences that familiarised him with Israel, its mechanisms and policies. Moreover, he worked as assistant for an MEP, a key position from which to learn how the European Parliament works and what the best strategies are to lobby MEPs. Finally, he previously worked as director of the European Friends of Israel (EFI), the Brussels-based NGO that unites MEPs and MPs sympathetic to Israel's cause (D&D Consulting Service 2012). Importantly, his experience provided him with connections with MEPs and EU officials, and this was likely to contribute to an easier and more informal access to the European Parliament.

In the initial stages of the preparation and negotiation of the ACAA, the Brussels office of Teva was not particularly involved, and mainly worked to ensure that the negotiations were moving forward and to liaise between Israeli officials and the European Commission. Teva in Israel was by contrast directly engaged in the technical side of the negotiations, providing data and information to both the EU and the Israeli Ministry of Health (Interviewee 63). The involvement of Teva was important in order to ensure the correct application of the legislative changes made by Israel to comply with EU law. Moreover, the Commission organised meetings with the parties affected by the ACAA, especially pharmaceutical companies, in order to ensure a smooth implementation of the ACAA and a real benefit to trade relations (Interviewee 55). Therefore, Teva also contributed to the preparation and drafting of the agreement.

Once the ACAA reached the European Parliament and the dossier was frozen by the INTA Committee, Teva started lobbying MEPs, both those sitting on the

INTA Committee and those who were influential in their political group, in order to convince them to support the ACAA. More importantly, Teva arranged several meetings with MEP Andrikiene, the first rapporteur for the ACAA, who was very active on this dossier from the very beginning (Interviewee 63). She was very interested in receiving information and getting to know the implications of the ACAA in detail. She contacted the representative of Teva on her own initiative in order to get additional information and explanations on the ACAA, showing how NSAs and EU policy-makers are dependent on each other (Interviewee 63). Her interest was also reflected in her support for the ACAA in the INTA Committee, as will be shown in a later section of this chapter. At the same time, Teva benefited from this well-established relationship as Andrikiene played an important role within the Committee because she, as the rapporteur of the dossier, was in charge of drafting the report.[15] The two sides thus developed mutual trust, viewed each other as partners and their interactions were consensual and cooperative. Interestingly, even when Andrikiene pulled out in July 2010, she remained very active on the issue, continuing to support the ACAA both in parliamentary debates and through articles in newspapers (Andrikiene 2011a) and to keep in touch with Teva representatives (Interviewee 63).

In spring 2011, Teva started to target ALDE MEPs more strongly, given that there were hints that they might change their views on the ACAA. What created tensions inside the group was the fact that the decision about freezing the ACAA in the Committee was taken by the Coordinators, without any previous consultation inside the group. As a result of these dynamics, ALDE decided to 'unfreeze' the ACAA and place it again on the agenda of the INTA Committee (Interviewees 36, 70). Meetings with MEPs and officials working in the European Parliament continued. In 2012, when the AFET Committee was asked for an opinion on the ACAA, Teva began a new round of behind the scenes meetings with MEPs to expose its view on why the ACAA needed to be supported by the European Parliament (Interviewee 45). Oral interactions were always complemented by the provision of written material on the company itself and on the reasons why the Parliament should give its consent to the agreement (Interviewees 45, 70).

The other NSA who was very active on the ACAA, the MATTIN Group, also played the role of dialogue-builder. Its initial lobbying on the Commission did not lead to significant results (Interviewee 1). Once the ACAA reached the European Parliament, the MATTIN Group intensified its lobbying with a view to sending it back to the Commission and the Council to change some of its provisions.[16] As confirmed in interviews (Interviewees 45, 57), the MATTIN Group relied on an access approach, arranging meetings with MEPs and officials in the European Parliament and sending documents and policy briefs explaining why the European Parliament should not give its consent to the agreement as drafted.

Like Teva, the MATTIN Group's consensual role favoured the establishment of a dialogue with officials and MEPs aimed at reaching a mutual understanding on the ACAA. Given its long lobbying experience in the EU, the MATTIN Group had already established its professional reputation and its credibility (Interviewee 45). This facilitated dialogical interactions with EU officials and MEPs, as it was viewed as a trustworthy NGO and as a partner. In particular, the involvement of the AFET opened a new context for the MATTIN Group, who could also rely on the already existing contacts with the rapporteur, MEP De Keyser. The latter had always been sympathetic to the cause of the Palestinian people and she had known the MATTIN Group from previous meetings. They had, therefore, already established working relationships and perceived each other as trustworthy inter-locutors even before the ACAA. This made the exchange of information and knowledge between them easier (Interviewee 45).

Unlike Teva and the MATTIN Group, other NSAs played less consensual roles, including the ones of the voice-articulator and the opponent. Their actions were based on information politics such as publishing articles in newspapers or organising workshops, and on protest politics like letter campaigns involving public opinion. On the same side of Teva in terms of their position with regard to the ACAA, the EFI worked on this dossier when it reached the European Parliament. Interestingly, the EFI coordinated its actions with the Israeli Representation in Brussels, which was also very active in lobbying MEPs to persuade them to support the ACAA.[17] In light of its composition based on MEPs and European MPs, the EFI worked as a liaising actor between the Israeli Representation in Brussels and the MEPs to ensure that the latter would be exposed to the Israeli view on the ACAA. While these actions mainly took place behind the scenes and implied the establishment of direct contacts with MEPs, the EFI also played the role of the voice-articulator based on information politics, publishing short articles on its website in support of the ACAA. For example, on 8 February 2012, the EFI commented on the session of the AFET Committee of 6 February, and the discussion of the working document presented by De Keyser (European Friends of Israel 2012), and on 20 April 2012 it published an article by MEP Inese Vaidere, who argued in favour of the ACAA (Vadeire 2012). Moreover, in February 2011, the EFI accompanied MEPs to the areas where Israeli pharmaceutical companies are located in order to raise MEPs' awareness concerning the ACAA and what it means in practice (Interviewee 62).

Swinging between the dialogue-builder and the voice-articulator was also the form chosen by the EJC. While its lobbying efforts on the ACAA were more limited than those of Teva or the MATTIN Group, the EJC met several MEPs, especially of the ALDE Group. It prepared a summary of the argument in favour of the European Parliament's support to the agreement, and also organised meetings with them to further discuss the issue (Interviewee 77).

Similar to the lobbying conducted by the EFI and EJC, other NGOs and soli-darity movements carried out their activities in a less systematic way, acting sporadically and at moments of crisis, when there were crucial events in the European Parliament. Among these NSAs, the Council for European Palestinian Relations (CEPR), the European Coordination of Committees and Associations for Palestine (ECCP), APRODEV, the EMHRN, CIDSE, the Quaker Council for European Affairs and some NSAs based in member states were active. In some cases, they relied on information politics, thus playing the role of voice-articulator: they issued public statements or wrote articles to raise public awareness. For example, the CEPR and the ECCP co-wrote an article for *EUobserver* on 23 April 2012, in which they made the case for the rejection of the ACAA (Lemanska and Reigeluth 2012). Similarly, the ECCP issued a statement on its website calling on MEPs to reject the ACAA in order to ensure that the EU pursued a consistent foreign policy.[18] In April 2012, APRODEV, the EMHRN, CIDSE and the Quaker Council for European Affairs also called on MEPs in the INTA Committee to postpone the vote on the ACAA (APRODEV *et al.* 2012). This letter was also accompanied by more inside lobbying, whereby representatives of the NGOs met with MEPs and officials to support their cause against the approval of the ACAA (Interviewee 4).

Forms of protest politics were also used to lobby on the ACAA. In particular, the ECCP launched a letter campaign mobilising its member organisations in EU member states in 2012 in an attempt to exert pressure on MEPs from constituencies. Similarly, an online petition called 'PASS ACAA' collected signatures from EU citizens to go to the European Parliament and present the 'voice' of EU peoples on the matter.[19] These two examples of the role of the opponent did not allow for the establishment of dialogue and an exchange between the parties; they involved the public at large and made use of constituencies as a way to 'blackmail' policy-makers. Unlike information politics, therefore, they enlarged the scope of the conflict and targeted politicians indirectly (Beyers 2004). These confrontational social interactions did not lead to any shared understanding of the situation, but caused a mutual delegitimation.

As shown, NSAs played various roles in the EU's decision-making process. While the MATTIN Group and Teva relied on the role of dialogue-builder, which allowed them to have many contacts with officials and MEPs and to be involved in the decision-making process leading to the ACAA, those NSAs using less consensual approaches played a less significant role.

A battle of frames

In the case of the ACAA, various types of frames were used. Teva and the MATTIN Group employed technical frames. The EFI and EJC almost copy-pasted Teva's argument, although theirs was not well-developed or particularly sophisticated. The EMHRN and the other NGOs used a mixed frame, while the ECCP and the people behind the online petition PASS ACAA proposed political frames.[20] As will be shown, the technical and, to a certain extent, the mixed frames gave NSAs the possibility of playing a significant role in the policy-making process and of contributing to the development of new frames in EU foreign policy.

Teva developed its lobbying around a technical frame. First of all, the frame disentangled EU–Israel bilateral relations from the political aspects of the Middle East Peace Process. Teva highlighted that the ACAA was not an upgrade for Israel, because, as provided for in the Action Plan, it only 'constitutes an implementation of an existing framework agreement and therefore does not exceed the political framework'.[21] There was indeed a clear attempt to avoid being trapped into political and ideological debates and to only discuss the issue in technical and economic terms. Second, Teva referred to key principles at the basis of the EU's integration project, namely the idea of free trade, market access and benefits for EU consumers. More specifically, Teva maintained that the ACAA was in the interest of the EU in general, and of its patients and health care providers in particular. The removal of trade barriers would increase the offerings on the market: the entire chain of production in the EU would be positively affected through an increase in the number of jobs. There would also be savings for both EU consumers and health care systems. According to Teva's figures, between €100–250 million per year could be saved, if access to generic medicines was speeded up. Teva argued that health care authorities face costs due to delays in entry of these products, so that '[o]n average, one day of delay corresponds to about €10 million of missed savings'.[22] Moreover, generic medicines would enter EU markets and be available to patients more quickly. Finally, the authorities' inspectorates would greatly benefit from the ACAA, as people and resources could be freed up and employed on other tasks, such as the assessment phase.

By highlighting the negative repercussions on trade and consumers due to delays in the approval of the ACAA, relying on the key EU principles of free trade and consumer rights and showing the benefits for the EU, Teva was proposing a technical frame. Its argument was also supported by empirical evidence, such as figures concerning the delays and losses for the EU's economic system. These technical details and the empirical evidence provided were complemented by the provision of an alternative policy option to the issue. Instead of linking the MEPP and EU–Israel bilateral relations, the two aspects needed to be kept separate and policy actions carried out independently.

This technical frame was reflected in Andrikiene's speeches and articles, which confirm the interactions taking place between Teva and Andrikiene as well as the circularity that characterises the relationship between the EU and NSAs. As explained in Chapter 1, knowledge and frames are the results of social interactions, whereby the parties reach a common understanding of the topic and a shared view on how to approach an issue. For example, Andrikiene wrote an article for the *EUobserver* on 28 February 2011, complaining about the fact that the ACAA was blocked in the INTA Committee 'due to the position of certain political groups which think there should be no upgrade of EU–Israel relations until Israel takes a more committed stance in peace talks with Palestinians and improves its human rights record' (Andrikiene 2011a). Andrikiene's argument in favour of the ACAA was based on three points: 1) the ACAA is a foreign policy tool that can help to bring Israel closer to EU legislation; 2) the Israeli human rights situation is not comparable to that of other countries in the region and around the world; 3) European consumers are damaged by the freezing of the ACAA, as they cannot get access to cheaper pharmaceutical products. This last point, which was also the main part in the article, mirrored the frame presented by Teva, as mentioned above. Similarly, during the debate on the ACAA which took place in the INTA Committee in October 2011, Andrikiene maintained that the INTA Committee needed to speed up the procedure and give its consent to the ACAA. Not only was the agreement already provided for in the Action Plan, but by withholding its consent negative repercussions would be felt by European consumers and health care providers, with around 100–250 million per year of wasted money. Interestingly, both these figures and the gist of the argument resembled the frame proposed by Teva (Interviewees 45, 63). The same position had already been stated by Andrikiene in the *EUobserver* of 6 October 2011, in which she highlighted the technical nature of the ACAA and the damage that the European Parliament was inflicting on EU consumers and health care providers who were forced to incur additional and unnecessary costs. In her view, 'by having the ACAA, generic products could enter the EU market much more quickly [and] the national medicines evaluation agencies within the EU would be able to free up resources currently employed to do the unnecessary additional checks and tests could be employed to evaluate new innovative medicines faster' (Andrikiene 2011b).[23]

The technical frame was also voiced by the ALDE MEP Marietje Schaake during the INTA session of 11 October 2011, when arguing that the ACAA was not the proper tool to deal with Israeli violations of human rights. She maintained that political and technical aspects should not be blurred and, therefore, the ALDE group was in favour of adopting a timetable to discuss and vote on the dossier. Similar points on the technical nature of the agreement were also raised by the ECR Group.[24] During this debate, some MEPs countered this argument by presenting a mixed frame based on legal and political considerations. In particular, Social and Democrats (S&D) MEP Arif argued that coherence among EU external relations policies, namely trade and human rights issues, was a necessity. Other S&D MEPs and European United Left/Nordic Green Left (GUE/NGL) MEP Scholz also supported this position. The EPP MEP Caspary also highlighted the need for coherence, but he argued that the latter had to be applied consistently, given that the INTA had recently discussed the agreement with the Palestinians on agriculture and fisheries.[25]

The gist of this argument reflected the mixed frame revolving around the concepts of coherence and consistency in EU foreign policies, which was proposed by the EMHRN, APRODEV, the Quakers and CIDSE. According to Article 21 TEU, the EU has the obligation to 'ensure consistency between the areas of its external action', meaning that its trade and human rights policies as well as its other foreign policy positions have to be in line with each other and go in the same political direction. Against this backdrop, it would be inconsistent to sign another agreement with Israel, given that its policies in the OPTs in terms of violations of human rights and international law have not changed. Moreover, it would be incoherent to condemn Israeli policies and violations of human rights and international law, on the one hand, and then adopt an accommodating policy leading to more cooperation, on the other hand. This frame did not, however, offer a new lens to the debate, as its core elements referred to the widespread view on the Israeli–Palestinian conflict which is frequently heard in the European Parliament – for instance, in parliamentary questions to the Commission and the Council. This argument based on the violations of human rights and international law by Israel and the need for policy coherence was already applied in other cases, such as when the European Parliament decided to freeze its approval on the Protocol on Israeli participation in Community programmes in 2008. The frame resonated with many MEPs, as it was in line with their views and their perceptions of the situation. Yet it did not provide an alternative perspective on how the European Parliament could deal with the issue, nor was this frame likely to favour dialogue due to the political component which risked alienating those MEPs who were supporters of Israel.[26]

Other NSAs also relied on mixed frames, by proposing a political/technical argument based on the frame proposed by Teva, but with a less sophisticated technical component. For example, in February 2012 the EFI strongly criticised De Keyser's working paper because she was politicising an agreement that had only a technical and commercial nature, and was beneficial for both sides. The EFI called on MEPs to keep the debate within technical and economic terms and to avoid political implications irrelevant to the issue at stake (European Friends of Israel 2012). Similarly, on 20 April 2012, it published an article by MEP Inese Vaidere, arguing that the agreement would bring important economic benefits for the EU and it could not be related to political issues (Vadeire 2012). In the same way, the EJC also supported the approval of the ACAA on the basis of the benefits for EU consumers and health care providers. Although the EFI and EJC's frame was akin to Teva's one, the level of precision and technical detail was lower. In some parts, there were even political argumentations related to the issue of discrimination that Israel suffered from due to the link that the EU made with the MEPP (Interviewee 77).

In contrast to these mixed frames, the MATTIN Group relied on a technical frame with a legal perspective (instead of the economic one used by Teva) and lobbied the European Parliament to vote against the agreement as drafted and to send the text back to the Council and the Commission for the necessary legal changes. The frame adopted recalled arguments akin to those employed in the case of the rules of origin, namely the idea of the 'territorial scope' of the Agreement. More specifically, the MATTIN Group argued that the problem of Israel's different interpretation of its territory was also present in the ACAA, in particular in Article 9(1). This provision concerns the recognition of the responsible authority, meaning the authority that is in charge of permitting pharmaceutical products to be placed on the market or requiring their withdrawal. The problem lies in the fact that Israel is asked to nominate these authorities according to its domestic law, namely following how it defines the territorial scope of its internal market. Israel will therefore notify the EU that the Ministry of Health is the responsible authority, thereby notifying the territorial scope of its market regulatory jurisdiction. However, under Israeli law, the Ministry's jurisdiction also includes East Jerusalem, the Golan Heights and all those areas of the West Bank that Israel has not placed under Palestinian economic administration. This notification would amount to the statement of a fact, which implies that it cannot be subject to different interpretations.[27] The acknowledgement of Israel's factual statement of territorial jurisdiction without the explicit exclusion of the OPTs from the territorial scope of the Ministry's jurisdiction implies that the EU would no longer be in a position to challenge Israeli interpretation of the territorial scope of applicability of the EU–Israel Association Agreement.[28]

By legally framing its arguments and pointing to the risks that such an agreement would have for the EU's legal system, the MATTIN Group relied on one of the key principles of the EU, namely the need to ensure the integrity of its legal framework and respect for international law, humanitarian law and its obligations thereunder. If the EU were to recognise Israeli jurisdiction over the OPTs, it would violate its own law and international law. Coming so close to the *raison d'être* of the EU itself, this argument had the potential to resonate in MEPs' minds. Instead of aiming to block the ACAA *tout court*, the MATTIN Group aimed to persuade MEPs and officials of the necessity of amending Article 9(1) of the ACAA Agreement to ensure that the position of the EU and its legal framework would not be compromised. Basically, it suggested that the European Parliament withhold its consent and send the dossier back to the Commission and the Council for the appropriate amendments via an interim report in which the conditions for the European Parliament's approval are listed (Interviewee 1).

While this frame was presented to various MEPs and EU officials (Interviewee 57), it definitely emerged as a key component of the parliamentary debate thanks to MEP De Keyser in the AFET Committee. In the working document that De Keyser presented in AFET on 6 February 2012, she raised two points: one was a political argument, the other referred to the legal dimension of the ACAA (De Keyser 2012a). In particular, she argued that 'a legal interpretation of certain articles of the Protocol might allow Israel to implement the Protocol on the basis of its national law defining the territorial scope of its domestic market, in other words including the territories occupied since 1967 not under Palestinian economic administration' (ibid.: 5). She also inserted the text of Article 9(1) as an annex, highlighting the legal problem of the formulation of the article.[29] In her view, it was necessary to request an opinion from the European Parliament legal service to have guarantees about the legal accuracy and implications of the agreement. Although the legal argument filtered through and became part of the frames used by MEPs, it was usually combined with the mixed frame, stressing the obligations of coherence and consistency that impinge upon EU foreign policy, as explained above.

Interestingly, the debate that followed De Keyser's presentation was defined along the mixed vs technical frames.[30] One group of MEPs argued that political and commercial aspects are entangled and cannot be dealt with separately, especially in the case of Israel and its violations of human rights and international law. The EU should ensure coherence in its foreign policies. Another group of MEPs supported the view that political and technical aspects should not be mixed: the ACAA is a technical agreement which cannot solve the political problems related to the Israeli–Palestinian conflict. Requesting a legal opinion from the European Parliament legal service to ensure that the ACAA contained no legal inconsistencies, as pointed out in the opinion by MEP De Keyser, was viewed as another way to delay the approval of the agreement and to gain time.[31] Thus, the MATTIN

Group managed to introduce the legal frame into the parliamentary debate, but its idea was not easily picked up by MEPs due to its complex nature. The political character of the European Parliament also meant that MEPs needed political arguments to use with their constituencies (Interviewee 45).

Nevertheless, the lack of expertise by MEPs and EU officials in technical and legal issues makes them dependent on external sources. MEPs need to rely on NSAs in order to get information on various issues. Framing is therefore a process of common construction and interpretation of the issue at stake between MEPs and NSAs. As the case of De Keyser shows, she used the legal frame proposed by the MATTIN Group, but also integrated it with her views and perspectives, including political aspects, as her knowledge was developing over time and on the basis of interactions with NSAs (Interviewee 45). The frame proposed by the MATTIN Group still shaped the policy process, as the Chair of AFET requested a legal opinion from the European Parliament legal service. The draft opinion by De Keyser, discussed on 27 March 2012, suggested that the INTA Committee draw up an interim report under Rule 81(3) of the European Parliament Rules of Procedure to propose amendments to the Commission and the Council to solve any legal issue (De Keyser 2012b).[32]

Finally, the CEPR and the ECCP also took part in the lobbying efforts, advocating the rejection of the ACAA. In a co-written article in the *EUobserver* of 23 April 2012, they made the case for the rejection of the ACAA on the basis of the political argument of coherence and consistency (Lemanska and Reigeluth 2012). While there were some attempts to deal with the legal frame proposed by the MATTIN Group, these points were not fully developed and explained. The main points of the articles revolved around the use of conditionality and the need to reject the ACAA in order to unblock the status quo in the West Bank. This argument was reiterated in another joint article published on *European Voice* on 26 April 2012, in which the representatives of the ECCP and CEPR argued that it was not only in the economic and security interests of the EU to block the agreement, but also a moral imperative that needs to be followed (*European Voice* 2012).

In summary, various NSAs were active at the EU level, especially in the European Parliament, with Teva and the MATTIN Group lobbying constantly and systematically. The frames proposed, as visualised in Table 6.3, covered the entire spectrum of frame types identified in Chapter 1. While technical frames, either with an economic or legal perspective, tended to be more effective, the European Parliament, due to its more political nature, was also open to mixed frames, which resonated with MEPs. This type of frame was not used with the Commission, where lobbying was limited to the activities carried out by the MATTIN Group and Teva.

Playing the 'national level' card

This section analyses the use of the national level by Brussels-based actors, paying particular attention to the examples of protest politics carried out by the ECCP and by the group organising PASS ACAA in the form of letter campaigns

Table 6.3 Frames used in the ACAA case

		Content	NSAs using frame
Technical frame	**Legal perspective**	- Legal problem in the formulation of the text (Art. 9(1)) - Risk of the EU violating international law and human rights	MATTIN Group
	Economic perspective	- ACAA is a technical agreement - No upgrade - Benefits for EU consumers and health care systems (save time and money)	Teva
Mixed frame	**Political/legal argument**	- Need for coherence and consistency in European foreign policy - Israel keeps violating international law and human rights/no changes on the ground	APRODEV, EMHRN, CIDSE, Quaker Council for European Affairs
	Political/ technical argument	- ACAA is a technical agreement - Benefits for EU consumers and health care systems (save time and money) - No discrimination against Israel and links to the Middle East Peace Process	EFI, EJC
Political frame	**Political argument**	- Reject the ACAA to unblock the stall in the West Bank - Predominantly focusing on coherence and consistency	ECCP, CEPR, PASS ACAA

Source: Author's own compilation.

and petitions respectively (opponent role). These forms of lobbying are relevant in this context as they relied on the involvement of national constituencies as ways to exert pressure on MEPs.

The ECCP, an umbrella organisation that comprises solidarity movements around Europe, published on its website a call for action entitled 'Ask your MEP to reject the agreement'. Working through its member organisations, it circulated an appeal among activists, asking them to direct a prepared letter to the MEP representing their constituency in Brussels to call on him/her to vote against the ACAA. Member organisations were also invited to create online petitions and be engaged in writing letters and articles to newspapers or online publications. For example, the Irish member organisation, Ireland Palestinian Solidarity Campaign, encouraged its members to take part in an e-action and send an email to their MEPs. Similarly, the UK-based Palestinian Solidarity Campaign called on people to become active and get in touch with their MEPs to convince them about the rejection of the agreement. As explained in Chapter 1, letter campaigns are protest politics forms of lobbying (opponent role), based on a confrontational approach that mobilises public opinion. By mobilising its member organisations and their activists, the ECCP aimed at confronting MEPs with the position of their constituencies against the approval of the agreement by the EU.[33]

Another initiative that saw the involvement of the national level has been the PASS ACAA campaign. More precisely, this campaign consisted in a petition addressed to EU citizens and aimed at pressing MEPs to give their consent to the ACAA during the plenary in October 2012. The PASS ACAA campaign had a website, a Facebook page and a Twitter account, all means through which the organisers mobilised the public. Despite various searches, it was not possible to identify who the promoters of this initiative were. However, analysis of their documents and messages suggested that the campaign was orchestrated from Brussels, as there are referrals to this initiative on the EFI and EJC's websites.[34] Through online social networks and the online petition, the PASS ACAA aimed at collecting as many signatures as possible with a view to giving the petition to MEPs on the day of the vote in Strasbourg.[35] The motto of the campaign was 'Putting European Patients Before Politics' and, as this suggests, it made a case for supporting the ACAA in light of the benefits that this would grant to EU citizens. It recalled the idea that the agreement is in the interest of EU citizens and national health care systems which would benefit from Israeli pharmaceutical products and medical innovation. In the petition, it is also argued that 'the ACAA complies with EU law, EU policy, EU principles and, most importantly, serves the interests of Europeans and their healthcare, first and foremost'.[36] The argument resembled the mixed frame proposed by the EFI and the EJC, as it recalled the idea that the ACAA is a technical agreement, is not an upgrade of the EU–Israel bilateral relationship and would benefit EU consumers. However, the argument had a strong political argument and no credible evidence in support of the claims: there were no precise references to back their claims and even inaccuracies, reducing the credibility of these messages. This petition, which was handed in to MEPs on the day of the plenary in October 2012, aimed at using constituencies as leverage on MEPs and pushing them to vote according to the preferences of PASS ACAA. It has to be noted that this form of involvement did not seem to have tipped the balance of the vote in the European Parliament, as decisions were already taken and the report of the INTA Committee was in favour of the ACAA, following the assurances of the Commission that the EU would check the legally correct implementation of the agreement.

Conclusions

This chapter has focused on the roles played and the frames used by NSAs when lobbying the EU, especially the European Parliament, on the case of the ACAA. In contrast to Chapter 4, where the European Parliament was only used by NSAs to ask questions to the Commission and the Council, and to Chapter 5, in which it had a more symbolic role, in this case it was a crucial actor in the decision-making process. Lobbying was mainly concentrated on this institution, as its consent was required for the ACAA to enter into force. In particular, lobbying was central to give further impetus to the discussion on the dossier, which had been 'buried' in the INTA Committee for almost two years. Had NSAs remained silent, the issue would have likely remained stuck in the Parliament for long time. Not only were NSAs particularly active on the issue and able to raise the attention of policy-makers, but their contribution to the policy-making process was crucial in shaping the frame that was at the basis of the final decision. Interestingly, this frame consists in a mix of elements that combine and reinterpret the different inputs provided by NSAs (especially the MATTIN Group and Teva) and on which MEPs made their final decision.

More specifically, Teva and the MATTIN Group were the most active NSAs on the issue of ACAA. Both of them played the role of dialogue-builder based on inside lobbying and direct contacts with EU officials and politicians. They relied on meetings behind the scenes with EU officials and MEPs during which they explained their interpretation of the ACAA and the reasons why the EU should or should not approve the agreement. More specifically, Teva and the MATTIN Group used a technical frame, with an economic and a legal perspective respectively. Teva supported the ACAA and based its frame on economic aspects. It disentangled the ACAA from the peace process, stressing its technical nature as a commercial agreement, which was also part of the 2005 EU–Israel Action Plan. It further highlighted the benefits that would accrue to the EU by signing the ACAA, with evidence and figures to support the claim. By showing the importance of free trade and the advantages for EU consumers and health care providers, Teva was also relying on key principles that shape EU identity and nature, thus ensuring that its frame would resonate with policy-makers' views. In contrast, the MATTIN Group framed its argument with reference to the legal implications of Article 9(1) of the Protocol. In light of this article, Israel could nominate the responsible authority to issue the certificate of conformity required under the ACAA. Given that Israel will nominate the Ministry of Health to carry out this task and that this ministry also has jurisdiction over the OPTs, the EU would violate its own law and international law. Acknowledging the Ministry's authority would amount to the recognition of Israel's jurisdiction over the occupied territories and, therefore, the impossibility of contesting the territorial scope of applicability of all other EU–Israeli agreements. Thanks to their consensual approach based on cooperative and dialogical interactions, both Teva and the MATTIN Group managed to develop shared views with EU officials and MEPs on the basis of their respective frames. Their frames became part of the debate within the INTA and AFET Committees first, and the European Parliament plenary later on. Through interactions between the EU and NSAs, new frames to interpret the events were produced.

The other NSAs presented in the chapter such as the EMHRN, APRODEV, the EJC and the EFI used mixed frames. Not only did these NSAs rely on frames that contained political elements, they also adopted a different approach from Teva and the MATTIN Group. They swung between the roles of dialogue-builder and voice-articulator and, in certain cases, even of opponent, making the definition of common meanings and interpretations more difficult. Their frames were also used in parliamentary discussions, as the European Parliament is open to frames that have political aspects, which are necessary in face of constituencies for electoral purposes. These frames were, however, not particularly new in terms of what the EU could do and how the argument was presented. While the EFI and EJC copied the frame of Teva, but in a more simplified version, the other NSAs stressed the aspect of coherence and consistency of EU external relations. It seems plausible to argue that these frames became part of the debate when the NSAs used the access approach more than when they relied on information politics, as the former allowed for the definition of common ideas and meaning, which reliance on newspaper articles makes more difficult. It is also necessary to note that the political references in the frames had already been used in previous debates in the European Parliament when discussing the Israeli–Palestinian conflict. Therefore, there was not much new added to the debate.

Finally, the chapter has also shown that some Brussels-based NSAs relied on the national level to carry out their lobbying. In this case, attention has been paid to the protest politics approach adopted by the ECCP and the group organising the online petition PASS ACAA. With letter campaigns and petitions, these NSAs aimed at raising the attention of the public in MEPs' constituencies with a view to exerting pressure on MEPs indirectly via the use of national NSAs. However, these efforts did not seem particularly significant in the case of the ACAA, especially if compared to the cases discussed above. The discussion on the use of the national level and the Europeanisation of NSAs based in member states will be developed in the following chapter.

Notes

1 It has to be remembered that these goods can be traded even without the ACAA, but their access to each other's market requires double-checks and certifications due to the lack of an agreement on conformity assessment and acceptance.
2 While the consent procedure provides the European Parliament with some leverage, in practice the real room for manoeuvring is limited (Interviewees 45, 57).
3 This date was found on the Legislative Observatory of the European Parliament before it moved to the new system. This information was retrieved in April 2011, but is no longer available.
4 A similar situation occurred in December 2008, when the European Parliament decided to block the 'Protocol to the Euro-Mediterranean Agreement establishing an association between the European Communities and their Member States, of the one part, and the State of Israel, of the other part, on a framework Agreement between the European Community and the State of Israel on the general principles governing the State of Israel's participation in Community programmes' due to the continuation of the siege on Gaza. The Protocol is, however, partially implemented (see Euro-Mediterranean Human Rights Network and APRODEV 2012).
5 During the INTA meeting of 13 July 2010, Andrikiene asked that the ACAA be placed onto the agenda again. The Chair of INTA MEP Moreira replied that the decision was taken by the Coordinators' meeting, within which the EPP coordinator also voted in favour of freezing the ACAA, and the decision would not change unless the Coordinators change their minds (see the record of the meeting in the archive of the

EP-Live: www.europarl.europa.eu). What followed was that, due to the 'point system' for assigning reports, the EPP decided to give this report back because it was interested in another one (Interviewee 57).

6 In the ALDE group it was felt as undemocratic that only a few people (coordinators) could decide on the dossier (whether to discuss it in the committee and plenary), so they wanted to discuss it. However, the group was divided on the content of the agreement and within ALDE no common position was reached on how to vote (Interviewee 70).

7 One dossier goes by default to the Chair of the Committee if no political party requests it or the point system does not allow any political party to take it (Interviewees 45, 57).

8 For the debate, see the record of the meeting in the archive of the EP-Live: www. europarl.europa.eu

9 In some cases the ACAA was wrongly associated with the issue of the rules of origin (Chapter 4) in terms of traded goods from settlements. This is, however, incorrect, as the ACAA concerns certification procedures.

10 The details of these events can be found in the minutes of the Committees (available at: http://www.europarl.europa.eu/committees/en/full-list.html). See also European Parliament (2013), where all the documents mentioned in this section can be found.

11 See the text of the amendments to the report of the INTA Committee at this link: http://www.europarl.europa.eu/sides/getDoc.do?type=AMD&reference=A7-2012-0289&secondRef=001-002&language=EN&format=PDF (accessed 30 November 2014). The amendment indicated that the Council should issue an interpretative declaration stating the different view on the jurisdiction of the Israeli Responsible Authority, as indicated in article 9(1). It was basically aimed at qualifying the territorial scope in order to ensure compliance with EU legislation. See the rest of the chapter for more details.

12 Interviewees at the national level did not mention any pharmaceutical company that lobbied on the ACAA in capitals.

13 According to Teva Factsheet (document given to the author by Teva representative in October 2011), the company spans across 26 European countries. Teva is a leading company in many European markets and also has 12 manufacturing facilities for the production of active pharmaceutical ingredients, generic research and development. For further information on the company, see also the Transparency Register of the EU.

14 This was confirmed during interviews with both Teva representative and EU officials. Moreover, the name of Teva is listed among the clients of the D&D Consulting Service (2013). See also the Transparency Register: http://ec.europa.eu/transparencyregister/public/consultation/displaylobbyist.do?id=40855887550-54 (accessed 17 April 2013). The D&D Consulting Service has not been included in the database, as lobbying was carried out on behalf of, and together with, Teva.

15 Despite numerous attempts, Andrikiene refused to be interviewed. The facts presented here are based on the other interviews carried out, the articles she wrote for newspapers and the positions she had in the debates in the INTA Committee and the plenary.

16 Documents supplied to the author by the MATTIN Group.

17 According to interviews, Teva also coordinated its lobbying strategy with the Israeli Representation in Brussels (Interviewees 56, 59, 63, 70).

18 See http://www.eccpalestine.org/the-eu-israel-acaa-agreement-legally-flawed-encouraging-impunity/ (accessed 20 March 2013). The ECCP changed its website recently, so many blog posts and articles that were published in previous years now have a more recent date due to the new website.

19 See www.passacaa.com (accessed 15 April 2013).

20 It was not possible to identify who the people promoting the PASS ACAA petition were.

21 Teva Position Paper, 10 February 2012. Document given to the author by an EU official.

22 Ibid.

23 As mentioned above, Teva's position paper argued that: 'Generic medicines' lower prices provide healthcare authorities with significant savings on their healthcare budgets by speeding up access to affordable generic medicines. ... With the ACAA, generic products could enter the market much more quickly. ... Specialist resources could thus be freed up and deployed to reduce the workload for assessment.'

24 For the debate, see the record of the meeting in the archive of the EP-Live: www.europarl.europa.eu

25 Ibid.

26 While this frame is clearly articulated in the document published in April 2012 on the EMHRN website, the same NGOs started their lobbying earlier and did so via an access approach (Interviewee 4). This frame was not particularly new, so MEPs were already familiar with it. There seems to be a circularity between the argument used by NSAs and MEPs to the extent that they influence each other.

27 Documents supplied to the author by the MATTIN Group.

28 Documents supplied to the author by the MATTIN Group and Interviewee 1.

29 This part of the Working Paper uses the same argument presented by the MATTIN Group. The documents seen by courtesy of the MATTIN Group cannot be reproduced here.

30 For the debate, see the record of the meeting in the archive of the EP-Live: www.europarl.europa.eu

31 Ibid.

32 In the European Parliament legal service's opinion, the legal problems related to Article 9(1) could be solved at the implementation stage. The Commission, which cannot acknowledge a Responsible Authority nominated by Israel which has jurisdiction over the areas covered by the EC–PLO Interim Agreement, is in the position to refuse to acknowledge any Authority whose responsibility exceeds the internationally recognised territory of Israel (internal document seen by the author during interviews).

33 See http://www.eccpalestine.org/864/ (accessed 20 March 2013). The ECCP changed its website recently, so many blog posts and articles that were published in previous years now have a more recent date due to the new website.

34 In an article published by the European Jewish Press on 22 June 2012, the PASS ACAA was described as 'a grassroots initiative for Europeans concerned about the politicization of their healthcare'. See Reyness (2012). However, interviews carried out at the national level did not lead to identifying this initiative as a spontaneous citizen-based campaign.

35 See www.passacaa.com (accessed 15 April 2013).

36 Ibid.

References

Al Jazeera. 2009. 'The Palestinian Papers'. 14 October. http://transparency.aljazeera.net/ar/projects/thepalestinepapers/20121911258828123.html

Andrikiene, Laima. 2011a. 'EU Parliament is Damaging EU–Israel Relations'. *EUobserver*, 28 February. http://euobserver.com/opinion/31886

———. 2011b. 'International Trade: Israel Should Not be Discriminated Against'. *EUobserver*, 6 October. http://euobserver.com/opinion/113820

APRODEV, CIDSE, Euro-Mediterranean Human Rights Network and Quaker Council for European Affairs. 2012. 'Human Rights and Development NGOs Ask MEPs to Suspend the Vote of the EU–Israel ACAA Protocol', 12 April. http://euromedrights.org/publication/human-rights-and-development-ngos-ask-meps-to-suspend-the-vote-of-the-eu-israel-acaa-protocol/

Beyers, Jan. 2004. 'Voice and Access: Political Practices of European Interest Associations'. *European Union Politics* 5 (2): 211–40.

Council of the European Union. 2010. 'Council Decision of 22 March 2010 on the Signing, on Behalf of the European Union, of a Protocol to the Euro-Mediterranean Agreement Establishing an Association between the European Communities and Their Member States, of the One Part, and the State of Israel, of the Other Part, on Conformity Assessment and Acceptance of Industrial Products (CAA), 2010/319/EU'. Brussels.

D&D Consulting Service. 2012. 'About us' http://www.ddconsult.eu/about-dd-consulting/
———. 2013. 'Clients'. http://www.ddconsult.eu/our-clients/

De Keyser, Veronique. 2012a. 'Working Document. Additional Protocol to the Euro-Mediterranean Agreement Establishing an EC–Israel Association on an EC–Israel Agreement on Conformity Assessment and Acceptance of Industrial Products (ACAA)'. European Parliament, Committee on Foreign Affairs.
———. 2012b. 'Draft Opinion of the Committee on Foreign Affairs for the Committee on International Trade on the Draft Council Decision on the Conclusion of a Protocol to the Euro-Mediterranean Agreement Establishing an Association between the European Communities and Their Member States, of the One Part, and the State of Israel, of the Other Part, on the Conformity Assessment and Acceptance of Industrial Products (CAA)'. European Parliament, Committee on Foreign Affairs.

Euro-Mediterranean Human Rights Network and APRODEV. 2012. *EU–Israel Relations: Promoting and Ensuring Respect for International Law.* Brussels.

European Commission. 2003. 'Commission Directive 2003/94/EC Laying down the Principles and Guidelines of Good Manufacturing Practice in Respect of Medicinal Products for Human Use and Investigational Medicinal Products for Human Use'. Brussels.
———. 2005. 'EU–Israel Action Plan'. Brussels.
———. 2009. 'Proposal for a Council Decision on the Conclusion of an Additional Protocol on the Euro-Mediterranean Agreement Establishing an Agreement between the European Community and the State of Israel on Conformity Assessment and Acceptance of Industrial Products COM(2009)559final'. Brussels.
———. 2013. 'Single Market for Goods Agreements on Conformity Assessment and Acceptance of Industrial Products (ACAA)'. 5 February. http://ec.europa.eu/enterprise/policies/single-market-goods/international-aspects/acaa-neighbouring-countries/index_en.htm

European Friends of Israel. 2012. 'ACAA Agreement and the Lost Time'. http://www.efi-eu.org

European Parliament. 2012. 'Rules of Procedure of the European Parliament'. http://www.europarl.europa.eu/sides/getDoc.do?pubRef=-//EP//TEXT+RULES-EP+20120417+RULE-081+DOC+XML+V0//EN&language=EN&navigationBar=YES
———. 2013. 'Procedure File – 2009/0155(NLE) – EC/Israel Agreement: Conformity Assessment and Acceptance of Industrial Products (ACAA). Additional Protocol to the Euro-Mediterranean Agreement'. http://www.europarl.europa.eu/oeil/popups/ficheprocedure.do?reference=2009/0155%28NLE%29&l=en

European Parliament and Council of the European Union. 2001. 'Directive 2001/83/EC of the European Parliament and of the Council on the Community Code Relating to Medicinal Products for Human Use'. Brussels.

European Voice. 2012. 'Stuck at the Borders'. 26 April. http://www.europeanvoice.com/article/imported/stuck-at-the-border/74217.aspx

Hania, Evelyne. 2010. 'New Legislation in the Internal Market'. Presented at the TAIEX Seminar, Brussels, 16 April. http://ec.europa.eu/enlargement/taiex/dyn/taiex-events/library/detail_en.jsp?EventID=41170

Lemanska, Katarzyna and Stuart Reigeluth. 2012. 'Why EU Should Reject New Israeli Trade Pact'. *EUobserver*, 23 April.

Ludford, Sarah. 2011. 'MEPs Finally to Get Chance to Approve EU–Israel Medicines Trade Agreement'. http://enfieldlibdems.org.uk/en/article/2011/0489446/meps-finally-to-get-chance-to-approve-eu-israel-medicines-trade-agreement

Reyness, Shari. 2012. 'European Petition Launched over Delayed EU–Israel Healthcare Trade Agreement'. 22 June. http://ejpress.org/index.php?option=com_content&view=article&id=26231&catid=25:israel&Itemid=18

Vadeire, Ines. 2012. 'ACAA – Between Trade and Politics'. http://www.efi-eu.org

VoteWatchEU. 2012. 'VoteWatch Europe: European Parliament, Council of the EU'. http://www.votewatch.eu/en/protocol-to-the-euro-mediterranean-agreement-establishing-an-association-between-the-ec-and-israel-o-2.html (authorisation required to access website).

7 Using the national level to lobby the EU

Member states are obviously one of the levels at which NSAs can decide to lobby on EU foreign policy issues. Foreign policy is indeed a domain in which national capitals still have a great deal of power. It is therefore important for NSAs to have member states on their side. In the previous chapters it has been shown how NSAs that are based or active in Brussels use the national level to complement their activities at the EU level. In contrast, this chapter focuses on the activities carried out by NSAs based in member states and how they lobby on issues related to EU foreign policy towards the Israeli–Palestinian conflict. More specifically, two aspects will be investigated here. First, Europeanisation patterns will be analysed with the aim to understand whether NSAs take the EU dimension into consideration and, if so, how they do that. Second, this chapter will compare the types of roles and frames used at the national level to those employed at the EU level.

These two aspects will be investigated in the case of three EU member states, namely the United Kingdom, Germany and France. The choice of these cases is related to their crucial role in the definition of EU foreign policy towards Israel and Palestine. Not only are they the 'big' member states in the EU, with a significant weight when decisions need to be taken, but they are also perceived as such by many NSAs (e.g., Interviewees 2, 4, 60). Similarities among these member states are also matched by different historical and institutional features in foreign policy, especially when it comes to the Israeli–Palestinian conflict (see Chapter 2). This variation is therefore useful to understand the extent to which domestic conditions influence and shape lobbying and advocacy activities by NSAs.

Against this backdrop, this chapter shows that NSAs based in member states lobby their governments when it comes to the Israeli–Palestinian conflict, but they tend to do so mainly in relation to national foreign policies. The EU dimension does not always figure among their priorities or their lobbying actions. Partial Europeanisation of lobbying on foreign policy can be observed, but the national and EU arenas still remain rather isolated from each other. In terms of roles and frames, at the national level the role of opponent is used more frequently than at the EU level. This is often combined with the use of political frames, which is not surprising. Given the politicised nature of national politics, political frames resonate well with politicians and their constituencies. Political frames are also used by NSAs to start lobby campaigns and demonstrations with the aim of directly influencing national policy-making. This approach makes, however, the definition of common frames a very difficult enterprise.

The chapter is structured as follows. First, the NSAs active in the United Kingdom, Germany and France are presented, together with an overview of the context in which they operate. Second, Europeanisation patterns of lobbying activities are described and discussed. The following two sections discuss the roles and frames that NSAs use at the national level. The final section summarises the key findings of the chapter.

Policy-making and NSAs in the United Kingdom, France and Germany

The United Kingdom, France and Germany display similarities in the institutional features of their foreign policy-making process, which is centralised in the hands of the government. In contrast, their interest intermediation systems and their historical legacies with Israel and the Palestinians differ quite significantly, thus confronting NSAs with different contexts and situations to deal with. As shown in this section, these features determine the differences among the population of NSAs in these countries and also in their lobbying activities.

In the United Kingdom foreign policy is decided by the party in power. The House of Commons is only informed by the government about the decisions taken in foreign policy. MPs, who rarely vote against the party line, can ask questions to ministers in order to keep them accountable, to convey the mood of public opinion and to raise issues and problems to the government, without actually having any power to change the course of the government's decisions (Williams 2004; Interviewee 87). Foreign policy is also centralised in London, so that instructions on issues referring to EU foreign policy are not decided by the Permanent Representation, but come directly from the government (Foster 2000).

France has also a strongly centralised foreign policy, which is normally the *domaine réservée* of the President. In Risse-Kappen's (1991) terms, the policy network that links the state and society is state-dominated, so that the government is in the position to ignore pressure coming from public opinion and the media to a larger extent than in contexts that are society-dominated or in which there is a weak state. Foreign policy is defined and conducted in symbiosis between the Elisée and the Quai d'Orsay, especially due to the links between the elites that work in the two. The Parliament plays a negligible role (Blunden 2000).

Similarly, the German Bundestag also has a minimal weight in foreign policy decisions. The Grundgesetz attributes power to the executive branch (and therefore the Chancellor's cabinet) in this policy domain. Party politics plays a role in the system, as the Ministry of Foreign Affairs is normally assigned to a representative of the junior coalition party (as governments are usually based on coalitions). Nevertheless, there is a substantial continuity in foreign policy, which is aimed at consensus-building among the parties, and popular involvement is very limited (Harnisch 2013; Risse-Kappen 1991).

While all three states have centralised foreign policy-making, the system of interest intermediation differs. Although NSAs face similar institutional constraints due to the centralisation of power in the hands of the executives, the context of interest intermediation offers them different room for manoeuvre. The United Kingdom has been described as a pluralistic system, France is known for a more statist approach to interest intermediation and Germany is between these two models, displaying the features of a corporatist system (Eising 2009). These differences clearly influence the role that state actors and interest groups play in policy-making and shape their interactions. In a pluralist model, the state simply moderates among different and competing interest groups, each of them representing a diffuse or concentrated interest of society. State actors are open to listening to different voices and interests. In a pluralist system NSAs actively lobby to pursue their interests and are more likely to find a context that is receptive and open to their requests. At the opposite side of the spectrum, in the statist model, NSAs are normally involved later in the process and play a minimal role. The state pursues the national interest in view of its democratic legitimacy and defines the boundaries of policies. Like the pluralist model, fragmentation characterises this system, but participation in the policy-making process is more limited. As a middle way, in a corporatist system, representation occurs through peak associations that represent and speak in favour of the factors of production or big sectors of society. These associations tend to be on an equal footing with state actors in terms of bargaining power, and the state mediates among these associations and tries to build consensus on shared positions.

While all these features are generally applied to state–business relations, this also tends to be the general context in which NSAs and state representatives interact in the domain of foreign policy. According to some representatives of NSAs (Interviewees 4, 60, 103), the United Kingdom's system is the most open to NSAs. British officials and MPs are used to interacting with them. In contrast, France is perceived as a state without a culture of engagement with NSAs. While many NSAs are active there, the context in which they operate is considered less favourable to their activities. Germany's system of interest intermediation shows that the state is used to dealing with interest groups, but there is not the same plurality as in the British system.

An additional factor that influences the context shaping the types of interactions between NSAs and state officials are the historical legacies of the three states towards Israel and Palestine, the relations between EU and national policies, and interest-related factors. The United Kingdom's presence in the region dates back to its colonial past, especially during its League of Nations mandate over Palestine, during which the establishment of a Jewish homeland was enabled (Hollis 2010). Paraphrasing Geoffrey Edwards (as quoted in Musu 2010: 91), 'there has been an essential duality of purpose in British policy irrespective of the political complexion of the government; this has been to influence the Arabs as far as possible to take a more conciliatory attitude and to influence the Americans to press the Israelis to the same end'. The United Kingdom has often been torn between supporting the EU's stance and being in line with the American ally. On the one hand, it supports the EU's role in the region and shares the EU's stance based on the two-state solution and respect for international law, humanitarian law and human rights. On the other hand, however, its strong ties with the USA prevent the United Kingdom from pushing for a completely independent EU foreign policy in the region. Referring to an interview with Sir Malcom Rifkin, Musu (2010: 92) further maintains that

> the British position differs from that of some other member states (France in particular) in that it sees increased EU involvement in the political negotiations as a 'distraction' in a domain that should be left to the Americans. The EU's involvement should be limited to those activities that are welcomed by the Arabs, the Israelis and the Americans, first among them the economic support provided to the Palestinian Authority.

British policy has thus been characterised by a strong link to Israel in line with the US stance and, at the same time, friendly relationships with Arab countries for economic and geopolitical reasons. Economic ties are significant not only with Arab states, but also with Israel. Bilateral trade with the latter amounted to £3.85 billion in 2011, making Israel the United Kingdom's largest individual trading partner in the Near East and North Africa region and its twenty-ninth largest market worldwide. Moreover, many British companies (e.g., HSBC) have significant interests in Israel due to its developed market and its potential in the R&D sector (Foreign Office 2012).

France's foreign policy towards Israel/Palestine has been marked by some *ruptures*, but also by a significant degree of continuity. Following the French colonial past in the region, Arab–French relations went through troubled times in the 1950s, while at the same time bilateral relations with Israel improved significantly, especially in terms of military cooperation (above all nuclear) and arms trade. Under De Gaulle, however, this military cooperation was interrupted and a deterioration of French–Israeli relations was sped up after the Six-Day War in 1967. This led to a clear pro-Palestinian stance, and a more balanced position emerged only when Mitterand took power. Chirac went even further with his 'philosémite pro-arabe' policy, as he tried to be seen as a mediator between the parties (Hecker 2010: 117). Since 2000 French politicians have steadily worked to improve bilateral relations with Israel, reaching a peak under Sarkozy's presidency (Interviewees 79, 80, 85). Despite some points of rupture, French policy has mainly been characterised by an attempt to have balanced relations with both Arab countries and Israel, and to pursue a European foreign policy independent from the USA, also with a view to promoting French interests (Musu 2010).

This median position is probably also the result of the composition of French society. France hosts the largest Jewish and Muslim communities in Europe, so that French governments have attempted to find a middle ground that meets the need and demands of both groups (Interviewees 79, 81). Economically, bilateral trade has been strengthened, totalling around €2.3 billion (Trésor 2012b). French business groups, however, tend to adopt a very cautious approach to investing in Israel due to the instability caused by the conflict and the idea that this would be counterproductive for their bilateral relationships with Arab countries. The government has tried to boost these economic ties, also sponsoring events such as the Day of French–Israeli innovation in December 2011 (Interviewees 80, 85). Some big companies like Veolia and Alstom have been active in Israel, but French FDI is low for the size of the economy and French companies do not seem to exploit Israeli potential in the field of technology and research (Trésor 2012a).

Finally, German Middle Eastern policy is heavily influenced by its sense of guilt towards Israel, which has led to a special relationship between Germany and Israel. In the 1950s and 1960s bilateral relations between the two countries were strengthened by signing economic agreements and establishing institutional fora such as the bilateral Chamber of Commerce or the German–Israeli Parliamentary group. This special relationship has also favoured significant commercial relations. In 2011 the volume of trade between the two amounted to $6.51 billion, covering 15 per cent of all EU–Israel bilateral trade (International Monetary Fund 2012). While supporting the EU's position based on the two-state solution, successive German governments have always worked for better bilateral relations with Israel (Asseburg and Busse 2011). Only recently have there been signals of less unconditional support to Israel and some discontent with Israeli policies. The war in Gaza in 2008/9 was probably the turning point and the subsequent policies of the Netanyahu administration surely helped to slightly shift German position towards a tougher stance towards Israel (Interviewees 4, 91). Nevertheless, the policy space for NSAs is limited, as every position, declaration etc. on Israel/Palestine has to be calibrated to ensure that no connections to German historical past can be drawn. This has also led to a gap between German political elites, who prefer to avoid certain topics (e.g., ban or labelling of settlement goods), and the German society/public, which is increasingly critical of current Israeli policies (Interviewees 108, 109). Germany remains a key partner for Israel and, as such, a key player in EU foreign policy-making towards Israel/Palestine. Not only is Germany in the position to block a decision, it is also able to influence the decisions of other countries, especially the new member states (Interviewee 60).

Who are the NSAs based in these three member states?

On the basis of the mapping presented in Chapter 3,[1] a first aspect that deserves attention is the geographical distribution of NSAs among the three countries. Out of a total of 130 NSAs with their headquarters located in any of the three countries, the United Kingdom has the highest number of NSAs (74), mainly due to business groups, which are between five and six times more numerous there than

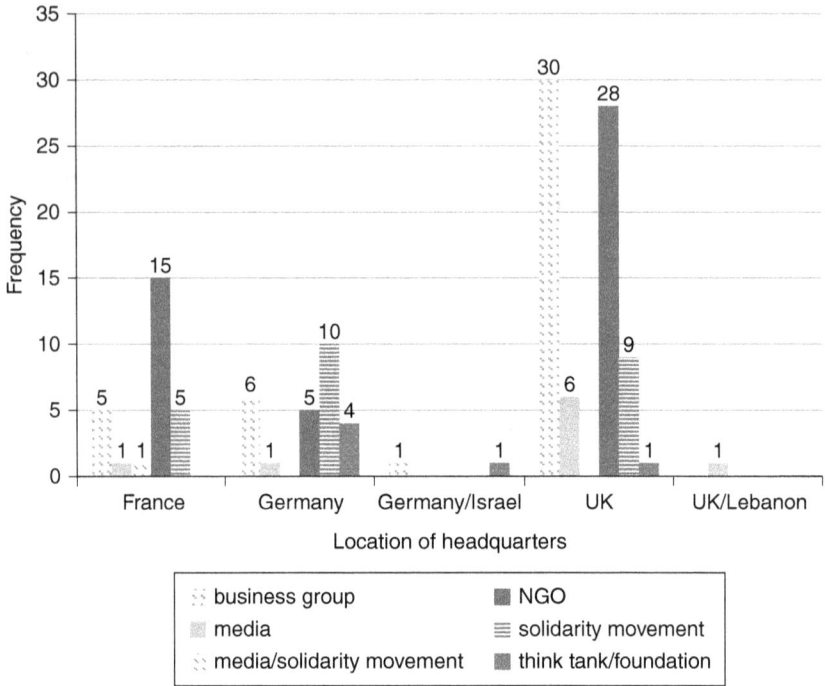

Figure 7.1 Frequency of NSAs divided by category and location

in the other two countries (see Figure 7.1). Such a strong presence of British business groups might be the result of the different access to sources, which might have inflated the figures and would therefore explain this significant difference among the three countries.[2]

Three further aspects are worth mentioning in this respect. First, according to several interviews (Interviewees 91, 95, 96, 98, 100, 101, 103, 107, 108), German history and the political sensitivity to the topic make it difficult for NGOs to work on issues related to Israel and Palestine. As a result, many German NGOs tend to avoid the issue, which becomes more discussed at the level of solidarity groups, whose role is, however, perceived as limited (Interviewee 98). Those NGOs working on Israel/Palestine mainly work on the ground through the implementation of projects of cooperation. For example, forumZFD dispatches peace experts to conflict areas like Israel/Palestine and aims to spread the concept of 'Civil Peace Service' among citizens (Interviewee 102). In contrast, British NGOs are widely recognised as very professional, well-organised and capable NSAs that can carry out effective advocacy and lobbying work (Interviewees 4, 96). Working in these organisations normally requires specific skills and capabilities in areas like communication, fund raising, etc. This significant professionalisation of these NGOs is likely to be determined by the fact that many international NGOs are headquartered in the United Kingdom. Similarly, French NGOs are relatively active on issues related to Israel/Palestine, as public opinion is very sensitive to the topic. While some NGOs are relatively big and with ramifications world- or Europe-wide (e.g., EJC, FIDH), the majority of NGOs are not professional groups with expertise in lobbying (Interviewee 81). Moreover, NSAs perceive a significant difference between pro-Israel or Jewish groups and pro-Palestinian groups in terms of their respective access to high-level officials and politicians. For example, the CRIF is seen as a powerful NSA in the French context, with strong ties with the President and his staff and the ability to influence decisions (Interviewees 81, 83; Ghiles Meilhac 2011).

The second aspect concerns solidarity movements. In particular, solidarity movements account for a large proportion of NSAs dealing with Israel/Palestine in Germany, unlike NGOs which are relatively limited in number (Interviewees 91, 98). Although there are some Europe-wide or worldwide movements or groups (e.g., BDS movement), solidarity groups tend to focus on and target their national audiences.

Third, German foundations, which are here considered as think tanks, are a particular form of NSA and play a significant role in Germany, but have no equivalent in other European states. While German foundations have often been mentioned in interviews, the same cannot be said for French and British think tanks. German political foundations are important NSAs that, together with activities on the ground, lobby the politicians of their political party and the German public.[3] As far as media-related actors are concerned, the existence of a national public sphere makes their work easier at the national level. While it has been difficult to assess the role of the media, the focus here has been given to those media-related NSAs that are clearly committed to lobbying and advocacy activities (e.g., BICOM).

This brief overview of the NSA population in the United Kingdom, France and Germany has shown that lobbying at the national level takes place in three different contexts. While foreign policy-making is centralised in all three member states, the interest intermediation system and the culture of interacting with NSAs are different. This affects the nature of NSAs and the activities they can carry out. While business groups tend to behave in a similar way at all levels, NGOs can encounter some problems in Germany, where the political elites are not particularly willing to deal with certain topics. More in general, solidarity groups are more present at the national level than at the EU level and they work to raise public awareness and affect politicians indirectly.

EU and national level: two disentangled arenas?

The analysis of patterns of Europeanisation of lobbying by NSAs based in member states is not only an important indicator of the development of lobbying in the EU, but also gives us an idea about the level of EU integration. The more lobbying on EU foreign policy is carried out at the two levels and links between national and EU lobbying activities are established, the more the EU foreign policy system is integrated. This section sheds light on this aspect by analysing the patterns of Europeanisation (or lack thereof) of lobbying of NSAs based in

NO INTEREST	• Lobbying on issues of national foreign policy • National level
INTERNALISATION	• Lobbying on EU issues • National level
SUPRANATIONALISATION	• Lobbying on EU issues, but delegated to umbrella organisations • EU level
EXTERNALISATION	• Lobbying on EU issues through direct representation • EU level

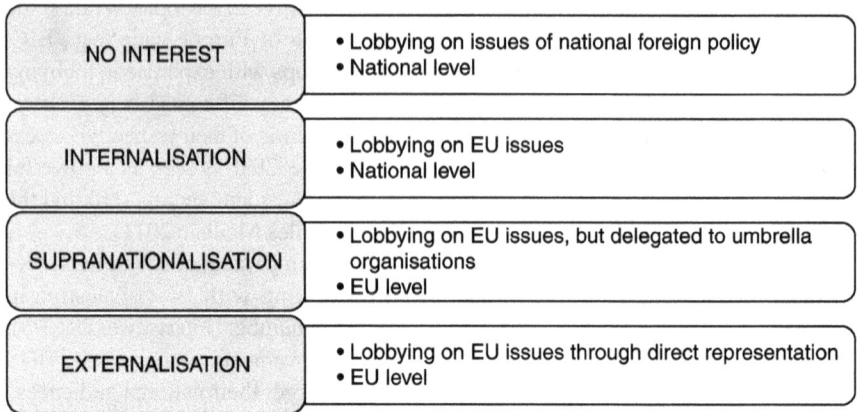

Figure 7.2 Patterns of Europeanisation among NSAs based in member states

Source: Adapted from Balme and Chabanet (2002).

member states. Four patterns have been identified. The first option is a form of non-Europeanisation – that is, NSAs based in member states show a lack of interest in EU foreign policy. The other three modes of Europeanisation, as highlighted in Figure 7.2 are internalisation, supranationalisation or externalisation (Balme and Chabanet 2002; Saurugger 2005; see also Chapter 1).[4]

Not surprisingly, all four modes of Europeanisation are present. Many NSAs do not take EU foreign policy towards the Israeli–Palestinian conflict into consideration, but focus exclusively on national foreign policies. In contrast, other NSAs display at least a partial Europeanisation of their lobbying activities. In some cases, there is an internalisation of EU issues into their lobbying at the national level. In others, NSAs based in member states delegate the activities of lobbying on EU issues to umbrella organisations based in Brussels (supranationalisation). Finally, other actors go directly to Brussels to represent their interests in the EU context (externalisation). More importantly, Brussels-based NSAs are crucial in shaping and directing the activities of many NSAs based in member states when it comes to lobbying on EU issues.

Many NSAs lobby exclusively on national policies towards the Israeli–Palestinian conflict. They do not include the EU dimension into their lobbying at the national level, nor do they go to Brussels to interact with EU officials and MEPs directly. Their priority is to change national foreign policy, and the national level is rarely conceived as a way to indirectly influence EU policies (Interviewees 4, 78, 82, 84, 95, 103). For instance, the German NGO Medico International lobbied the German government on the issue of Israeli demolition of infrastructures and buildings in Area C (West Bank) (Interviewee 91). The focus was exclusively on the German position and what the German government should do in this regard, instead of addressing the broader dimension of EU policies concerning Area C. Other examples of lobbying concern the actions taken against business groups working or involved with the settlements, such as Deutsche Bahn or Veolia. In both cases, NSAs' activities targeted the German and French governments respectively, without involving the EU dimension in this issue (Interviewees 84, 103). In another case, the French NGO CRIF lobbied the French government on the kidnapping by Hamas of the Israeli soldier Shalit due to his French–Israeli citizenship (Interviewee 78). Similarly, business groups or business-related NSAs target a specific national government to increase and strengthen the economic relations between the two countries. For instance, the German Deutsch–Israelische Wirtschaftsvereinigung (DIW) lobbies the German government with a view to favouring business relations between Israeli and German enterprises. It is usually consulted before the bilateral consultations between Israel and Germany in order to give indications of the main issues of concern for German firms (Interviewee 93).

Paraphrasing McCauley (2011), two explanations can account for this lack of Europeanisation: EU opportunities are 'out of reach' and 'out of focus'. The former explanation refers to lack of resources and limited understanding of how the EU works; the latter instead points to a form of disinterest and deliberate distancing of NSAs with regard to EU issues. Both aspects have been confirmed during interviews: on the one hand, many NSAs based in member states do not have enough resources in terms of money and staff or enough knowledge as far as EU institutions and policies are concerned (Interviewees 95, 103, 105, 109). In other cases, NSAs clearly expressed their preference for lobbying at the national level (Interviewees 82, 91, 100).

Despite this lack of interest on the part of some NSAs, forms of Europeanisation are in place. A possible way to lobby on EU issues is internationalisation, namely that NSAs based in member states include issues related to EU foreign policy in their lobbying actions at the national level. Internalisation is likely to be determined by two factors. First, many issues that fall within the remit of interest of NSAs based in member states have an EU dimension in that they are dealt with at the EU level. This is, for example, the case of EU bilateral agreements with Israel and Palestine. This explains why the United Kingdom Palestine Campaign,[5] the French Association France Palestine Solidarité (AFPS) (2012b) and the German KOPI[6] each promoted a petition in their respective country against the approval of the ACAA by the European Parliament. Similarly, the French groups Jforum, SIONA and BNVCA, with the support of CRIF, launched a petition to ask for the abrogation of the Goldstone Report after Goldstone partially retracted his conclusions on the war in Gaza in the pages of the *Washington Post* in April 2011 (CRIF 2011a). Similarly, the German NGOs EED/Misereor and Medico International and the French Plateforme des ONG françaises pour la Palestine and AFPS attempt, from time to time, to tackle EU issues in their lobbying efforts at the national level. For example, EED/Misereor lobbied the German government on issues related to settlement goods, the ACAA, the Europol Agreement between the EU and Israel, and the labelling of settlement goods, linking the German and EU dimensions of the issue at stake (Interviewee 100).

Second, and more frequently, internalisation is the consequence of the inputs coming from Brussels-based NGOs (especially umbrella groups), which push NSAs based in member states to lobby their governments and parliaments on issues related to EU foreign policy. Brussels-based NSAs confirm that there is a gap between the lobbying carried out at the national and EU levels, with the former being often unaware of what happens in Brussels and not understanding the complementarity of the two levels (Interviewee 2). In light of their expertise, Brussels-based NSAs help national actors to lobby at the national level or they carry out direct lobbying there (see Chapters 4–6). For example, the EMHRN organised, together with APRODEV, a training programme in which national NGOs were taught how to lobby and what they can do at the national level to influence EU policies. They also prepared a toolkit for NGOs, strategies and recommendations that national NGOs can use in their advocacy work at the national level (Euro-Mediterranean Human Rights Network 2013). There has been, therefore, a clear attempt to develop a methodology of lobbying that can be employed by NSAs at both the EU and national levels, as Brussels-based NSAs consider the national arena as necessary in order to exert influence on EU foreign policy (Interviewees 2, 4, 60). Another example of Brussels-based NSAs providing NSAs based in member states with inputs on EU policies is offered by the ECCP. This group identifies the priorities and sends relevant information to the national groups, suggesting how they can lobby their governments in order to influence their position in the EU. In the case of the ACAA (see Chapter 6), the ECCP prepared an open letter that national solidarity groups were supposed to disseminate among their members, inviting them to send it to their MEPs to show public opposition to the approval of the agreement.

This top-down instruction from Brussels-based to member state-based NSAs is also related to another mode of Europeanisation, namely supranationalisation. Some NSAs based in member states have recognised the relevance of the EU and have, therefore, decided to pool and share their resources by creating umbrella organisations in Brussels (Interviewee 4). This has generated a sort of division of labour between national and EU levels, whereby Brussels-based NGOs focus on EU issues, and national groups on national concerns (Interviewee 82). Moreover, umbrella organisations are meant to help NGOs and solidarity movements to overcome the problem of not being present in Brussels, as they represent national NSAs and forward their requests at the EU level. They also, however, collect information at the EU level and pass it on to national groups, thus guaranteeing that the national level is not completely cut off from the events in Brussels. For example, CIDSE asks its member organisations in member states to lobby their parliaments and governments: it provides them with parliamentary questions, letters for campaigns etc. Lobbying at the EU level is mainly used as an added-value to the work done at the national level (Interviewee 5). Similarly, the EJC also does strong lobbying at the national level via its national organisations, as member states are considered central in EU foreign policy (Interviewee 52). However, coordination between the activities carried out at the two levels and across EU member states is not always easy. On the one hand, NSAs based in member states do not lobby on the same issues that are dealt with in Brussels and focus on national concerns, unless explicitly asked to do otherwise (Interview 2). On the other hand, NSAs have different priorities and different contexts in which to operate, so that this diversity does not always allow for coordinated and shared lobbying actions (Interviewee 61).

Finally, some NSAs represent their interests directly in Brussels and lobby the EU on EU-related aspects of foreign policy. This fourth mode of Europeanisation, which often includes the opening of an office in Brussels to ensure a constant presence in the EU, is not the most common option. The majority of NSAs based in member states are relatively small, carry out activities on the basis of volunteers and have limited financial resources. Not only does this lack of resources prevent them from being able to go to Brussels, it can also hamper their ability to develop expertise as far as EU-related issues are concerned. Due to their familiarity with their own government and national context, they prefer to work at their local/national level. Brussels remains a second choice, if at all (Interviewee 87). Among British, French and German NSAs, NGOs such as Oxfam, Amnesty International or FIDH have an international outreach and, normally, an office in Brussels. These NSAs are big enough to conduct lobbying at different levels and use the national channel as a way to lobby the EU as well (Interviewees 8, 52, 89). Other cases of partial externalisation are isolated lobbying actions in the EU when specific topics are considered. For example, the Plateforme des ONG françaises pour la Palestine and its member organisations bombarded French MEPs with emails and letters in order to convince them not to vote in favour of the EU–Israel agreement on Community programmes in December 2010 (Hecker 2010).

To summarise, NSAs based in EU member states have Europeanised their lobbying, but only to a limited extent. The majority of them still focus on national foreign policies towards Israel and Palestine and conduct lobbying only with this national dimension in mind. There are examples of Europeanisation patterns along the forms of internalisation, supranationalisation and externalisation, but links between the EU and national arenas remain relatively weak and are generally established by Brussels-based NSAs, more than as a bottom-up movement coming from NSAs based in member states.

Adversarial roles at the national level?

NSAs lobbying in member states are considered important actors able to provide information and knowledge to national officials and politicians. In particular, NGOs are seen as crucial sources of information (Interviewees 79, 87, 88, 98, 101, 106, 107, 109), which provide early warning of coming problems or changes in the situation on the ground. NGOs from Israel and Palestine have frequently been mentioned in interviews: they offer updated information and a first-hand view on the facts taking place on the ground. Similarly, big NGOs that have branches around the world, like Oxfam and Amnesty International, are seen as credible partners that national officials and politicians trust and rely on. Therefore, there is a constant dialogue between national officials/MPs and NSAs (Interviewees 79, 87, 88, 98, 101, 106, 107, 109).

NSAs also rely on inside lobbying based on face-to-face meetings, email exchanges, etc., with intensification in the number of contacts and interactions when specific events take place. For example, NGOs were particularly active in France on the issue of the flotilla in May/June 2010 and on the vote on Palestinian statehood in September 2011: this translated into more pressure on policy-makers than the normal routine (Interviewee 79). However, NSAs in member states play the role of opponents and voice-articulators more often than NSAs based in Brussels. Instead of working behind the scenes, NSAs frequently rely on voice approaches which convey information and knowledge in public spheres and involve a larger audience than only policy-makers and officials. The involvement of the public and the increase in the awareness of people about the situation in Israel/Palestine is seen as crucial by many NSAs, to the extent that some of them argued that their main task is the education of civil society, an aspect that some of them consider as more relevant than direct lobbying (e.g., Interviewee 84).

Many NSAs also express their dissent to EU and national policies through letter campaigns, demonstrations and other forms of public protest, using litigation and protest politics as their main approach. This way, NSAs aim to exert pressure on policy-makers by exploiting the direct link between politicians and their constituencies. The blockade of Gaza is an example of an adversarial role played by NSAs. In particular, solidarity movements and NGOs organised a variety of initiatives aimed at demonstrating their opposition to the blockade of Gaza and pushing for a change of the situation on the ground. For instance, the French Plateforme des ONG françaises pour la Palestine organised a campaign called 'Un bateau français pour Gaza' in order to send two boats as part of this international flotilla (Plateforme des ONG françaises Pour la Palestine 2012). The UK-based Palestine Solidarity Campaign (PSC) organised a rally on the 18 January 2011 asking for the end of the siege of Gaza with a view to demonstrating public support to the people in Gaza.[7] Every year, this solidarity group also organises the 'National Lobby of Parliament for Palestine'. People are invited to lobby their MPs on topics that are decided by the PSC, such as the settlements, the expulsion of Palestinians from their homes, the rights of Palestinian prisoners and child prisoners and so on. The aim of these forms of protest politics is to show politicians that they do not have the support of public opinion, a fact that might work against their popularity and their electoral success. Therefore, these confrontational forms of social interactions are based on the NSAs' belief that the power of public opinion and the strength of public opinion can exert pressure on the government, given the politicisation of national political systems (e.g., Interviewees 79, 80, 81, 98, 101).

A strongly confrontational form of social interaction is also used by the BDS campaign, namely the Boycott, Divestment and Sanctions movement born in 2005 in Palestine, which soon spread out around the world. By targeting individuals, business groups and states, the BDS movement calls for boycotting Israeli goods, divesting from and sanctioning Israel until it withdraws from the OPTs and acknowledges the rights of the Palestinian people. There are BDS branches in all the three states analysed in this chapter and, in each of them, lobbying has been based on confrontational interactions, but has taken slightly different forms and targets. For example, in Germany, where the BDS movement is still very limited, there is a day of protest per year against Galerie Kaufhof, which sells agricultural, Ahava and Soda Stream products coming from the settlements. Protesters stage a peaceful protest by going to the Galerie wearing red t-shirts with messages against settlements and in favour of Palestine, with a view to raising customers' attention and to explaining them why they should boycott certain goods (Interviewee 96; BDS 2012). In contrast, the French branch of the BDS has mostly been active as far as the divestment part of the BDS campaign is concerned. In particular, their actions and leaflets targeted two French companies, Connex and Alstom, involved in the construction of the railway between Jerusalem and Tel Aviv. Besides providing information concerning the railway and the related problems, the movement also invited French citizens to get in touch with the French government and the public authorities responsible for transport asking for the withdrawal of the contract with Connex, and to write to newspapers and other media outlets to make bad publicity for these two companies (BDS 2009).

Linked to the issue of settlements and the boycott, the German branch of Pax Christi launched a campaign in 2012 called 'Besatzung schmeckt bitter' (Occupation tastes bitter), in which they called for an appropriate labelling of goods and for a boycott of those goods that are not clearly identifiable as Israeli or Palestinian and might come from the settlements. The campaign has some public support, but it has remained a niche issue, without managing to generate a public debate in the media. According to German officials (Interviewees 98, 101, 107), the discourse on goods coming from the settlement has slowly become an issue of public concern, but it still raises suspicion not only among officials and policy-makers, but also among German citizens due to the legacy of the Nazi period.

Finally, another form of confrontational interaction characterising the role of opponent is litigation. This approach is used more frequently at the national level than at the EU level. Unlike the case of Brita GmbH, many NSAs do not target a national court to challenge EU legislation or policies, and direct their attention only to national policies and issues related to the national context. For example, the French AFSP employed the legal pathway to force certain French companies to divest from the settlements. By targeting business groups, they were also challenging the state for not intervening in cases of violations of human rights and humanitarian concerns. The group presented a claim against Veolia and Alstom for their involvement in the construction of the railway between Jerusalem and Tel Aviv on the basis of violations of the Geneva Conventions and the French Civil Code (articles 6, 1131 and 1133), according to which economic contracts contrary to public order and good morals can be cancelled (Interviewee 84; Nieuwhof and Lherm 2007; Association France Palestine Solidarité 2011; Lacorie 2012). Although the case was submitted in 2007, it was some years before it was established whether it fell under the competence of French tribunal to decide on the case. The first judgment given by the Tribunal de grande instance of Nanterre in 2011 maintained that international law is not applicable to private actors, but the AFPS appealed the decision. The case was finally concluded on 22 May 2013, with the Cour d'Appel de Versailles confirming the previous decision (Veolia 2013).

While NSAs in member states played various roles, the role of the opponent was played more frequently than at the EU level. This is likely to reflect the higher level of politicisation at the national level which favours a more adversarial approach than in the EU context, where NSAs prefer to opt for a more consensual stance.

Lobbying through political frames?

In all three member states NSAs rely on political frames to a greater extent than NSAs based in Brussels. Sometimes mixed frames are also used, especially by the big NGOs, while the employment of technical frames is more rare. In the majority of cases, as indicated above, NSAs based in member states pay more attention to national foreign policies, paying marginal attention to the EU dimension.

Political frames are quite evident when it comes to the topic of settlements. NSAs working at the national level tend to rely on emotional and ideational aspects that resonate with public opinion and to offer arguments that suit the competition among politicians. Therefore, these frames are based on the idea of injustice and discrimination or on the fact that there is inconsistency between the declared and implemented policies. A clear example of this type of frame is provided by the BDS movement, whose name (Boycott, Divestment and Sanctions) has already a strong political connotation that resonates in people's minds. Moreover, the BDS campaign refers to Israel as an apartheid state and urges people and politicians to take action against the state on the basis of its wrongdoings, as it was done in the case of South Africa.[8] The points presented are not supported by strong empirical credibility, but work mainly on the ideational centrality of shared beliefs. This also explains why the focus on the three member states is slightly different: the context of action shapes the type of issue that can be raised and how this can be done. The British branch tends to support all three actions of boycott, divestment and sanctions, with a strong engagement from the public. In contrast, the German context poses severe limits to the ability of NSAs to use this type of argument due to the historical legacies. The image of boycott is still strongly associated with the boycott imposed by the Nazi regime on Jewish shops and products. There is little resonance for this argument not only among politicians and officials, but also among the public. France is a middle-way case, as part of the society is receptive to this campaign, but there are legal constraints to what can be done in practice.[9] Together with the call for boycott, the French NGO AFPS also focuses on divestment by taking actions against French companies that are involved in the settlements, such as Veolia and Alstom.

Similarly, Pax Christi launched a campaign against settlement products under the slogan 'Besatzung Schmeckt Bitter'. In a short document explaining the goals of the campaign, there were references to the problem of labelling and the deprivation of the Palestinian people of their natural resources and proper conditions of living due to Israeli policies. By communicating ideas of injustice and exploitation, emotional links were raised among the people. It also stressed that the boycott of Jewish products in 1933 and the current call for boycott were very different: 'Boycottmassnahmen, die Menschen Unrecht antun, und zivilgesellschaftiche Aktionen, die Menschen Recht verschaffen wollen, sind jedoch zwei unterschiedliche Dinge. Menschen- und vöelkrechtswidrigen Umständen seine Unterstützung zu verweigern, ist eine legitime ethische Entscheidung'[10] (Pax Christi Deutschland 2012). There is a clear reference to the moral value of choosing products in light of the protection of human rights, an argument that corresponds to the features of political frames.

In relation to the settlements, NSAs also raise concerns about the negative implications on the ground. Not only do settlements lead to the fragmentation of what should be the territory of a future Palestinian state, but they have also created systems that differentiate between the rights of Israelis and Palestinians. Israeli citizens have better infrastructures and services, while Palestinians are often denied basic services and access to their own land. In this regard, the AFSP campaigned against the construction of the 'wall' or 'separation barrier' that Israel started building in 2002 along its border with the West Bank, defining it as the 'Mur d'Apartheid' (Association France Palestine Solidarité 2012a). By drawing clear references to ethical principles, issues were framed in such a way as to raise parallels to the South African apartheid regime in order to mobilise more people. In other cases, NGOs stress the inconsistency of their government's foreign policy towards settlements. For example, in July 2012 Christian Aid asked the British government to 'ban settlement produce by putting in place effective legislation to stop products reaching our markets' on the basis of the condemnation by the international community of settlements as illegal and the United Kingdom's declaration that describes them as "the greatest obstacle to peace" between Israel and the Palestinians'.[11]

Those NSAs that support Israel in their lobbying activities tend to adopt political frames referring to Israel's security, to the idea of discrimination against Israel and to anti-Semitism. For example, the CRIF strongly criticised France for its vote in favour of the admission of Palestine at UNESCO in December 2011. It argued that this vote was not in line with President Sarkozy's declaration in the General Assembly, according to which the admission would be conditioned upon the restart of peace negotiations, the renunciation of terrorism and the acceptance of a two-state solution. It further stressed the danger of cultural negationism made by Muslim states that try to appropriate Jewish cultural heritage (CRIF 2011c). Another important point has been the fight against anti-Semitism. The CRIF has been vocal about this risk in France, but it has also referred to it in cases of criticisms towards Israeli policies (CRIF 2011b). The Iranian nuclear problem has also been an issue of lobbying, with a specific focus on the dangers that a nuclear

Iran entails for Israel and a request for a tough stance from the West against Iran. For instance, in the October 2012 Hannover Declaration the Deutsche–Israelische Gesellschaft (DIG) called on the EU and the German government to exert pressure on Iran, given Iran's 'persistent refusal to comply with the five United Nations resolutions and suspend their uranium enrichment program until the allegations have been clarified'. In the DIG's view, '[t]he Iranian nuclear weapons program is not only a threat to Israel ... but also endangers the balance of global security and peace in the region'. Thus, the DIG pushed the German government to 'urgently call for further stricter sanctions to be declared against Iran on all levels', both within the European Union and in other international fora (DIG 2012).

Similarly, some groups ask for a stronger bilateral relationship between their country and Israel by emphasising the advanced and democratic status of Israel. This way, they try to disentangle Israel from the broader context of the conflict, which they do not see as a fair yardstick with which to deal with Israel (Interviewee 104). For example, the DIW aims to further develop the trade relationship between Germany and Israel, without linking commercial aspects with the advancement of political issues.[12] Similarly, the Association France–Israël states that:

> France–Israël doit faire connaître les vérités d'Israël et, en même temps, lutter contre l'entreprise de délégitimation qui en fait un coupable permanent devant les nations, ... agit pour défendre l'image et les droits d'Israël. ... aujourd'hui, les nations française et israélienne sont menacées par des ennemis identiques: la détestation de l'État-Nation, l'islamo-fascisme et l'extrémisme de droite et de gauche. Le mot d'ordre de France–Israël est donc: 'Quand nous défendons la France nous défendons Israël, et quand nous défendons Israël nous défendons la France!'[13] (Association France–Israël 2013)

In other words, these examples show how the proposed frames are not supported by empirical, technical or legal elements, but rely on ethical, moral and emotional aspects that stress ideas of shared values, discrimination and threats to people, with a view to mobilising the public in support of their view. Given that politicians are elected by citizens and have to ensure that the interests of their constituencies are pursued, political aspects are useful to get the attention of policy-makers and to help them 'sell' some policies to their constituencies (Interviewee 106).

Although the majority are political frames, there are also instances of mixed frames. For example, a coalition of UK NGOs published a report in March 2008, highlighting the consequences of Israeli blockade of Gaza as far as basic public and medical services for the Gazans were concerned (Oxfam GB 2008).[14] Figures and data backed up the argument of the report and the sources of information were properly referenced. Unlike technical frames, however, there was also a political argument. To start with, the title was evocative, as it referred to a 'humanitarian implosion', conveying the idea of a failure of the international community to prevent a humanitarian disaster. In the final recommendations to the British government and the EU, there were the classical recommendations of exerting pressure on Israel, condemning Israeli policies, etc., thus failing to frame the discourse differently from the usual view of the debate on the Israeli–Palestinian conflict. Similarly reports such as *Failing Gaza: No Rebuilding, No Recovery, No More Excuses* and *Dashed Hopes: Continuation of the Gaza Blockade* refer to the lack of development in Gaza. Again, the titles aim to send a political message and to make claims related to the inconsistencies and failures of the policies implemented by the international community to deal with the situation in Gaza. Claims are supported by data and various sources, but they do not offer a new lens through which the issue can be considered (Oxfam International 2009, 2010).

Finally, the only NSA found that used technical frames (with a legal perspective) at the national level was the German NGO EED/Misereor, which conducted its lobbying on the basis of the concept of third state responsibility. This legal argument revolves around the obligations of the EU and its member states under international law, international humanitarian law and EU law. The EED/Misereor interacts with German policy-makers by stressing the need for Germany to comply with international law. The adoption of a legal perspective triggers interest in officials and policy-makers and, at the same time, offers a shield against criticisms of anti-Semitism or guilt for historical reasons, thus being a way to overcome some of the obstacles of the German context (Interviewee 100).

Overall, the majority of NSAs based in member states rely on political frames based on emotional or moral issues. This seems to reflect the politicised nature of national political systems. By using these political frames, NSAs aim to educate public opinion and make it more attentive to certain issues. This way, they try to lobby national officials and policy-makers indirectly, through the pressure exerted by the public. Political frames are therefore suited for this purpose. MPs are more likely to use these arguments, as they provide features that they can sell to their constituencies. Furthermore, these arguments have a clear political stance that is easily transferable to a political debate, thus making them more suitable for parliamentary settings. For example, a member of the Bundestag (Interviewee 106) recalls issues such as the destruction of German-funded constructions in Area C or the issue of the involvement of Deutsche Bahn in the construction of the Tel Aviv–Jerusalem train. These topics were discussed in the Bundestag thanks to the input given by NGOs (a similar view was also confirmed by Interviewee 109, who mentioned the issue of the 'separation barrier' in 2002–3). Some NGOs, especially big international ones or coalitions, also employ mixed frames, supporting their argument by empirical evidence and detailed analysis, but always keeping a political component that tends to reproduce the mainstream approach and discourse on the Israeli–Palestinian conflict.

Conclusions

Lobbying in member states is important. NSAs provide information that national officials and MPs can use in their work (Interviewees 87, 98, 101, 107). Moreover, they raise attention on specific issues, especially inside national parliaments (Interviewees 87, 106). However, the majority of NSAs tend to concentrate their efforts on national foreign policies, paying marginal attention to the EU dimension. While lobbying has been partially Europeanised (as the previous chapters have also shown), EU and national lobbying activities are only partially integrated. This leads to the idea that the EU and member states are often two disentangled arenas. This means that some NSAs based in member states occasionally include EU issues in their lobbying, that some of them lobby directly the EU on its foreign policy towards Israel–Palestine and that they have created umbrella organisations that represent their interests in Brussels. There are, however, some caveats to be made in this regard. As shown, internalisation – that is, the inclusion of EU issues in their lobbying actions – is often the consequence of inputs that NSAs based in member states receive from Brussels-based NSAs: the latter push the former to include EU issues in their lobbying at the national level.

Supranationalisation, the creation of umbrella organisations to represent their interests in Brussels, does not necessarily bring about coordinated efforts between the EU and national levels. It often seems as if the two arenas are completely separated, with Brussels-based and member state-based NSAs working on different issues. Finally, externalisation (direct lobbying in Brussels) is limited and generally confined to big NGOs or business groups. The majority of NSAs do not have the capacity to conduct direct lobbying in Brussels, much less to have a permanent office there.

When lobbying, NSAs based in member states predominantly play the role of opponent and use political frames. Unlike the EU level, the reliance on forms of protest politics such as letter campaigns and demonstrations, or litigation are more common at the national than at the EU level, where a consensual approach tends to be the predominant mode of interaction. While the use of more confrontational approaches is in line with the higher level of politicisation of national arenas, this form does not lead to constructive interactions between policy-makers and NSAs. At the same time, however, political frames with a strong ideational centrality and evoking values, historical events and common image are likely to resonate at the national level, especially among MPs and public opinion.

Notes

1 Location of NSAs is based on the location of their headquarters. The data are taken from the database presented in Chapter 3, thus some of the problems and limitations identified there also apply here. First, French, German and British NSAs have been identified on the basis of secondary sources, existing databases and through a snowball process. This implies that the amount of retrieved data might be unbalanced due to the different access to sources. Second, some NSAs have been excluded from the dataset, whenever they were not relevant to this study, as they were not engaged in any lobbying activity (e.g., some cultural groups). Despite possible mistakes in the inclusion of NSAs in the database, the mapping is as comprehensive as possible. It might still be the case that those NSAs with a low level of activities or those working in a very secretive and non-public way are not included, but interviews and the other sources ensured that the most important NSAs are listed.

2 While reports on British business group involvement exist (e.g., Van Gelder and H. Kroes 2009), similar analysis for France and Germany has not been found. Therefore, the figures for French and German groups are probably underestimated. This is especially true for the German case, given the fact that Germany is the biggest trading partner of Israel among EU countries.

3 Each foundation is linked to one political party. The funding system is indeed based on the share of votes that political parties receive. Although there is a clear connection between parties and foundations, the latter are independent from political control.

4 In order to identify the Europeanisation patterns, an analysis of lobbying activities has been conducted. First, the mapping described in the previous section has allowed for the identification of NSAs. Second, the websites of these NSAs have been analysed to understand their nature and explore the issues they work on. Third, 30 interviews with NSAs, national officials and experts were carried out between 2011 and 2012. In addition, umbrella organisations based in Brussels have been asked about their member organisations and how they work with NGOs based in member states. The combination of these three steps has made it possible to identify the key trends and features of the population of NSAs active in the United Kingdom, Germany and France and the type of activities they carry out.

5 http://www.palestinecampaign.org/Index5b.asp?m_id=1&11_id=3&12_ id=137&Content_ID=2829 (accessed 15 October 2012; web address no longer live).

6 http://www.kopi-online.de/joomla/ (accessed 13 October 2012).

7 http://www.palestinecampaign.org/index9b.asp?m_id=1&11_id=4&12_ id=99&Content_ID=1648 (accessed on 23 October 2012; web address no longer live).

8 See www.bdsmovement.net

9 Some courts prohibited the boycott according to the anti-discrimination act of 1981, as 'incitement to discrimination, hatred or violence against a person or a group of persons on the basis of descent, ethnicity and nationality or the fact whether or not one belongs to a race or a religion'. In other cases, the courts acquitted the defendants on grounds of freedom of expression (Interviewee 83; BDS 2011).

10 Boycotts that are unjust and civil society actions aiming at bringing about justice are two different endeavours. Not to support human rights and public international law is thus a legitimate and ethical decision (author's translation).

11 See http://www.christianaid.org.uk/whatwedo/middle-east/take-action-to-ban-israeli-settlement-produce.aspx (accessed 20 June 2013).

12 See their website, www.d-i-w.de (accessed 20 June 2013).

13 France–Israël must make known the truths of Israël and, at the same time, fight against the attempt at delegitimation that would make Israel a permanent guilty party in the view of the nations, … act to defend the image and the rights of Israel. … today, the French and Israeli peoples are menaced by the same enemies: hatred of the nation-state, Islam-Fascism and the right and left extremisms. The word of action of France–Israël is therefore: 'When we defend France, we defend Israel; and when we defend Israel, we defend France!' (author's translation).

14 The coalition of NGOs presenting the report was composed of Amnesty International UK, CARE International UK, Christian Aid, CAFOD, Medicins du Monde UK, Oxfam, Save the Children UK and Trocaire. The last of these is the only Irish organisation of the coalition.

References

Asseburg, Muriel and Jan Busse. 2011. 'Deutschlands Politik Gegenueber Israel'. In *Deutsche Außenpolitik, Sicherheit, Wohlfahrt, Institutionen, Normen*, by Thomas Jaegen, Alexander Hoese and Kai Oppermann. Wiesbaden: VS Verlag für Sozialwissenschaften. 693–716.

Association France–Israël. 2013. 'L'assoc'. http://www.france-israel.org/page. ahd?idrub=5

Association France Palestine Solidarité. 2011. *Dossier de Presse. Tramway de Jérusalem: Des Entreprises Françaises Complices de La Colonisation*. Paris.

———. 2012a. 'Israël va reprendre la construction du mur d'apartheid autour de Jérusalem'. http://www.france-palestine.org/Israel-va-reprendre-la

———. 2012b. 'Eurodéputés français, dites non à l'ACAA!' http://www.france-palestine. org/Eurodeputes-francais-dites-non-a-l

Balme, Richard and Didier Chabanet. 2002. 'Action collective et gouvernance de l'Union européenne'. In *L'action collective en Europe*, edited by Richard Balme, Didier Chabanet and Vincent Wright. Paris: Presses de Sciences Po. 21–120.

BDS. 2009. 'Tract contre Connex et Alstom'. 9 December. http://www.bdsfrance.org/ index.php?option=com_content&view=article&id=15&Itemid=17&lang=fr (web address no longer live).

———. 2011. 'France: Yes, the Boycott of Israel Is Legal'. 17 September. http://www. bdsmovement.net/2011/france-yes-the-boycott-of-israel-is-legal-17sep11-8121

———. 2012. 'BDS Activists in Germany Target Galeria Kaufhof'. 2 April. http://www. bdsmovement.net/2012/8830-8830

Blunden, Margaret. 2000. 'France'. In *The Foreign Policies of European Union Member States*, edited by Ian Manners and Richard Whitman. Manchester: Manchester University Press. 19–43.

CRIF. 2011a. 'Pétition internationale pour l'abrogation du Rapport Goldstone'. http:// www.crif.org/fr/lecrifenaction/Petition-internationale-pour-l-abrogation-du-rapport-Goldstone24421

———. 2011b. 'Lutter contre le racisme et l'antisémitisme'. 11 October. http://www.crif. org/fr/lecrifenaction/lutter-contre-le-racisme-et-l%E2%80%99antis%C3%A9mitisme/ 5?language=fr

———. 2011c. 'UNESCO: le CRIF déplore le vote de la France'. http://crif.org/fr/ communiquedepresse/UNESCO-le-CRIF-deplore-le-vote-de-la-France26687

DIG (Deutsche–Israelische Gesellschaft). 2012. 'Hannover Declaration of the German–Israeli Association on the Current Situation in Israeli and Middle-East'. http://www. deutsch-israelische-gesellschaft.de/bund/im-fokus/showme/hannoveraner-erklaerung

Eising, Rainer. 2009. *The Political Economy of State–Business Relations in Europe*. Abingdon/New York: Routledge.

Euro-Mediterranean Human Rights Network. 2013. 'EMHRN Training Guide and Advocacy Toolkit'. 15 January. http://euromedrights.org/publication/emhrn-training-guide-and-toolkit-on-eu-advocacy/

Foreign Office. 2012. 'Israel'. http://webarchive.nationalarchives.gov.uk/20121212135632/ http://www.fco.gov.uk/en/travel-and-living-abroad/travel-advice-by-country/country-profile/middle-east-north-africa/israel/?profile=tradeInvestment

Foster, Anthony. 2000. 'Britain'. In *The Foreign Policies of European Union Member States*, edited by Ian Manners and Richard Whitman. Manchester: Manchester University Press. 44–65.

Ghiles Meilhac, Samuel. 2011. *Le CRIF: de la résistance juive à la tentation du lobby, de 1943 à nos jours*. Paris: Robert Laffont.

Harnisch, Sebastian. 2013. 'Germany Foreign Policy: Gulliver's Travails in the 21st Century'. In *Foreign Policy in Comparative Perspective: Domestic and International Influences on State Behaviour*, edited by Ryan Beasley, Juliet Kaarbo, Jeffrey S. Lantis and Michael T. Snarr, 2nd edn. Thousand Oaks, CA: SAGE.

Hecker, Marc. 2010. 'Les acteurs transnationaux face à l'état: l'exemple du militantisme, en France, lié au conflit Israélo-Palestinien'. Doctorat de science politique, Paris: Université Paris 1 Panthéon-Sorbonne.

Hollis, Rosemary. 2010. *Britain and the Middle East in the 9/11 Era*. Chichester: Wiley-Blackwell.

International Monetary Fund. 2012. 'Direction of Trade Statistics. Edition October 2012'. Mimas, University of Manchester.

Lacorie, Pascal. 2012. 'Veolia jette l'éponge en Israël dans les transports en commun'. *AFPS – Groupe Local de l'Hérault*. 28 May. http://afps34.wordpress.com/2012/05/29/veolia-jette-leponge-en-israel-dans-les-transports-en-commun/

McCauley, Darren. 2011. 'Bottom-Up Europeanization Exposed: Social Movement Theory and Non-State Actors in France'. *Journal of Common Market Studies* 49 (5): 1019–42.

Musu, Costanza. 2010. *European Union Policy towards the Arab–Israeli Peace Process: The Quicksands of Politics*. Basingstoke: Palgrave Macmillan.

Nieuwhof, Adri and Maria Lherm. 2007. 'PLO Takes Veolia Transport and Alstom to Court in France'. *Electonic Intifada*, 20 November. http://electronicintifada.net/content/plo-takes-veolia-transport-and-alstom-court-france/7219

Oxfam GB. 2008. *The Gaza Strip: A Humanitarian Implosion*. http://policy-practice.oxfam.org.uk/publications/the-gaza-strip-a-humanitarian-implosion-126094

Oxfam International. 2009. *Failing Gaza: No Rebuilding, No Recovery, No More Excuses*. http://www.oxfam.org/policy/failing-gaza-no-rebuilding-no-recovery-no-more-excuses
———. 2010. *Dashed Hopes: Continuation of the Gaza Blockade*. http://www.oxfam.org/en/policy/dashed-hopes

Pax Christi Deutschland. 2012. 'Infoblatt: Besatzung Schmeckt Bitter'. http://www.paxchristi.de/fix/files/doc/Infoblatt_Webversion.pdf

Plateforme des ONG françaises Pour la Palestine. 2012. 'Un bateau français pour Gaza'. http://www.plateforme-palestine.org/spip.php?rubrique127

Risse-Kappen, Thomas. 1991. 'Public Opinion, Domestic Structure, and Foreign Policy in Liberal Democracies'. *World Politics* 43 (4): 479–512.

Saurugger, S. 2005. 'Europeanization as a Methodological Challenge: The Case of Interest Groups'. *Journal of Comparative Policy Analysis* 7 (4): 239–78.

Trésor. 2012a. 'Israël'. http://www.tresor.economie.gouv.fr/Pays/israel
———. 2012b. 'Le Commerce Bilatéral Entre Israël et La France en 2011'. February 10. http://www.tresor.economie.gouv.fr/4771_le-commerce-bilateral-entre-israel-et-la-france-en-2011

Van Gelder, J. W. and H. Kroes. 2009. *UK Economic Links with Israeli Settlements in Occupied Palestinian Territories*. Profundo. www.profundo.nl

Veolia. 2013. 'Projet de Tramway de Jérusalem'. http://www.veolia.com/fr/medias/dossiers/tramway-jerusalem.htm

Williams, Paul. 2004. 'Who's Making UK Foreign Policy?' *International Affairs* 80 (5): 911–29.

8   Conclusions

The Israeli–Palestinian conflict and lobbying are two issues of paramount importance in the study of the European Union (EU). On the one hand, the Israeli–Palestinian conflict has been on the EU's agenda since the beginning of European Policy Cooperation in the 1970s. Much has been written on EU policies on conflict resolution as well the EU's bilateral relations with the parties to the conflict. On the other hand, lobbying in the EU has received increased attention over the past decade. However, these two stories have not been told together. Scholars working on interest groups and lobbying have focused on several EU policies areas but not foreign policy (with the partial exception of EU foreign economic relations). Their attention has been on various facets of interest group activities, ranging from influence, civil society participation and the EU's democratic deficit, to the Europeanisation of interest representation and the differences between national systems of interest intermediation. While often treated as a special policy area where different rules apply, foreign policy is actually a policy domain where lobbyists are active, and understanding their involvement in the policy-making process is a key concern for both the scholarly community and public opinion. While some attention has been paid to non-state actors (NSAs) on the output side of EU external policy-making, as beneficiaries of EU funding or in implementing EU projects (Tocci 2011; Jünemann 2002), not much is known in terms of their work on the input side – that is, as far as their contribution to the formulation and shaping of EU external policy is concerned.

While the USA remains the most influential player in the Middle East Peace Process, and several scholars have investigated the influence of interest groups in shaping its policies (Goldberg 1990; Mearsheimer and Walt 2007), the EU has also progressively established a well-defined position towards the Israeli–Palestinian conflict and, despite strong criticisms for its rhetoric–practice gap (e.g., Tocci 2005), it has nonetheless established its presence in the region and is part of the efforts of the international community to solve the conflict (see Chapter 2). Because of its involvement in the Peace Process and the well-developed bilateral relationships that the EU has established with most of its southern neighbouring countries – including Israel and the Palestinians – the EU is an important target for NSAs, which aim at influencing its policies according to their preferences. Investigating who these NSAs are, and how they work and interact with the EU, is therefore an important academic task that tackles recurrent questions in the academic debates about who has influence in the policy-making process and how. Starting with the question of whether NSAs matter in the EU's foreign policy-making process, this book has thus told the story of lobbying in EU foreign policy, using the case of the Israeli–Palestinian conflict. This has been organised around three interrelated dimensions. First, the book has asked *what role, if any, NSAs play in EU foreign policy-making*. Second, it has investigated *what type of frames NSAs use in their lobbying actions*. Finally, it has analysed *at what level NSAs exert their lobbying and how the EU and national levels are linked in lobbying activities*.

By conducting an exploratory case study, this book has made both theoretical and empirical contributions. Theoretically, it has demonstrated that NSAs are very active in the foreign policy domain and contribute substantially to the formation of EU policies. While they are not the only actors shaping EU policies, they still need to be included in the analysis, as their contribution to framing EU foreign policy can be – on the basis of the roles played, the frames proposed and the levels at which they act – significant. By shedding light on NSA lobbying, this book thus challenges the widespread view that NSAs do not matter in foreign policy and it broadens the debates in both the literature on interest groups and that on EU foreign policy by adding to the predominant rational-choice perspective of the former and to the more state/institution-centred studies of the latter. Moreover, by building on insights from constructivism, it has shed light on the embeddedness of the actors involved in lobbying and the social interactions that NSAs and the EU develop. Metaphorically, this idea has been visualised by comparing lobbying to a performance on the stage of a theatre: the actors perform a script and the performance itself is based on the interactions among the different players and the context as well. Actors are interdependent, with each of them needing the others in order to perform their own part. The final outcome is the result of what develops on the stage, with the boundaries set by the script, but the actions and modes of expressions depending on those performing and on the stage itself. The 'whos' (the other actors) and 'wheres' (which context) are going to shape the performance itself, the role each actor plays and the frames that are used.

This book has not taken a black-or-white view on NSAs, arguing that they are all-powerful or are completely without influence. In contrast, it has adopted a more nuanced reading of EU foreign policy and of who plays a role in its policy-making. Lobbying is a very complicated issue which requires a nuanced and multifaceted understanding of how NSA–EU relations develop. NSAs play various roles within the EU foreign policy-making process, with some of them being able to develop cooperative social interactions with EU officials and politicians, which can lead to the mutual understanding of the issue at stake and to the reframing of EU policies. In contrast, other NSAs challenge the EU and the legitimacy of its policies: common understanding and a reframing of policies are less likely to happen. Counterfactuals showing what would have happened in the absence of lobbying are not easy to determine. As said, the book does not want to draw the conclusions that it was only because of NSAs that the EU took certain decisions. What it aims to show is that the role of NSAs cannot be ignored, as they, together with other actors at the EU and national levels, contributed to the final outcome by playing a role in the framing processes which are at the basis of the decisions taken.

Empirically, this book broadens our knowledge of EU foreign policy and of lobbying in two ways. First, the book provides an original dataset composed of over 300 NSAs, which allows us to have a better understanding of the types of NSAs involved or potentially interested in EU foreign policy towards the Israeli–Palestinian conflict. Second, the book provides an in-depth analysis of three crucial issues related to the EU's foreign policy towards the Israeli–Palestinian conflict, namely the issue of trade between the EU and Israel that involves goods produced in the settlements, the case of the Goldstone Report following the Gaza war in December 2008–January 2009, and the EU–Israel Agreement on Conformity Acceptance and Assessment of pharmaceutical products. By analysing issues that have not received systematic attention in the literature on the EU and the Israeli–Palestinian conflict, this research offers new insights into the relations that the EU has with the parties to the conflict and into its broader role in the Peace Process.

This chapter summarises and compares the main findings of the empirical analysis in light of the framework proposed in Chapter 1. The first section discusses the roles and frames that shape NSA lobbying and how this impacts on their ability to influence EU foreign policy towards the conflict. It then elaborates on the levels used by NSAs, reflecting on how this aspect deserves further research to highlight the links between venues and the differences between lobbying at the national and EU levels. The final section reflects on the implications of these findings and proposes new avenues for further research.

NSAs in EU foreign policy: roles and frames

Roles and frames are two critical dimensions that allow us to investigate lobbying in EU foreign policy, by highlighting the social interactions that develop among the EU and NSAs and the potential (re)framing of EU policies. In the case studies, it has been shown that conceiving lobbying exclusively as a strategic behaviour does not capture the entire story. Social interactions between the EU and NSAs shape how actors understand a situation, make sense of information and (re)frame EU policies towards Israel and Palestine. The main finding is that roles and frames need to be considered together. Adopting a consensual approach that does not challenge EU legitimacy and using a technical frame makes NSA involvement in and contribution to the policy-making process more likely. In contrast, the more political the argumentation used and the more confrontational NSAs are, the less likely it is for the EU to be responsive to their pressures.

The concept of role is useful to encapsulate the relationship between the EU and NSAs, as it defines the features that characterise actors' behaviours (and performances) and clearly conveys the idea of social embeddedness through the metaphor of the 'stage'. As explained in Chapter 1, the different types of roles allow us to highlight the level of contention between the EU and NSAs and the

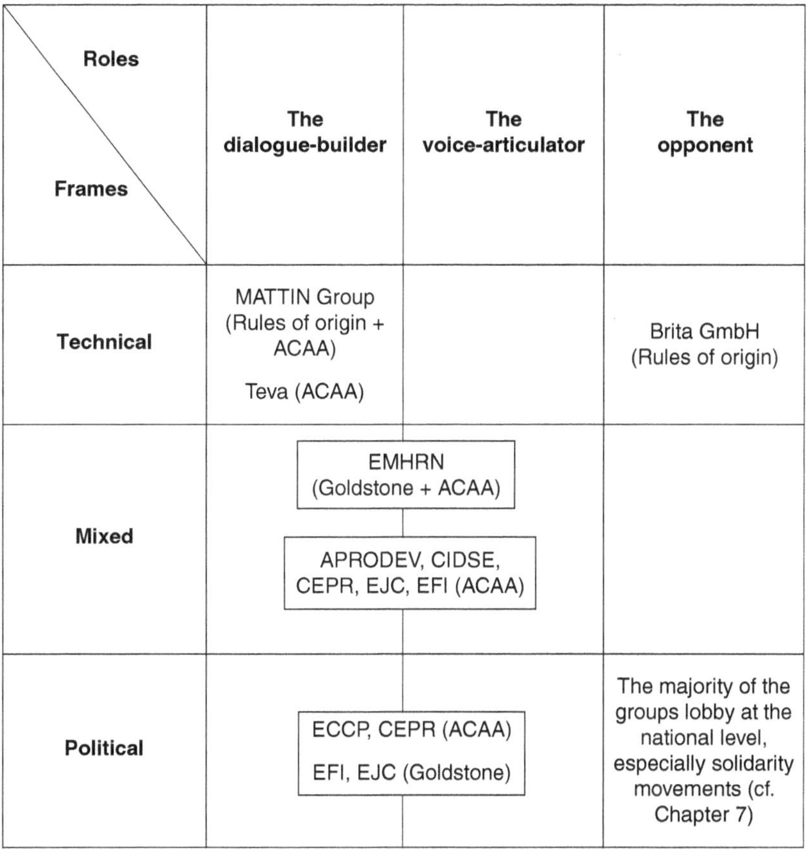

Roles / Frames	The dialogue-builder	The voice-articulator	The opponent
Technical	MATTIN Group (Rules of origin + ACAA) Teva (ACAA)		Brita GmbH (Rules of origin)
Mixed		EMHRN (Goldstone + ACAA) APRODEV, CIDSE, CEPR, EJC, EFI (ACAA)	
Political		ECCP, CEPR (ACAA) EFI, EJC (Goldstone)	The majority of the groups lobby at the national level, especially solidarity movements (cf. Chapter 7)

Figure 8.1 Matrix of roles and frames in NSA lobbying in the case of EU foreign policy towards the Israeli–Palestinian conflict

modes through which they interact. As summarised in Figure 8.1, the cases of the rules of origin in EU–Israel trade relations, of the Goldstone Report and of the EU–Israel ACAA have shown that the majority of NSAs active at the EU level play the roles of dialogue-builder or voice-articulator. This means that NSAs rely on either an access approach or a voice approach based on information politics. By adopting a consensual role, NSAs can establish cooperative interactions with EU officials and policy-makers and, through dialogue, they can achieve a shared understanding of the situation at stake. This is clearly demonstrated in the case of the MATTIN Group which, in both the cases of the rules of origin and the ACAA, interacted with EU officials and policy-makers and established a dialogue that led to the common understanding of the situation at stake and of how to interpret it. Through cooperative interactions, the MATTIN Group and the EU created the basis on which frames could travel and be developed.

Similarly, Teva played the role of dialogue-builder in the case of the ACAA: it worked behind the scenes, arranging meetings with EU officials and MEPs with a view to convincing them that parliamentary consent to the ACAA was in the EU's interest. By adopting an access approach, Teva managed to build working relations with some EU officials and to establish a dialogue through which the parties built up their knowledge and understanding on the ACAA. Both the MATTIN Group and Teva played a role that did not challenge the legitimacy of EU policies. In contrast, their approach was based on the idea of contributing to developing a shared understanding of EU policies.

Unlike the MATTIN Group and Teva, other NSAs swung between the roles of dialogue-builder and voice-articulator – that is, between a form of lobbying that takes place behind the scenes and an approach based on the involvement of the public. In this latter case, dialogue and the definition of a shared understanding on an issue is still possible, but it is more difficult to achieve. In the case of the Goldstone Report and the ACAA, the EMHRN, EFI and EJC relied on these two approaches in their lobbying actions. As explained in Chapter 5, the EMHRN was widely involved in the parliamentary works on the Goldstone Report, but the interactions leading to a common understanding of the problem occurred in meetings and discussion behind closed doors. This NGO was successful in bringing to the European Parliament a frame based on the concept of impunity, which found positive responses among MEPs. This was, however, the consequence of direct and constant contacts with the people involved and not so much due to the voice-articulator role based on press statements (information politics), with much less room for manoeuvre and for negotiating the meaning of issues.

In contrast, the role of opponent based on protest politics or litigation leads to confrontational interactions and mutual delegitimisation between NSAs and the EU. This is evident in the case of Brita GmbH, which relied on a litigation approach. By challenging EU policies via judicial means, there was no possibility for significant interaction between the EU and Brita GmbH that could bring about a different understanding of the problem. While examples of the role of opponent at the EU level are limited, there are various instances of it at the national level: NSAs based in member states rely on a confrontational stance more often than the NSAs based in Brussels, as shown in Chapter 7. Although the higher degree of politicisation at the national level would potentially make the national arena more responsive to a confrontational approach based on public campaigns, boycott actions and the mobilisation of public opinion, there was no strong evidence that the role of opponent has actually led to policy change. The role of NSAs was seen in a positive light in the member states analysed, but policy-makers and officials still seemed to prefer those NSAs that were not too challenging and confrontational.

Roles need to be analysed in conjunction with frames to have a clear understanding of lobbying actions and EU–NSA interactions. While frames are often conceived as strategic instruments used by NSAs to influence EU policies, this book has offered a more complex understanding of framing processes. Frames were not simply taken and accepted by the EU, but became the object of discussion, dialogue and reinterpretation that gave rise to new and shared views of EU foreign policy towards the Israeli–Palestinian conflict. As shown, technical frames are particularly suited to favour the reframing of EU foreign policy, although the European Parliament is also receptive to mixed frames. This can be explained on the basis of the nature of the institutions, namely the more technical nature of the Commission, which is also the guardian of the Treaties, and the more political features of the European Parliament, which is composed of elected members who need to respond to their constituencies.

Teva and the MATTIN Group provided the EU with frames characterised by strong empirical credibility and evidence, as these NSAs supported their claims with data, figures, legal and economic references and precise analyses of the issues at stake. Their frames also made clear references to key principles and values of the EU. For instance, Teva relied on the idea of free trade and the benefits of the ACAA to EU consumers and health care providers. The MATTIN Group instead based its argument on the legal obligations of the EU and the risks of violating its commitments under international law, international humanitarian law and human rights, as well as its own legislation. The EU legal framework and free trade represent two of the constituting elements and principles of the EU itself, so that they cannot be easily ignored by policy-makers. More importantly, these NSAs did not challenge the EU's legitimacy, but used their frames to develop a common understanding and shared knowledge with EU policy-makers. Through these frames, Teva and the MATTIN Group constructively engaged with EU policy-makers with the aim of providing an alternative view to the predominant lens through which the EU's policy towards the Israeli–Palestinian conflict is considered.

The cases of the Goldstone Report and of the ACAA have shown that mixed frames can also resonate with policy-makers, especially when the European Parliament is involved. In the former case, the EMHRN used a mixed frame based on the concepts of impunity and accountability, arguing that the EU should support the Goldstone Report in line with its commitments to respecting human rights. While the frame offered some legal references and the argument was properly supported with evidence and appropriate sources, the argument also relied on the political dimension of a rhetoric–practice gap in EU foreign policy. Therefore, this frame did not provide the EU with alternative views on how to deal with the issue at stake. Nevertheless, the argument presented by the EMHRN was brought forward into the debate in Parliament concerning the resolution on the Goldstone Report issued in 2010, and the resolution ultimately contained elements recalling that argument. This demonstrates that mixed frames containing both political and technical/legal arguments resonate with MEPs. In the case of the ACAA, similar trends were at work. The mixed frames used by the EMHRN, the EFI and EJC entered the debate in the European Parliament and played a role in shaping the understanding of MEPs on the issue.

In contrast, political frames did not play a significant role, as purely political arguments did not lead to a reframing of EU foreign policy. In Chapter 5 it was demonstrated that the EFI and EJC's lobbying based on the idea that the

Goldstone Report was inherently biased against Israel and was an attempt to discredit Israel's stance in the international arena, did not shape the content of the Resolution of the European Parliament. This type of frame, based on the use of certain words and concepts of discrimination, of democracy as a distinctive feature of Israel, and of anti-Semitic policies, aimed at exerting leverage on emotional aspects. While this type of ideological claim might have persuaded some MEPs, the resolution passed by MEPs did not contain these references, but instead referred to the political-legal argument presented by the EMHRN.

Compared to the EU level, NSAs active in member states have relied on political frames to a larger extent. Given the ideational centrality and the constant reference to values and historical legacies, political frames resonate with national policy-makers as well as with public opinion. Thanks to the reliance on public mobilisation, the mood of public opinion was often included in the frames used at the national level. Given the more politicised nature of policy-making and the stronger link between politicians and their constituencies at the national level, political frames are more likely to be included in political debates in member states than at the EU level, where political feelings are diverse and member states differ in terms of historical legacies and political context (e.g., minority groups present in one state).

More importantly, the analysis also highlighted the existence of a link between roles and frames. At the EU level, the role of dialogue-builder combined with technical frames allows NSAs and the EU to engage in cooperative relations and develop a common understanding of the issue at stake. This in turn can lead to the reframing of EU policies towards Israel/Palestine on the basis of new views and alternative perspectives. This link between roles and frames clearly emerged in Chapter 4. Although both the MATTIN Group and Brita GmbH made use of a legal frame, they played different roles. The former based its lobbying on a consensual role, while the latter challenged the EU in court. While the MATTIN Group managed to establish a dialogue with EU officials and policy-makers and to interact in a way leading to the definition of the problem of the territorial scope in EU–Israel agreements, Brita GmbH challenged the legitimacy of EU policies through judicial means, which did not allow the parties to discuss what the issue at stake was and how to deal with it. This points to how a legal frame, in itself, is not sufficient to play a role at the EU level; it needs to be combined with a cooperative approach that does not challenge the EU's legitimacy, but establishes good working relationships between the EU and NSAs. In contrast, at the national level officials and politicians are more receptive to political frames, but the role of opponent does not appear to be better suited to favour a redefinition of policies. NSAs in member states are more likely to play this type of role, but there is no clear evidence that this allows them to contribute to policy-making.

The question is why NSAs tend to play a more consensual role and use technical frames at the EU level compared to NSAs based in member states. In Chapter 1, it was suggested that the role of dialogue-builder suits the EU political system better. In a comparison between the EU and the USA, Woll (2012) explains that the difference in lobbying styles between American and European interest groups is determined by divergence in the nature of the two political systems. In the USA, the system favours a more adversarial approach, while the consensual nature of the EU context leads to the adoption of a soft-spoken approach by NSAs. The idea of the EU as a consensual system, where cooperation and compromise prevail and where the level of politicisation is lower, is also supported by various scholars (e.g., Mahoney 2008; Hix and Hoyland 2011; Lewis 2008), suggesting that a consensual approach fits into the system more easily than a confrontational stance. The same argument could also work when we discuss the preference for technical frames compared to political ones. Again, this is linked to the nature of the EU system in relation to member states: in the former, the Commission and, to a large extent, the European Parliament need information and knowledge that is technical, legal and that contributes to the formulation of policies that guarantee the EU's output legitimacy (Woll 2012; Scharpf 1999). The level of political contestation and polarisation of political parties is not the same as in member states: political arguments resonate less in Brussels than in national capitals (cf. Woll 2012; Radaelli 1999; Follesdal and Hix 2006).

For Woll (2012), the choice of lobbying styles is the result of a strategic choice by NSAs to exert influence in the system: NSAs lobbying the EU use a 'soft-spoken' style which gives them the potential to be able to influence EU policies. However, evidence in the empirical chapters does not highlight this strategic adaptation. In contrast, we observe a tendency to stick to the same role and frame in all venues/levels where NSAs lobby. A possible explanation, which, however, deserves further investigation, is that NSAs are socialised to the rules and the context where they play most often (Lewis 2005; Checkel 2005). By using the metaphor of the stage again, the performance of each actor is also shaped by the others and by the setting in which they act. Therefore, NSAs that are predominantly active at the EU level are progressively socialised to adopt a more consensual role and rely on technical frames. Their embeddedness in the system and the constant interactions with certain types of actors shape their identity and preferences, leading to a progressive change and adaptation to the context in which they play most of the time.

The MATTIN Group is a good example in this sense, as its lobbying has evolved over the decades. Some EU officials (Interviewees 13, 17) recalled the first meetings they had with this NGO as characterised by an aggressive and accusatory approach. In their view, it was as if the NGO had not understood how the EU functions, giving extra work to officials without obtaining much. Furthermore, an EU official (Interviewee 20) also argued that the frame used was quite complicated and was not pointing in the direction of how the EU could intervene concretely. If we look at the situation now, we can see how the frame proposed by the MATTIN Group has slowly begun to shape the way the EU looks at the policies towards Israel, as illustrated by the cases of Europol and the ACAA. The MATTIN Group's lobbying has evolved: constant interactions with EU officials have progressively developed its approach into a more consensual path, and its frame has been refined and tailored in line with the interlocutor. Interestingly, this combination of consensual role and legal frame does not change when the MATTIN Group targets the European Parliament and/or the national level. While it might still work when national officials are involved (e.g., officials working for national customs authorities), MEPs and MPs also need political elements that can be used with their constituencies (Interviewees 45, 87). A strategic choice would imply that the MATTIN Group adapts and modifies its style according to the context in which it operates, which does not seem to be the case.

Similarly, other groups define their identity and their behaviour on the basis of the context in which they are embedded and the interactions they develop. This is particularly evident in the case of Brussels-based umbrella organisations and their member organisations based at the national level. For example, the ECCP is composed of various associations and solidarity movements across Europe and represents them in Brussels. Interestingly, it mainly plays the role of voice-articulator in Brussels, while its member associations use a more confrontational stance. While the ECCP still relies on frames that contain a political element, it has internalised the rules of Brussels and adapted its identity and style accordingly.

A similar line of explanation can be applied to the national level, where political frames are largely used. NSAs based in member states have internalised the rules of the game of this 'stage', where the level of politicisation and polarisation are higher than in the EU political system. The fact that the role of opponent is often employed reflects a socialisation of NSAs to the political context, which is more confrontational. Yet, this role does not seem to lead to a strong involvement in policy process or to any significant change. If actors were only acting strategically, then they would probably opt for an approach that is more conducive to success. They are, therefore, likely to have internalised the patterns of interaction of a politicised context, without strategically adapting when their actions are not conducive to results.

This point about socialisation is only a suggestion about how we might interpret the differences in roles and frames used at the EU and national levels. In this regard, it is important to stress that the embeddedness of actors and a form of circularity between the EU and NSAs cannot be dismissed. This aspect, however, requires further research in order to advance these exploratory findings.

The levels of lobbying

The literature on EU lobbying stresses the relevance of the national level as an important venue where lobbying takes place (Mazey and Richardson 2006; Saurugger 2009). Given that member states are crucial actors in EU policy-making, especially in EU foreign policy, NSAs can use member states to lobby on issues related to EU policies. Chapters 4 to 7 have done an exploratory analysis of this issue, with the aim of identifying some key trends that can provide us with some answers in relation to the levels of lobbying and the Europeanisation of NSAs in the field of foreign policy. As shown in Chapters 4 to 6, most NSAs based in Brussels, or predominantly active in this arena (e.g., MATTIN Group), rely on the national channel as a complementary way to conduct their activities at the EU level. For instance, the MATTIN Group developed contacts with both national parliaments and customs authorities in member states on the issue of the rules of origin. Similarly, the EMHRN went to member states in order to explain its position on the Goldstone Report and to persuade member states to support a certain position or policy. In certain cases, Permanent Representations in Brussels are also targeted, although this option has not been mentioned so frequently.

The analysis of the national level has also aimed at understanding how NSAs based in member states lobby on EU foreign policy and whether their lobbying has been Europeanised. While Europeanisation is in part evident (there is lobbying on EU foreign policy), it is interesting to understand the patterns that explain the behaviour of NSAs based in member states. By referring to forms of internalisation, supranationalisation and externalisation (Saurugger 2005; Balme and Chabanet 2002), Chapter 7 has shown that there is only partial Europeanisation of lobbying. For example, internalisation – that is, the inclusion of EU issues in the lobbying carried out at the national level – is not extensive, as NSAs based in member states tend to focus their attention on national foreign policies, lobbying their governments and MPs on EU policies and using the national channel to exert influence at the EU level on a more sporadic basis. There are also instances of supranationalisation, as some umbrella organisations have been created in Brussels to conduct lobbying at the EU level on behalf of their member organisations. The EMHRN and APRODEV are examples of this trend and are supposed to represent their member organisations on the Brussels stage. Finally, some NSAs based in member states, such as the big NGOs like Oxfam and Amnesty International, have also opened offices in Brussels and are able to conduct direct lobbying there (externalisation). It has to be noted, however, that most NSAs based in member states are still more preoccupied with the policies of their respective member state, thus concentrating their lobbying actions at the state level. The EU was mainly taken into consideration at the national level when Brussels-based NSAs exerted pressure in this regard and asked NSAs in member states to conduct lobbying on certain issues that were addressed in Brussels at the same time.

The link between lobbying at the national and EU levels also provides indications of integration in the field of EU foreign policy. Although we would expect existing links across levels, due to the patterns of Europeanisation highlighted, in reality the EU and national arenas remain quite separate. Umbrella organisations, despite representing their member organisations, act in Brussels and recognise the importance of involving the national level in their activities, while those based in member states are much less aware of the EU level and what they can do there. This is also one of the reasons why some NGOs, such as the EMHRN, have been developing a training programme and toolkit for NSAs based in member states.

Implications for the literature and the way forward

This book has provided an exploratory research of lobbying in EU foreign policy, which is a topic that has received limited attention in the literature. First of all, it has proposed a theoretical framework to analyse the issue, which can be used to investigate lobbying in other EU policy areas. Two crucial dimensions to understand lobbying are indeed the approach used by NSAs (roles) and the knowledge they bring to policy-making (frames). As demonstrated, it is not information per se that matters, but the frames through which policies or events are understood. Framing does, however, make a difference when combined with a role that fits with the features of the political system. By playing a consensual role, NSAs and EU policy-makers can interact in a cooperative way that leads to a new understanding of the issue at stake. Dialogue and mutual legitimisation become the basis on which frames can travel and be developed.

Second, the key finding that NSAs matter in EU foreign policy-making and are involved in the policy process contributes to our understanding of how EU foreign policy comes about and which actors and factors determine its content. While it has not been argued that NSAs are all-powerful and steer decisions, it has been demonstrated that NSAs matter in EU policy-making and need to be taken into account to have a better understanding of where EU policies come from, why certain issues are on the agenda and why certain frames prevail over others. Member states and EU institutions remain key players, but complementing the analysis by including NSAs in the equation gives us a deeper understanding of the process. Building on a constructivist understanding of lobbying and framing, this book has aimed at showing that the circularity and embeddedness between the EU and NSAs cannot be neglected. The focus of the book has predominantly been on the role that NSAs play in EU foreign policy-making, looking at 'one side' of the co-constitutive relationship that constructivism stresses (the impact of NSAs on the EU). The analysis clearly needs a more in-depth investigation of the other part of this circular relationship, namely how the EU has contributed to shaping the preferences and identities of NSAs. Nevertheless, it has offered inputs to use this perspective in the study on lobbying.

The third dimension referring to the level of lobbying has provided preliminary findings that show how and where NSAs lobby. The empirical analysis has sketched some interesting points that need further research. In particular, a detailed comparison between lobbying at the EU and national levels is much needed. This book has started to highlight some patterns, but a more in-depth analysis is necessary to have a better sense of how lobbying in member states works, as well as the use of the national channel (which includes the Council and the Permanent Representations). Moreover, understanding what happens at the EU level and in member states is also relevant to identify the extent of integration between the EU and the national arenas in foreign policy. Given the differences across political systems, we would expect different roles and frames, but it is less clear whether this is always the case and what reasons explain this difference. For example, are political frames the most chosen ones at the national level due to the fact that politicians and the incumbent administration at the national level need public support, or are technical frames likely to be successful as well? To what extent would the electoral dynamics determine policy choices compared to the EU level?

In relation to this point, the discussion on Europeanisation patterns can be further developed. In this sense, it would also be important to understand why certain NSAs in member states Europeanise, while others do not. While some scholars link it to the resources available (Klüver 2010; Beyers and Kerremans 2007), it might well be that the EU is not perceived as an important actor or that NSAs do not have sufficient knowledge to deal with the EU level as well. Most of the interviewees at the national level mentioned at least one or all of these reasons, but a systematic investigation of what drives NSAs' decision to take the EU dimension into account (Europeanisation) would also contribute to our understanding of how lobbying in a multi-venue setting works and the extent of integration of the EU political system with that of its member states.

Moreover, this book has analysed the role of NSAs in EU foreign policy-making from the agenda-setting stage to the decision-making stage. The analysis would, however, benefit from a clearer distinction between the different policy stages in order to test whether there is a relationship between the three analytical dimensions presented in the theoretical framework and the various stages of the policy-making process. It would also be interesting to develop the analysis at the agenda-setting stage and investigate how issues are placed on the agenda and how frames and roles are relevant in this regard.

Future research should also include a more fine-grained distinction of the different institutions targeted by NSAs. In the book, there is the implicit assumption that all DGs and all Committees in the European Parliament behave and interact with NSAs in a similar way. While this might be the case, as a result of a form of organisational culture, it would be worth seeing whether the EEAS follows the same logics as the Commission or is more in line with the Council. The Council has been considered as part of the national level/venue, as decisions in the working groups, COREPER etc. are taken by representatives of member states and, quite often, by following instructions from their capitals. The national level has been viewed as the use of the national channel and no distinction in this sense has been made. However, it might be worth exploring this dimension to see if and how NSAs distinguish between lobbying member states in Brussels (Permanent Representations) and in the capitals. Moreover, almost no space has been given to the Delegations on the ground, although it might be that the framing that NSAs on the ground use when lobbying EU officials and member state representatives is different from that used in Brussels or Europe, as the reality of the situation is evident to everyone and there might be a different sensitivity to the problems at stake.

Finally, framing has recently been accorded increased attention by scholars of interest groups. While there is a predominant attempt at analysing frames through quantitative approaches and to consider them as strategic tools, this book suggests that a more constructivist approach that pays attention to the ways in which framing processes occur and shape EU policies is conducive to new findings on the ways in which lobbying acts and policies are formulated and implemented. Further attention is therefore needed to develop this aspect of the research on interest groups and EU foreign policy in order to identify how processes of knowledge construction take place and shape EU policies and outcomes.

References

Balme, Richard and Didier Chabanet. 2002. 'Action collective et gouvernance de l'Union Européenne'. In *L'action collective en Europe*, edited by Richard Balme, Didier Chabanet and Vincent Wright. Paris: Presses de Sciences Po. 21–120.

Beyers, Jan and Bart Kerremans. 2007. 'Critical Resource Dependencies and the Europeanization of Domestic Interest Groups'. *Journal of European Public Policy* 14 (3): 460–81.

Checkel, Jeffrey T. 2005. 'International Institutions and Socialization in Europe: Introduction and Framework'. *International Organization* 59 (4): 801–26.

Follesdal, Andreas and Simon Hix. 2006. 'Why There is a Democratic Deficit in the EU: A Response to Majone and Moravcsik'. *Journal of Common Market Studies* 44 (3): 533–62.

Goldberg, David Howard. 1990. *Foreign Policy and Ethnic Interest Groups: American and Canadian Jews Lobby for Israel*. New York/London: Greenwood Press.

Hix, Simon and Bjorn Hoyland. 2011. *The Political System of the European Union*. London: Palgrave Macmillan.

Jünemann, Annette. 2002. 'From the Bottom to the Top: Civil Society and Transnational Non-Governmental Organizations in the Euro-Mediterranean Partnership'. *Democratization* 9 (1): 87–105.

Klüver, Heike. 2010. 'Europeanization of Lobbying Activities: When National Interest Groups Spill Over to the European Level'. *Journal of European Integration* 32 (2): 175–91.

Lewis, Jeffrey. 2005. 'The Janus Face of Brussels: Socialization and Everyday Decision Making in the European Union'. *International Organization* 59 (4): 937–71.

———. 2008. 'Strategic Bargaining, Norms, and Deliberation: Modes of Action in the Council of the European Union'. In *Unveiling the Council: Games Governments Play in Brussels*, edited by Daniel Naurin and Helen Wallace. Basingstoke: Palgrave Macmillan. 165–84.

Mahoney, Christine. 2008. *Brussels versus the Beltway: Advocacy in the United States and the European Union*. Washington, DC: Georgetown University Press.

Mazey, Sonia and Jeremy Richardson. 2006. 'Interest Groups and EU Policy-Making: Organizational Logic and Venue Shopping'. In *European Union: Power and Policy-Making*, by Jeremy Richardson. London/New York: Routledge. 247–68.

Mearsheimer, John J. and Stephen M. Walt. 2007. *The Israel Lobby and US Foreign Policy*. London: Allen Lane.

Radaelli, Claudio M. 1999. 'The Power of Policy Narratives in the European Union: The Case of Tax Policy'. In *Public Policy and Political Ideas*, edited by Dietmar Braun and Andreas Busch. Cheltenham/Northampton: Edward Elgar. 98–115.

Saurugger, Sabine. 2005. 'Europeanization as a Methodological Challenge: The Case of Interest Groups'. *Journal of Comparative Policy Analysis* 7 (4): 239–78.

———. 2009. 'COREPER and National Governments'. In *Lobbying the European Union*, by David Coen and Jeremy Richardson. Oxford: Oxford University Press. 105–27.

Scharpf, Fritz Wilhelm. 1999. *Governing in Europe: Effective and Democratic?* Oxford: Oxford University Press.

Tocci, Nathalie. 2005. *The Widening Gap between Rhetoric and Reality in EU Policy towards the Israeli–Palestinian Conflict*. 271. CEPS Working Paper Document. Brussels: CEPS.

———. 2011. *The European Union, Civil Society and Conflict*. Abingdon/New York: Routledge.

Woll, Cornelia. 2012. 'The Brash and the Soft-Spoken: Lobbying Styles in a Transatlantic Comparison'. *Interest Groups & Advocacy* 1 (2): 193–214.

Appendix 1

List of interviewees

Database of non-state actors (updated as of 22 December 2014)

See Chapter 3 for the relevant explanation of the database

Name	Category	BXL	Transparency Register	Location	Location of headquarters	Umbrella organisation
ACAT-France	NGO	NO	NO	Cross-country	France	NO
Achva-Achdut	Business group	NO	NO	Israel/Palestine	Israel	NO
ACRI – Association for Civil Rights in Israel	NGO	NO	NO	Israel/Palestine	Israel	NO
ACSUR – Las Segovias	NGO	NO	NO	EU/Europe-based	Spain	NO
ACT Alliance	NGO	YES	NO	Cross-country	Switzerland	YES
Actieplatform Palestina	Solidarity movement	NO	NO	EU/Europe-based	Belgium	YES
Adalah	NGO	NO	NO	Israel/Palestine	Israel	NO
Adama Agricultural Solutions	Business group	NO	YES	Israel/Palestine	Israel	NO
Adanim Tea	Business group	NO	NO	Israel/Palestine	Israel	NO
ADDAMEER Prisoners Support and Human Rights Group	NGO	NO	NO	Israel/Palestine	West Bank	NO
Adumim Food Additives/Frutarom	Business group	NO	NO	Cross-country	Israel	NO
Agrexco	Business group	NO	NO	Cross-country	Israel	NO
AgustaWestland	Business group	NO	NO	Cross-country	Netherlands	NO

(Continued)

Name	Category	BXL	Transparency Register	Location	Location of headquarters	Umbrella organisation
Ahava	Business group	NO	NO	Cross-country	Israel	NO
Airtechnology Group	Business group	NO	NO	EU/Europe-based	UK	NO
AJC – American Jewish Committee	NGO	YES	YES	Cross-country	USA	NO
Al-Haq	NGO	YES	NO	Israel/Palestine	West Bank	NO
Al Mezan Center for Human Rights	NGO	NO	NO	Israel/Palestine	Gaza Strip	NO
Al-Monitor – The Pulse of the Middle East	Media	NO	NO	Other	USA	NO
Al Dameer Association for Human Rights	NGO	NO	NO	Israel/Palestine	West Bank	NO
Aljamaheer Association for Development in the Arab and Jewish Sectors	NGO	NO	NO	Israel/Palestine	Israel	NO
Alstom	Business group	YES	YES	Cross-country	France	NO
Alternative Information Centre	Media	NO	NO	Israel/Palestine	Israel	NO
Amnesty International	NGO	YES	YES	Cross-country	UK	NO
Anglo-Israel Association	NGO	NO	NO	EU/Europe-based	UK	NO
Apax Partner	Business group	NO	NO	Cross-country	UK	NO
APRODEV	NGO	YES	YES	EU/Europe-based	Belgium	YES
Arab Association for Human Rights	NGO	NO	NO	Israel/Palestine	Israel	NO
Arava Export Growers	Business group	NO	NO	Cross-country	Israel	NO
Architects and Planners for Justice in Palestine	NGO	NO	NO	EU/Europe-based	UK	NO
ASDA	Business group	NO	NO	EU/Europe-based	UK	NO
Ashmore Investment Management	Business group	NO	NO	EU/Europe-based	UK	NO
Assa Abloy/Mul-T-Lock	Business group	NO	NO	Cross-country	Sweden	NO
Association belgo palestinienne	Solidarity movement	YES	NO	EU/Europe-based	Belgium	NO
Association France–Israël	NGO	NO	NO	EU/Europe-based	France	NO
Association France Palestine Solidarité – AFPS	Solidarity movement	NO	NO	EU/Europe-based	France	YES
Assopace	NGO	NO	NO	EU/Europe-based	Italy	YES
Avocats sans frontières	NGO	YES	NO	Cross-country	Belgium	NO
Badil – Resource Center for Palestinian Residency and Refuge	NGO	NO	YES	Israel/Palestine	West Bank	NO
BAE System	Business group	YES	YES	Cross-country	UK	NO

Name	Type			Category	Country	
Bank Leumi	Business group	NO	NO	Cross-country	Israel	NO
Barclays	Business group	NO	NO	Cross-country	UK	NO
BBC Watch	Media	NO	NO	EU/Europe-based	UK	NO
BDS – Boycott, Divestment and Sanctions	Solidarity movement	NO	NO	Cross-country	West Bank/Gaza	YES
Bertelsmann Stiftung	Think tank/Foundation	YES	YES	EU/Europe-based	Germany	NO
BICOM	Media	NO	NO	EU/Europe-based	UK	NO
BIMKOM – Planners for Planning Rights	NGO	NO	NO	Israel/Palestine	Israel	NO
B'nai B'rith	NGO	YES	YES	Cross-country	USA	NO
Board of Deputies of British Jews	NGO	NO	NO	EU/Europe-based	UK	YES
Boeing – Boeing International Corp.	Business group	YES	YES	Cross-country	USA	NO
Breaking the Silence	NGO	NO	NO	Israel/Palestine	Israel	NO
Brimar	Business group	NO	NO	Cross-country	UK	NO
Brita GmbH	Business group	NO	YES	Cross-country	Germany	NO
British–Israel Coalition Public Affairs Committee – BICPAC	NGO	NO	NO	EU/Europe-based	UK	NO
British Israel Investments	Business group	NO	NO	Israel/Palestine	Israel	NO
British–Palestine Twinning Network	Solidarity movement	NO	NO	EU/Europe-based	UK	YES
Broederlijk Delen	NGO	YES	NO	EU/Europe-based	Belgium	NO
Brot für die Welt	NGO	YES	YES	EU/Europe-based	Germany	NO
B'Tselem	NGO	NO	NO	Israel/Palestine	Israel	NO
Bureau de Vigilance Contre l'Antisémitisme – BNVCA	NGO	NO	NO	EU/Europe-based	France	NO
BusinessEurope	Business group	YES	YES	EU/Europe-based	Belgium	YES
Caabu – Council for the Advancement of Arab–British Understanding	NGO	NO	NO	EU/Europe-based	UK	NO
CAFOD	NGO	NO	NO	Cross-country	UK	NO
Campagne Civile Internationale pour la protection du peuple palestinien (CCIPPP)	Solidarity movement	NO	NO	EU/Europe-based	France	NO
Campaign Against Arms Trade	Solidarity movement	NO	NO	EU/Europe-based	UK	NO
CAPJPO – EuroPalestine	Solidarity movement	NO	NO	EU/Europe-based	France	NO
CARE	NGO	YES	YES	Cross-country	UK	NO

(Continued)

Name	Category	BXL	Transparency Register	Location	Location of headquarters	Umbrella organisation
Carnegie Endowment for International Peace	Think tank/Foundation	YES	NO	Cross-country	USA	NO
Caterpillar Belgium SA	Business group	YES	YES	Cross-country	Belgium	NO
CCDPRJ – The Civic Coalition for Defending Palestinians' Rights in Jerusalem	NGO	NO	NO	Israel/Palestine	Israel	YES
CCFD – Terre Solidaire	NGO	NO	NO	EU/Europe-based	France	YES
CEIA – Costruzioni Elettroniche Industriali Automatismi	Business group	NO	NO	EU/Europe-based	Italy	NO
CEJI – A Jewish Contribution to an Inclusive Europe	NGO	YES	YES	EU/Europe-based	Belgium	NO
Cement Roadstone Holdings	Business group	NO	NO	Cross-country	Ireland	NO
Centre on Housing Rights and Evictions – COHRE	NGO	NO	NO	Cross-country	Switzerland	NO
Centre Simon Wiesenthal Europe	NGO	NO	NO	EU/Europe-based	France	NO
CEPS	Think tank/Foundation	YES	YES	EU/Europe-based	Belgium	NO
Christian Aid	NGO	NO	YES	Cross-country	UK	NO
Christians for Israel International	NGO	NO	NO	Cross-country	Netherlands	NO
Christians for Zion	NGO	NO	NO	EU/Europe-based	UK	NO
Christian Friends of Israel	NGO	NO	NO	Cross-country	Israel	NO
Christian Middle East Watch	NGO	NO	NO	EU/Europe-based	UK	YES
CIDI – Centrum informatie en documentatie Israel	NGO	NO	NO	EU/Europe-based	Netherlands	NO
CIDSE	NGO	YES	YES	Cross-country	Belgium	YES
CiF Watch	Media	NO	NO	EU/Europe-based	UK	NO
Coalition of Women for Peace – Who Profits?	NGO	NO	NO	Israel/Palestine	Israel	NO
Collectif Urgence Palestine	Solidarity movement	NO	NO	EU/Europe-based	Switzerland	YES
Combatant for Peace – CFP	Solidarity movement	NO	NO	Israel/Palestine	n/a	NO
COMECE – Commission of the Bishops' Conferences of the European Community	NGO	YES	YES	EU/Europe-based	Belgium	NO

Comité pour une Paix Juste au Proche-Orient – CPJPO	Solidarity movement	NO	NO	EU/Europe-based	Luxembourg	NO
Concord	NGO	YES	YES	EU/Europe-based	Belgium	YES
Conflicts Forum	Media	NO	NO	Cross-country	UK/Lebanon	NO
Conservative Friends of Israel	NGO	NO	NO	EU/Europe-based	UK	NO
Cordaid	NGO	NO	YES	Cross-country	Netherlands	YES
Corporate Watch	Media	NO	NO	EU/Europe-based	UK	NO
Council for European Palestinian Relations	NGO	YES	YES	EU/Europe-based	UK	NO
CRIF – Conseil Représentatif des Institutions juives de France	NGO	NO	NO	EU/Europe-based	France	YES
Crisis Action	NGO	YES	YES	Cross-country	UK	YES
DanChurchAid	NGO	NO	NO	Cross-country	Denmark	NO
Dansk–Palaestinensisk Venskabsforening	Solidarity movement	NO	NO	EU/Europe-based	Denmark	NO
Defence for Children International	NGO	NO	NO	Cross-country	Switzerland	NO
Deutsch–Israelische Gesellschaft – DIG	Solidarity movement	NO	NO	EU/Europe-based	Germany	NO
Deutsch–Palaestinensichen Gesellschaft	Solidarity movement	NO	NO	EU/Europe-based	Germany	YES
Deutsche Bahn International	Business group	YES	YES	EU/Europe-based	Germany	NO
Deutscher Koordinationskreis Palaestina Israel – KOPI	Solidarity movement	NO	NO	EU/Europe-based	Germany	YES
Deutscher Koordinierungsrat	NGO	NO	NO	EU/Europe-based	Germany	YES
Development Company for Israel	Business group	NO	NO	EU/Europe-based	UK	NO
Dexia Group	Business group	NO	NO	Cross-country	France	NO
diAk	Solidarity movement	NO	NO	EU/Europe-based	Germany	NO
DIAKONIA	NGO	NO	NO	Cross-country	Sweden	YES
DiSTeK	Business group	NO	NO	Cross-country	Israel	NO
DIW – German–Israeli Economic Association	Business group	NO	NO	EU/Europe-based	Germany/Israel	YES
Eden Spring	Business group	NO	NO	Cross-country	Switzerland	NO
EDO-ITT	Business group	NO	NO	Cross-country	USA	NO
EED – Evangelischer Entwicklungsdienst	NGO	YES	NO	EU/Europe-based	Germany	NO
EEPA – European External Policy Advisor	NGO	NO	NO	EU/Europe-based	Belgium	NO
Egis Rail	Business group	NO	NO	Cross-country	France	NO

(Continued)

Name	Category	BXL	Transparency Register	Location	Location of headquarters	Umbrella organisation
EIPA – Europe Israel Press Association	Media	YES	NO	EU/Europe-based	Belgium	NO
El Al	Business group	YES	NO	Cross-country	Israel	NO
Electronic Intifada	Media	NO	NO	n/a	n/a	NO
Elnet	NGO	YES	NO	EU/Europe-based	Belgium	NO
EMHRN	NGO	YES	YES	EU/Europe-based	Denmark	YES
European Federation of Pharmaceutical Industries and Associations – EFPIA	Business group	YES	YES	EU/Europe-based	Belgium	YES
European Former Leaders Group	Individuals	n/a	NO	n/a	n/a	NO
European Jewish Development Fund	NGO	YES	NO	EU/Europe-based	Belgium	NO
Ensan Center for Human Rights and Democracy	NGO	NO	NO	Israel/Palestine	West Bank	NO
European Policy Centre – EPC	Think tank/Foundation	YES	YES	EU/Europe-based	Belgium	NO
EPLO – European Peace-building Liaison Office	NGO	YES	YES	EU/Europe-based	Belgium	YES
EUJB – EU Jewish Buildings	NGO	YES	NO	EU/Europe-based	Belgium	NO
Euro-Arab Forum	NGO	YES	NO	EU/Europe-based	Belgium	NO
Euro-Med Non-Governmental Platform	NGO	NO	NO	EU/Europe-based	France	YES
Euro Middle East Forum	NGO	YES	NO	EU/Europe-based	Belgium	NO
Europe Near East Forum	NGO	YES	NO	EU/Europe-based	Belgium	NO
European Coalition for Israel	NGO	YES	YES	EU/Europe-based	Belgium	YES
European Coordination Committee for Palestine – ECCP	NGO	YES	YES	EU/Europe-based	Belgium	YES
European Friends of Israel – EFI	NGO	YES	YES	EU/Europe-based	Belgium	YES
European Jewish Association	NGO	YES	YES	EU/Europe-based	Belgium	YES
European Jewish Community Centre	NGO	YES	YES	EU/Europe-based	Belgium	NO
European Jewish Press	Media	YES	NO	EU/Europe-based	Belgium	NO
European Jews for a Just Peace – EJJP	NGO	NO	NO	EU/Europe-based	Netherlands	YES
European Jewish Union	NGO	NO	NO	EU/Europe-based	Belgium	YES
European Muslim Network	Think tank/Foundation	YES	NO	EU/Europe-based	Belgium	YES
European Palestinian Campaign for the Cultural Boycott of Israel	Solidarity movement	NO	NO	EU/Europe-based	n/a	YES

European Jewish Congress – EJC	NGO	YES	YES	EU/Europe-based	France	YES
Federatie Nederlande Zionisten	NGO	NO	NO	EU/Europe-based	Netherlands	YES
FIDH – Fédération Internationale des Droits de l'Homme	NGO	YES	YES	Cross-country	France	YES
Finn Church Aid	NGO	NO	NO	Cross-country	Finland	NO
Fortis Investments – BNP Paribas	Business group	YES	YES	EU/Europe-based	Belgium	NO
Forum of Strategic Dialogue – FSD	NGO	NO	NO	Cross-country	Israel	NO
Fundacio Internacional Olof Palme	NGO	NO	NO	Cross-country	Spain	NO
Frauen in Schwarz	Solidarity movement	NO	NO	EU/Europe-based	Austria	NO
Free Gaza Movement	Solidarity movement	n/a	NO	EU/Europe-based	Cyprus	YES
Friedrich Ebert Stiftung	Think tank/foundation	YES	YES	Cross-country	Germany	NO
Friends of the Earth Middle East – FoEME	NGO	NO	NO	Israel/Palestine	Israel/West Bank/Jordan	NO
Front Line Defenders	NGO	YES	YES	EU/Europe-based	Ireland	NO
G4S – Group 4 Securicor	Business group	NO	YES	Cross-country	UK	NO
Geneva Initiative	NGO	NO	NO	Israel/Palestine	Israel/Palestine	NO
German Marshall Fund	Think tank/fund	YES	NO	Cross-country	USA	NO
Gisha	NGO	NO	NO	Israel/Palestine	Israel	NO
GRIP	Think tank/foundation	YES	NO	EU/Europe-based	Belgium	NO
Grupo de ONG por Palestina	NGO	NO	NO	EU/Europe-based	Spain	YES
HaMoked – Center for the Defence of the Individual	NGO	NO	NO	Israel/Palestine	Israel	NO
Heidelberg Cement	Business group	YES	YES	Cross-country	Germany	NO
Heinrich Boell Stiftung	Think tank/Foundation	YES	YES	Cross-country	Germany	NO
Henry Jackson Society	Think tank/Foundation	NO	NO	EU/Europe-based	UK	NO
Honest Reporting	Media	NO	NO	Cross-country	Israel	NO
Honestly Concerned	Media	NO	NO	EU/Europe-based	Germany	NO
HSBC	Business group	NO	NO	Cross-country	UK	NO
Human Rights and Democracy Network	NGO	YES	NO	EU/Europe-based	Belgium	YES
Human Rights Watch	NGO	YES	YES	cross-country	USA	NO

(Continued)

Name	Category	BXL	Transparency Register	Location	Location of headquarters	Umbrella organisation
IBEXPERTS Ltd	Business group	NO	YES	Israel/Palestine	Israel	NO
ICAHD – Israeli Committee against House Demolition	NGO	NO	NO	Israel/Palestine	Israel	NO
ICCO – Interchurch Organization for Development Co-operation	NGO	NO	NO	Cross-country	Netherlands	NO
IENP – Israeli–European Policy Network	Think tank/Foundation	NO	NO	Cross-country	Germany/Israel	YES
ILI – I like Israel	Solidarity movement	NO	NO	EU/Europe-based	Germany	NO
Independent Jewish Voices	Solidarity movement	NO	NO	EU/Europe-based	UK	NO
Info-Palestine.net	Media/Solidarity movement	NO	NO	EU/Europe-based	France	NO
Inform – International Forum on the Middle East	Media	YES	NO	EU/Europe-based	Belgium	NO
Initiative 27. Januar e.V.	Solidarity movement	NO	NO	EU/Europe-based	Germany	NO
The International Association of Jewish Lawyers and Jurists	NGO	NO	YES	Cross-country	Israel	YES
International Crisis Group	Think tank/foundation	YES	YES	Cross-country	USA	NO
International Solidarity Movement	Solidarity movement	NO	NO	Cross-country	West Bank/Gaza	YES
Interpeace	NGO	YES	YES	Cross-country	Switzerland	NO
Interwand Eibergen BV	Business group	NO	NO	Cross-country	Netherlands	NO
IPPNW	NGO	NO	NO	Cross-country	USA	YES
Ir Amim	NGO	NO	NO	Israel/Palestine	Israel	NO
Ireland–Palestine Solidarity Campaign	Solidarity movement	NO	NO	EU/Europe-based	Ireland	NO
Irish Friends for Israel (IF4I)	Solidarity movement	NO	NO	EU/Europe-based	Ireland	NO
Islamic Relief	NGO	YES	NO	Cross-country	UK	NO
Israel Advocacy UK	Solidarity movement	NO	NO	EU/Europe-based	UK	YES
Israel Aircraft Industries	Business group	NO	NO	Israel/Palestine	Israel	NO
Israel Allies Foundation	NGO	YES	YES	Cross-country	USA	YES
Israeli Center for Assistive Technology and Aging	Think tank/Foundation	NO	YES	Cross-country	Israel	YES

Israel Project	NGO	NO	NO	Cross-country	Israel/USA	NO
ISS	Business group	NO	NO	Cross-country	Denmark	NO
ITTIJAH – Union of Arab Community Based Organisations	NGO	NO	NO	Israel/Palestine	Israel	YES
JBC – Bamford Excavators	Business group	NO	NO	Cross-country	UK	NO
Jcall	Solidarity movement	YES	NO	EU/Europe-based	n/a	NO
Jerusalem Center for Legal Aid and Human Rights	NGO	NO	NO	Israel/Palestine	West Bank	NO
Jforum	Media	n/a	NO	EU/Europe-based	France	NO
Jnews	Media	NO	NO	EU/Europe-based	UK	NO
Jews for Justice for Palestinians – JFJFP	Solidarity movement	NO	NO	EU/Europe-based	UK	YES
John Lewis	Business group	NO	NO	EU/Europe-based	UK	NO
Joods Nationaal Fonds	NGO	NO	NO	EU/Europe-based	Netherlands	NO
Judische Stimme fuer gerechten Frieden in Nahost	Solidarity movement	NO	NO	EU/Europe-based	Germany	NO
Just Peace for Palestine	NGO	NO	NO	EU/Europe-based	UK	YES
Kav Laoved	NGO	NO	NO	Israel/Palestine	Israel	NO
Keshev – The Center for the Protection of Democracy in Israel	Media	NO	NO	Israel/Palestine	Israel	NO
Keter Plastic	Business group	NO	NO	Cross-country	Israel	NO
Konrad Adenauer Stiftung	Think tank/Foundation	YES	YES	EU/Europe-based	Germany	NO
Kvinna Till	NGO	NO	NO	EU/Europe-based	Sweden	NO
Labour Friends of Israel	NGO	NO	NO	EU/Europe-based	UK	NO
Labour Friends of Palestine and the Middle East	NGO	NO	NO	EU/Europe-based	UK	NO
Lawyers for Palestinian Human Rights – LPHR	NGO	NO	NO	EU/Europe-based	UK	NO
Levi Matusof	Individuals	YES	NO	n/a	n/a	NO
Leviev	Business group	NO	NO	Cross-country	UK	NO
Liberal Democrat Friends of Israel	NGO	NO	NO	EU/Europe-based	UK	NO
Liberal Democrat Friends of Palestine	NGO	NO	NO	EU/Europe-based	UK	NO
Liebherr	Business group	NO	NO	Cross-country	Germany	NO
Lockheed Martin	Business group	YES	NO	Cross-country	UK	NO
Machsom Watch	NGO	NO	NO	Israel/Palestine	Israel	NO

(Continued)

Name	Category	BXL	Transparency Register	Location	Location of headquarters	Umbrella organisation
Manitou	Business group	NO	NO	Cross-country	n/a	NO
Marks&Spencer	Business group	NO	NO	EU/Europe-based	UK	NO
MATTIN Group	NGO	NO	NO	Israel/Palestine	West Bank	NO
Mayanot Eden	Business group	NO	NO	Cross-country	Israel	NO
Medbridge	NGO	NO	NO	EU/Europe-based	France	NO
MEDEA	Think tank/Foundation	YES	YES	EU/Europe-based	Belgium	NO
Medical Aid for Palestinians	NGO	NO	NO	EU/Europe-based	UK	NO
MEDICO International e.V.	NGO	NO	NO	EU/Europe-based	Germany	NO
Meggit Avionics	Business group	NO	NO	Cross-country	UK	NO
Middle East Monitor (MEMO)	Media	NO	NO	EU/Europe-based	UK	NO
Mideast Freedom Forum Berlin	Solidarity movement	NO	NO	EU/Europe-based	Germany	NO
Misereor	NGO	NO	NO	EU/Europe-based	Germany	NO
Mossawa Center	NGO	YES	NO	Israel/Palestine	Israel	NO
Mouvement contre le racisme et pour l'amitié entre les peuples – MRAP	NGO	NO	NO	EU/Europe-based	France	NO
Mouvement de soutien à la résistance du peuple palestinien – MSRPP	Solidarity movement	NO	NO	EU/Europe-based	France	YES
Nahost Friedensforum	Solidarity movement	NO	NO	EU/Europe-based	Germany	NO
Netherlands Palestine Committee	Solidarity movement	NO	NO	EU/Europe-based	Netherlands	NO
New Israel Fund	NGO	NO	NO	Cross-country	USA	NO
NGO Monitor	NGO	NO	NO	Israel/Palestine	Israel	NO
Norwegian Church Aid	NGO	NO	NO	EU/Europe-based	Norway	NO
Oberthur Technologies	Business group	NO	NO	EU/Europe-based	France	NO
One Voice	Solidarity movement	NO	NO	Cross-country	n/a	NO
Oxfam	NGO	YES	YES	Cross-country	UK	NO
Page Aerospace	Business group	NO	NO	Cross-country	UK	NO
Palestinagrupperna I Sverige – Palestine Solidarity Association of Sweden	Solidarity movement	NO	NO	EU/Europe-based	Sweden	NO
Palestine Solidarity Campaign	Solidarity movement	NO	NO	EU/Europe-based	UK	YES

Palestinian Center for Human Rights – PCHR	NGO	NO	NO	Israel/Palestine	Gaza Strip	NO
Palestinian Hydrology Group for Water and Environmental Resources Development	NGO	NO	NO	Israel/Palestine	West Bank	NO
Palestinian Human Rights Organisation – PHRO	NGO	NO	NO	Other	Lebanon	NO
Palestinian Human Rights Monitoring Group – PHRMG	NGO	NO	NO	Israel/Palestine	Israel	NO
Palestinian Medical Relief Society – PMRS	NGO	NO	NO	Israel/Palestine	West Bank	NO
Palestinian International Business Forum	Business group	NO	NO	Cross-country	Sweden	YES
Palestinian Media Watch	Think tank/Foundation	NO	NO	Israel/Palestine	Israel	NO
Palestinian NGO Network – PNGO	NGO	NO	NO	Israel/Palestine	West Bank/Gaza	YES
PARC – Palestinian Agricultural Relief Committees	NGO	NO	NO	Israel/Palestine	West Bank	NO
Parsons Brinckerhoff – PB	Business group	NO	NO	Cross-country	USA	NO
Pax Christi	NGO	YES	NO	Cross-country	Belgium	NO
PCATI – Public Committee against Torture in Israel	NGO	NO	NO	Israel/Palestine	Israel	NO
Peace Now	NGO	NO	NO	Cross-country	Israel	NO
Penny and Giles Controls	Business group	NO	NO	Cross-country	UK	NO
Peres Center for Peace	NGO	NO	NO	Israel/Palestine	Israel	NO
Physicians for Human Rights Israel	NGO	NO	NO	Israel/Palestine	Israel	NO
Piattaforma delle ONG italiane per la Palestina	NGO	NO	NO	EU/Europe-based	Italy	YES
Pictet Asset Management	Business group	NO	NO	Cross-country	Switzerland	NO
Pizzarotti & Co.	Business group	YES	NO	Cross-country	Italy	NO
Plateforme des ONG françaises pour la Palestine	NGO	NO	NO	EU/Europe-based	France	YES
Popular Struggle Coordination Committee	Solidarity movement	NO	NO	Israel/Palestine	West Bank/Gaza	YES
Quaker Council for European Affairs	NGO	YES	YES	EU/Europe-based	UK	NO
Red Solidaria contra la Ocupacion de Palestina	Solidarity movement	NO	NO	EU/Europe-based	Spain	YES
Redress Information and Analysis	Media	NO	NO	n/a	n/a	NO
Redmayne Engineering	Business group	NO	NO	EU/Europe-based	UK	NO
Riwal	Business group	NO	NO	Cross-country	Netherlands	NO

(Continued)

Name	Category	BXL	Transparency Register	Location	Location of headquarters	Umbrella organisation
Robert Dyas	Business group	NO	NO	EU/Europe-based	UK	NO
Russell Tribunal on Palestine	Solidarity movement	NO	NO	n/a	n/a	NO
Sadaka – The Ireland Palestine Alliance	Solidarity movement	NO	NO	EU/Europe-based	Ireland	NO
Sainsbury's	Business group	NO	NO	EU/Europe-based	UK	NO
Save the Children	NGO	YES	YES	Cross-country	UK	NO
Search for Common Ground	NGO	YES	NO	Cross-country	USA	NO
Senior Aerospace Baxter Woodhouse & Taylor	Business group	NO	NO	Cross-country	UK	NO
Siemens	Business group	YES	YES	Cross-country	Germany	NO
Simone Susskind	Individuals	YES	NO	EU/Europe-based	Belgium	NO
Smiths Detection	Business group	YES	NO	Cross-country	UK	NO
Siona	NGO	NO	NO	EU/Europe-based	France	NO
Society for Austro-Arab Relations	NGO	NO	NO	EU/Europe-based	Austria	NO
Soda Stream/Soda Club	Business group	NO	NO	Cross-country	Israel	NO
Solidar	NGO	YES	YES	EU/Europe-based	Belgium	YES
Somerfield	Business group	NO	NO	EU/Europe-based	UK	NO
SPS Aerostructures	Business group	NO	NO	EU/Europe-based	UK	NO
Starbucks	Business group	NO	NO	Cross-country	USA	NO
State Street Corporation	Business group	NO	YES	Cross-country	USA	NO
Swedish Organisation for Individual Relief	NGO	NO	NO	EU/Europe-based	Sweden	NO
Tahal Group International	Business group	NO	NO	Cross-country	Netherlands	NO
Terrestrial Jerusalem	NGO	NO	NO	Israel/Palestine	Israel	NO
Tesco	Business group	NO	NO	EU/Europe-based	UK	NO
Teva	Business group	YES	YES	Cross-country	Israel	NO
The Rights Forum	NGO	NO	NO	EU/Europe-based	Netherlands	NO
Trocaire	NGO	NO	NO	EU/Europe-based	Ireland	NO
Tuv Nord Group	Business group	NO	YES	Cross-country	Germany	NO
UAV Engines Ltd	Business group	NO	NO	Cross-country	UK	NO
UK Lawyers for Israel	NGO	NO	NO	EU/Europe-based	UK	NO
UMTB	Business group	NO	NO	EU/Europe-based	UK	NO

Name	Type			Region	Country	
Un ponte per …	NGO	NO	NO	EU/Europe-based	Italy	NO
Unilever	Business group	YES	YES	Cross-country	UK	NO
Union des étudiants juifs de France – UEJF	NGO	NO	NO	EU/Europe-based	France	NO
Union des patrons et professionnels juifs de France – UPJF	NGO	NO	NO	EU/Europe-based	France	NO
Union juive française pour la paix – UJFP	Solidarity movement	NO	NO	EU/Europe-based	France	NO
United Civilians for Peace – UCP	NGO	NO	NO	EU/Europe-based	Netherlands	YES
United Synagogue	NGO	NO	NO	EU/Europe-based	UK	YES
UN Watch	NGO	NO	NO	EU/Europe-based	Switzerland	NO
Veolia Environment Europe Service	Business group	YES	YES	Cross-country	France	NO
Vlaams Palestina Komitee	Solidarity movement	NO	NO	EU/Europe-based	Netherlands	NO
Volvo AB	Business group	YES	YES	Cross-country	Sweden	NO
Waitrose	Business group	NO	NO	EU/Europe-based	UK	NO
War on Want	Solidarity movement	NO	YES	EU/Europe-based	UK	NO
We Believe in Israel	Solidarity movement	NO	NO	EU/Europe-based	UK	YES
Women's Centre for Legal Aid and Counselling	NGO	NO	NO	Israel/Palestine	Israel	NO
WIZO – Women's International Zionist Organisation	NGO	NO	NO	cross-country	Israel	YES
World Council of Churches	NGO	NO	NO	Cross-country	Switzerland	YES
World Jewish Congress	NGO	YES	NO	Cross-country	USA	YES
World Vision International	NGO	YES	YES	Cross-country	USA	YES
Yachad – Together for Israel; Together for Peace	Solidarity movement	NO	NO	EU/Europe-based	UK	NO
Young Israeli Forum for Cooperation	NGO	NO	NO	Israel/Palestine	Israel	NO
ZeLeM – Verein zur Foerderung des messanischen Glaubens in Israel e.V.	Solidarity movement	NO	NO	EU/Europe-based	Germany	NO
Zionist Federation of Great Britain and Ireland	NGO	NO	NO	EU/Europe-based	UK	YES

Appendix 2
List of interviewees

Interviewee no.	Role	Place	Date
1	Non-state actor representative	Brussels, Ramallah, Skype interview	February 2010; November 2010, several phone calls btw March 2010 and March 2011, phone call 22 April 2011; phone call 26 June 2012
2	Non-state actor representative	Brussels	12 February 2010; 29 November 2010; 23 June 2011
3	Journalist	London and Brussels	25 November 2010; 17 March 2011
4	Non-state actor representative	Brussels	29 November 2010; 17 February 2011; 21 March 2011; 20 June 2011; 6 February 2012 (email); 28 March 2012
5	Non-state actor representative	Brussels	30 November 2010
6	Non-state actor representative	Brussels	30 November 2010
7	Non-state actor representative	Brussels	2 February 2011
8	Non-state actor representative	Brussels	3 February 2011
9	Non-state actor representative	Brussels	4 February 2011
10	Non-state actor representative	Brussels	8 February 2011
11	EU official	Brussels	10 February 2011
12	Non-state actor representative	Brussels	11 February 2011

13	EU official	Brussels	11 February 2011
14	Non-state actor representative	Brussels	11 February 2011
15	Non-state actor representative	Brussels	14 February 2011
16	Non-state actor representative	Brussels	14 February 2011
17	EU official	Brussels	15 February 2011
18	European Parliament Political Advisor	Brussels	15 February 2011
19	Non-state actor representative	Brussels	16 February 2011
20	EU official	Brussels	16 February 2011
21	Non-state actor representative	Phone interview	17 February 2011
22	Non-state actor representative	Brussels	21 February 2011
23	EU official	Brussels	22 February 2011
24	Assistant of Member of European Parliament	Brussels	22 February 2011
25	Non-state actor representative	Brussels	22 February 2011
26	Non-state actor representative	Brussels	23 February 2011
27	EU official	Brussels	24 February 2011; 18 March 2011
28	EU official	Brussels	25 February 2011
29	EU official	Brussels	25 February 2011
30	EU official	Brussels	25 February 2011
31	Non-state actor representative	Phone interview	10 March 2011
32	Assistant of Member of European Parliament	Brussels	15 March 2011
33	Journalist	Brussels	16 March 2011
34	Non-state actor representative	Brussels	16 March 2011
35	EU official	Brussels	16 March 2011
36	Member of European Parliament	Brussels	16 March 2011
37	Non-state actor representative	Brussels	17 March 2011
38	Journalist	Brussels	17 March 2011
39	EU official	Brussels	17 March 2011
40	Member of European Parliament + Assistant	Brussels	18 March 2011

(Continued)

Interviewee no.	Role	Place	Date
41	European Parliament Political Advisor	Brussels	18 March 2011
42	Non-state actor representative	Brussels	18 March 2011
43	Non-state actor representative	Brussels	18 March 2011
44	Non-state actor representative	Brussels	18 March 2011
45	European Parliament Political Advisor	Brussels	21 March 2011; 24 June 2011; 19 October 2011; 15 February 2012 (phone); 28 March 2012
46	Former Assistant of Member of European Parliament	Brussels	21 March 2011
47	Member of European Parliament	Brussels	21 March 2011
48	Non-state actor representative	Brussels	22 March 2011
49	Former Assistant of Member of European Parliament	Brussels	22 March 2011
50	EU official	Phone interview	29 April 2011
51	Non-state actor representative	Email correspondence	3 may 2011
52	Non-state actor representative	Skype interview	4 June 2011
53	European Parliament Political Advisor	Brussels	20 June 2011
54	Non-state actor representative	Brussels	22 June 2011
55	Non-state actor representative	Brussels	22 June 2011
56	Israeli official	Brussels	22 June 2011
57	European Parliament Political Advisor	Brussels	22 June 2011; 19 October 2011
58	EU official	Brussels	23 June 2011
59	European Parliament Political Advisor	Brussels	24 June 2011
60	Non-state actor representative	London	4 July 2011
61	Non-state actor representative	Phone interview; Brussels	12 July 2011; 19 October 2011

62	Non-state actor representative	Phone interview	28 July 2011
63	Non-state actor representative	Brussels	17 October 2011
64	Member of European Parliament	Brussels	17 October 2011
65	Former EU official	Phone interview	18 October 2011
66	Assistant of Member of European Parliament	Brussels	18 October 2011
67	Jewish activist	Brussels	19 October 2011
68	EU official	Brussels	19 October 2011
69	Non-state actor representative	Brussels	20 October 2011
70	European Parliament Political Advisor	Brussels	20 October 2011
71	Non-state actor representative	Brussels	20 October 2011
72	National diplomat	Brussels	21 October 2011
73	Non-state actor representative	Brussels	21 October 2011
74	Non-state actor representative	Phone interview	25 October 2011
75	Non-state actor representative	Skype interview	25 October 2011
76	Non-state actor representative	Phone interview	2 November 2011
77	Non-state actor representative	Phone interview	2 November 2011
78	Non-state actor representative	Paris	8 November 2011
79	National official	Paris	17 November 2011
80	National official	Paris	17 November 2011
81	Expert	Paris	18 November 2011
82	Non-state actor representative	Paris	30 November 2011
83	Expert	Paris	30 November 2011
84	Non-state actor representative	Paris	2 December 2011
85	National official	Paris	6 December 2011
86	Member of European Parliament	Email correspondence	15 December 2011
87	Former Member of Parliament	London	7 March 2012
88	Former diplomat	Oxford	3 May 2012
89	Non-state actor representative	Oxford	3 May 2012
90	EU official	Phone interview	7 May 2012
91	Non-state actor representative	Berlin	26 May 2012

(Continued)

Interviewee no.	Role	Place	Date
92	Non-state actor representative	Phone interview	31 May 2012
93	Non-state actor representative	Phone interview	4 June 2012
94	Non-state actor representative	Phone interview	4 June 2012
95	Non-state actor representative	Berlin	5 June 2012
96	Non-state actor representative	Berlin	7 June 2012
97	Non-state actor representative	Berlin	8 June 2012
98	National official	Phone interview	12 June 2012
99	Non-state actor representative	Phone interview	18 June 2012
100	Non-state actor representative	Berlin	18 June 2012
101	National official	Berlin	20 June 2012
102	Non-state actor representative	Skype interview	22 June 2012
103	Non-state actor representative	Berlin	22 June 2012
104	Non-state actor representative	Berlin	27 June 2012
105	Non-state actor representative	Berlin	27 June 2012
106	Member of Parliament	Berlin	27 June 2012
107	National official	Berlin	28 June 2012
108	National political advisor	Skype interview	13 July 2012
109	Former Member of Parliament + former non-state actor representative	Phone interview	29 August 2012

Index

For Product Safety Concerns and Information please contact our EU
representative GPSR@taylorandfrancis.com
Taylor & Francis Verlag GmbH, Kaufingerstraße 24, 80331 München, Germany